The Age of Light, Soap, and Water

The Age of Light, Soap, and Water:

Moral Reform in English Canada, 1885 - 1925

Mariana Valverde

M&S

Canadian Cataloguing in Publication Data

Valverde, Mariana, 1955-
The age of light, soap, and water

(The Canadian social history series)
Includes bibliographical references and index.
ISBN 0-7710-8689-X

1. Canada – Moral conditions.   2. Canada – Social conditions –
1867-1918.*   I.   Title.   II.   Series.

HN110.Z9M64   1991   971.06   C91-093092-9

McClelland & Stewart Inc.
The Canadian Publishers
481 University Avenue
Toronto, Ontario
M5G 2E9

Printed and bound in Canada by John Deyell Company

Contents

In memory of Daniel
(1989-1990)

Acknowledgements

First things first. This book would not exist without the financial support given to me during a period of academic sub-employment by a Canada Council Non-Fiction Writers' Grant, in 1986-87. In the latter stages research assistance was provided by the Centre of Criminology at the University of Toronto, with funds from the Solicitor General of Canada; Lykke de la Cour, Carolyn Strange, and Cynthia Wright did invaluable research work. The Centre also provided much-needed moral and material support during the writing stage. This book has been published with the help of a grant from the Social Science Federation of Canada, using funds provided by the Social Sciences and Humanities Research Council of Canada.

Archivists, librarians, and staff at the Thomas Fisher Rare Book Room, Robarts Library, the British Library, the Salvation Army Heritage Centre, the Emmanuel College Library at Victoria College, the Queen's University Archives, the National Archives of Canada, the Public Archives of Ontario, and the City of Toronto Archives made their essential contribution to this book. Most of all I want to thank the generous and knowledgeable people at the United Church Archives, where the bulk of the research was done.

From the beginning to the end of the project, I was fortunate to receive essential support, criticism, and irony from the Informal Economy group (Karen Dubinsky, Ruth Frager, Franca Iacovetta, Lynne Marks, Janice Newton, Carolyn Strange, and Cynthia Wright). Many other people helped in various ways, including Frances Abele, Phyllis Airhart, Debi Brock, Matthew Clark, Philip Corrigan, Anna Davin, Lykke de la Cour, Tony Doob, Bryan Palmer, Ellen Ross, Joan Sangster, Carol Smart, and Judy Walkowitz. Angus McLaren allowed me to read the manuscript of his *Our Own Master Race* (1990) as my own research and writing were coming to an end; I am very thankful for his support and encouragement, and am very pleased that our two complementary books can appear in the same series. Greg Kealey was extremely generous in his support of a fuzzy idea by a non-historian and behaved as a model editor.

My deepest thanks go to three special people. Carolyn Strange gave me endless intellectual and practical support, but more crucially, has taught me much of what I know about historiography; Lorna Weir has been my best critic, sharing her sharp theoretical insights for over twelve years; and Clifford Shearing has taught me much about how to approach social theory grounded in concrete analysis. He also read the whole manuscript carefully. While not responsible for errors or unwise speculations, they made the writing process exciting rather than exhausting, and they deserve much of the credit for any contributions to theory and/or history made by this work.

Finally, I want to remember my son Daniel Valverde here in print. This book went through reviewers and funding agencies as he went from being a small but healthy baby, through being diagnosed as brain damaged, to his sudden death at eight months from the side effects of a drug. Friends and colleagues will in any case remember him when they read this book, but I want to publicly dedicate it to his memory.

Preface

A crisis of confidence is currently affecting both of the disciplines forming the intellectual context of this book, namely history and social theory. Historians, particularly social historians, are now asking themselves whether the traditional tasks of gathering facts and reconstructing the past are not perhaps somewhat illusory, given the findings of linguistic theory, discourse analysis, and studies in the sociology of knowledge. These approaches not only question the reliability of historians' sources by emphasizing the necessary theoretical bias of all records, but go on to argue that historians cannot gather facts because facts, as well as the subjects who think they know them, are generated and given meaning in discourses. What one should study, then, is the way various discourses – legal, political, familial – are put together. In this new approach, a few scholars have come close to the extreme point of view that the discourse is everything,[1] as Christine Stansell has pointed out in relation to Gareth Stedman Jones. As she cogently puts it, the simplistic negation of historical materialism in favour of a view of discourse (understood by Stedman Jones very narrowly as linguistic) as unilaterally creating the world is a mere inversion of the old model, and does not take current theories of language and textual analysis into account.[2]

Most scholars, however, and historians in particular, are not replacing one unidimensional determinism with its opposite, but are rather revamping their methods in the realization that the naive view of language as naming or reflecting a pre-existing reality is inadequate. The role of discourses, symbolic systems, images, and texts in actively organizing both social relations and people's feelings is now acknowledged by most social historians, even if there are great debates about the extent to which techniques of cultural analysis are useful or to what extent they imply an idealist diversion. Feminist social historians have made important contributions to this debate; recent works by Joan Scott, Mary Poovey, and Denise Riley have used deconstruction and other techniques of discourse analysis to critique the empiricist

9

historiography that sought to document the history of a pre-given category (such as "women").[3]

The present book is a contribution to this debate: one of my aims is to demonstrate that discourse analysis and some tools from literary theory (for instance, the study of rhetorical tropes) can indeed be used to shed light on historical processes, from moral reform to immigration policy, without thereby claiming that social and economic relations are created *ex nihilo* by words. In my view, the fundamental insight of twentieth-century theories of language, namely that language is not a transparent window giving access to the world but is rather itself a part of the world, a kind of object among objects, eliminates the old dichotomy between idealism and materialism, and hence makes the historians' fear of idealism redundant. Following but modifying Foucault's approach, I take the term "discourses" to refer not to language as separate from the real world but rather to organized sets of signifying practices that often cross the nineteenth-century boundary between "reality" and "language." The Salvation Army, for instance, largely organized itself through a discourse composed not only of slogans, speeches, and articles but also of uniforms, insignia, musical instruments, architectural designs for Army buildings, and so on. "Discursive relations" are thus, in my usage at least, much broader than simply relations among words. Insofar as material objects such as badges or clothes or church buildings function as signs, then the old dichotomy between idealism and materialism recedes from view.

This does not mean that the world is entirely composed of semiotic systems of signs, since there is obviously a material substratum (bricks making up the church, textiles making up uniforms, paper and ink of newspapers) without which the signifying practices of each semiotic system would not exist. But the technology involved in making these materials, important as it might be for a study of the economics of brick-making or the unionization of textile workers, is only marginally relevant to the study of the moral reform projects within which these physical entities gained their social meaning. These projects are best studied by reference to the non-verbal as well as verbal signs constituting particular discursive universes – always keeping in mind that discourses are not an absolute beginning point but are themselves shaped by pre-existing social relations (mainly of gender, race, and class), which historians overly enamoured of discourse analysis ignore at their peril.

It is this non-idealist sense of "discourses" that is relevant here. The present study reveals how particular discourses of moral reform were put together (specifically by the English-Canadian social purity movement). But, more generally, it shows that the practical institutional and even physical organization of class, race, and gender has been always articulated in and through discourse, with "articulation" meaning not only "expression" but also, in the structuralist usage, joining and organization. The class- and gender-specific practical work of "rescuing" "fallen" women, for instance, could not have taken place without a certain rhetorical system that defined "vice" and virtue" through both verbal and non-verbal signs.[4] The physical and administrative work of rescue homes was thus fundamentally defined and structured by discursive practices that made sense at the time but which now require some historically informed exegesis. (Homeless prostitutes in trouble are today perhaps sheltered in similar homes, but the discourse of social work structures today's shelters differently than those run by evangelical organizations eighty years ago.) In Chapter 2 the practical consequences of one particular set of discursive practices will be highlighted, namely the role of apparently confused metaphors and allegories in organizing and defining the practical work of moral reformers. This is not to suggest that verbal signs or pictures *create* certain social relations; it is rather to demonstrate that practical social relations are always mediated and articulated through linguistic and non-linguistic signifying practices.

If history as a discipline is in a methodological crisis, social theory is also in crisis: since the decline of structuralism (in both its liberal-functionalist and its Marxist varieties), no theoretical framework has emerged as dominant. The pluralism and eclecticism of most current social thought may be experienced by some as the slough of relativist despond; but it is in many ways a creative situation in which little is taken for granted and all assumptions are questioned. One route taken by some has been to cease producing new theoretical models, in favour of concrete studies of the historical emergence of both classical social theory and applied social sciences. These are usually undertaken in the belief, or hope, that understanding the origins of the theories now in crisis is the necessary precondition to overcoming that crisis. In researching the history of sociology, social work, philosophy, law, and even literature, scholars trained in theory are finding that they have to read a great deal of "ordinary" history, since part of the project to historicize theory involves acknowledging that political developments, career aspirations, economic contexts, and the emergence of particular professions and institutions are all relevant factors.

It is thus possible to say that history and social theory are perhaps coming closer now than they have been since the heyday of "grand history" in the nineteenth century. Nevertheless, the disciplines have a good century of separate and diverging growth, and they still speak different languages, even if there are more translators. I simply hope that "unilingual" readers will be open to the opportunity of becoming somewhat more fluent in the other language (much as dutiful Anglophone Canadians sometimes overcome their initial dislike of French messages on cereal packages and decide to turn breakfast into a learning opportunity).

Taken as a whole, the work at hand may seem quite unfamiliar to some historians. This is because I have attempted to use established techniques of historical research and writing for unusual purposes. For example, the occasional brief biographies do not imply that great individuals make history, or that those individuals about whom information is available are more important than those who left no records. Movements are composed of people and writing about movements can be enlivened and concretized by occasional forays into biography; but the political and philosophical assumptions of "Great Men" (or "Great Women") approaches to history are here firmly rejected.

Similarly, the description and analysis of ideas does not presuppose that ideas move the world or make this book traditional intellectual history. Traditional accounts of the history of ideas concentrate on major, systematic texts, whereas the texts analysed here are usually short, popular, and geared to action; many of the texts (newspaper articles or minutes of meetings) are without known author and purport to give news or formulate policy, not so much present ideas. Furthermore, more attention is paid to images and allegories than to abstract theory, partly because few people in any particular age ever read the abstract philosophical texts later consecrated as "the spirit of the age," and partly because, as I show in Chapter 2, metaphors and allegories work differently on people's consciousness than do systematic literary or philosophical texts.

The book may also sometimes sound like "history of women," a relatively new subfield seeking to restore women's presence in history. But it is not about women even though some care was put into finding out what women thought or did. Readers expecting it to be about women will be disappointed to hear so much about men; and even readers who see that feminist history is more important than women's history and who know that feminist history is about gender, not women, will perhaps be disappointed that the analysis claims that class, and more often race, was in many instances a more important social contradiction than gender even when women and sexuality are overtly the topic of concern.

The mix of methods and languages is the outcome of my intent to find adequate tools for understanding and explaining texts read in archives. A more elegant and consistent book possibly could have been produced if I had confined myself to one or two theoretical tool kits and had written a text that fit more neatly into an already established category of academic work. But, not finding life in the late twentieth century particularly consistent or elegant, I had no reason to think that eighty years ago people and organizations were any less complex and ambiguous. In my eclecticism as an historian, there is one assumption I have definitely rejected, namely, that the past is easier to describe than the present because people in the past were simpler than our own sophisticated and complicated selves. That assumption, flowing from what the great historian Edward Thompson dubbed "the enormous condescension of posterity," has prevented us from seriously considering people and discourses that seem naive or unscientific. I have tried to follow in his footsteps in this respect.

The book is organized as follows. An introductory chapter summarizes the main arguments – or more accurately, conclusions – about the character of moral reform and philanthropy and the role or non-role of the state in moral reform projects. The second chapter begins to re-create for contemporary readers the world view of social purity activists, concentrating on their myths and images. This is followed by an analysis of the term "moral and social reform" showing the inseparability of the two in the period under study as well as a sketch of the organizational form and practical work of the main institutions promoting moral reform. (The only exception is the Salvation Army, a description of which is delayed until the chapter on the moral problems of the city, given their unique role in moralizing the slums.) The final section of Chapter 3 stresses that social purity was in one sense an early sex education movement, contrary to the stereotype of moral reformers as censoring all discussions of sexuality.

The next chapters take up, one by one, some of the main concerns of moral reformers. One chapter explains the key place of prostitution in the thoughts and actions of social purity activists and analyses the "white slavery" panic, which was a specific form of the more general concern with prostitution. Two more chapters, on immigration and urbanization respectively, demonstrate the important moral and sexual dimensions of fundamental processes in Canadian history. Although the "white slavery" chapter highlights gender, the race/immigration chapter highlights the connection between racial and sexual purity, and the chapter on urbanization gives an opportunity to consider class, the emphasis throughout is on what I call "slippages." For example, a discourse on single women could easily have a strong and complex subtext on race, or a discourse apparently on race and immigration might slip into moral categories. This unexpected shift in the basic categories of a discourse helps us to understand how various moral panics are historically specific: for example, incest was in this time period a social problem primarily about or due to class problems, whereas in our own era incest is discussed almost wholly as a gender problem. The presence of constant slippages makes it impossible to determine whether a particular statement or a genre of statements (for instance, about the moral dangers posed to middle-class Canada by British female domestics) was *really* about class or about gender. Moral panics, I conclude, are by definition multidimensional, and the social anxiety associated with them is probably rooted in the unconscious coming together or condensation of different discourses, different fears, in a single image.

The final chapter, on the character of philanthropic work, puts social purity in its practical and intellectual context (most of the organizations doing purity work were philanthropies) and returns to the themes of morality, the state, and moral regulation outlined in the introduction.

1

Introduction

Practically all historians claim that the period of their particular interest is "a transitional age" witnessing profound changes in economy and society. At the risk of appearing both trite and self-serving, it can nevertheless be claimed that the decades from the 1880s to World War One saw major changes in Canadian society, many of which have had a lasting influence. It can also be claimed with some plausibility that these were in fact transitional decades: in the 1870s Canada was a very sparsely populated, barely post-colonial state where farming and staples production predominated; by the 1920s the Native populations had been firmly marginalized, the weight of the economy had shifted toward industry and finance, and urban living had become the rule rather than the exception. By the 1920s the Canadian state had developed, at least in embryonic form, most of the institutions it has today, and in English Canada a certain cultural consensus, based to a large extent on American and British influence but incorporating a new nationalism, had emerged and was being consolidated.

There were many different elements in this consolidation of a nation (an English Canada centred on and dominated by the Toronto-Ottawa axis) and a corresponding state:[1] this book is largely concerned with certain social and cultural aspects of this consolidation. The practices and discourses described herein were largely aspects of the class relations of the emerging urban and capitalist social formation.

As historians have pointed out, one important aspect of the growth of modern Canada was the development of an urban-industrial working class.[2] The correlate of that was the development of an urban bourgeoisie, certain sectors of which initiated a philanthropic project to reform or "regenerate" Canadian society. One strand of this book's argument is that the social reform movements of the turn of the century helped to shape the bourgeoisie, which led the movements, as well as the working class, toward which they were generally aimed. Although there is very little secondary literature on the constitution of the

English-Canadian bourgeoisie at the social and cultural levels (as opposed to the economic formations traced in business history), an attempt will be made to analyse, in however tentative a fashion, the making of the subclass involved in social reform. This was composed mostly of professionals and charity workers, who acted partly to uphold the specific interests and perspectives of their professions but who were also connected to the larger bourgeois culture of which they formed part.

This process of fragmented, interactive, and multiple class formation was in turn always gendered and racially specific. The process through which race, gender, and class were intertwined in what was known as "nation-building" is one of the main themes of this book. It is furthermore not assumed here that "gender" is merely a euphemism for women, "race" one for people of colour, and "class" one for working-class and poor people – just as class formation takes place in the bourgeoisie as well as in the proletariat, masculinity and Anglo-Saxon whiteness are as worthy of critical analysis as femininity and racial minorities.

The economic and cultural developments that form the background to the reform movement analysed here were not unique to Canada: similar developments in the northeastern United States and in urban Britain have been described by many historians. The ideas and practices of class formation that were popular in urban Canada were to a large extent adapted from English and American sources. The development of both unions and employers' associations, the workings of private charity and public relief, and the cultural practices of the various classes were all heavily influenced by the overall fact of Canadian dependence. In some cases, reformers imported certain ideas from abroad without reflecting on the extent to which Canadian realities made these ideas unsuitable. At other times, however, the uniqueness of Canada was highlighted by patriots who insisted that Toronto or Hamilton most definitely lacked the social evils plaguing Chicago or London.

It is very difficult if not impossible to make any general statements about the specificity of Canadian social reform movements; all that can be said is that the well-educated urban English Canadians who led these movements were definitely learning from English and, increasingly, American sources. Then as now, however, there was a constant tension between the temptation to copy or import and the equally strong temptation to claim that Canada was different – less corrupt, healthier – and that social remedies ought not to be imported for non-existent social ills. It would be impossible here to detail all the forms and channels of English and American influence on Canadian ideas about social and moral reform. The main point is that Canadians then (as now) tended to define themselves not so much positively but by way of a differentiation – from the Mother Country, first, and, in the twentieth century, from the United States. As we shall see, their self-image as healthy citizens of a new country of prairies and snowy peaks contributed both to twentieth-century nationalist ideas and to the success of the purity movement, one of whose symbols was pure white snow.

As Ramsay Cook has pointed out, at the turn of the century a large number of educated Canadians were interested in reforming their society and their state and building the foundations for what they thought could be a future of prosperity and relative equality. They envisaged this reform not as a series of small isolated measures but as a grand project to "regenerate" both society and the human soul.[3] Cook's analysis confines itself largely to theological and intellectual spheres, however, and leaves in the shadow one important component of the reform project – the effort undertaken by popular educators, temperance activists, and pamphlet writers, more than by either theologians or social theorists, to reshape the ethical subjectivity of both immigrants and native-born Canadians. They called their project "moral reform," usually linked to social concerns in the common phrase "moral and social reform."

To study moral reform at the turn of the century, it is appropriate to focus primarily on the self-styled "social purity movement," which, along with temperance and Sunday observance, helped to constitute a powerful if informal coalition for the moral regeneration of the state, civil society, the family, and the individual. The social purity movement was a loose network of organizations and individuals, mostly church people, educators, doctors, and those we would now describe as community or social workers, who engaged in a sporadic but vigorous campaign to "raise the moral tone" of Canadian society, and in particular of urban working-class communities. In 1895, a Canadian clergyman speaking at an important Purity Congress in Baltimore described "social purity work in Canada" as including the following issues: prostitution, divorce, illegitimacy, "Indians and Chinese," public education, suppression of obscene literature, prevention (of prostitution) and rescue of fallen women, and shelters for women and children.[4] These same issues were addressed from an American perspective by other speakers,[5] who all agreed that purity work was not simply a question of banning obscene books or suppressing prostitution but was rather a campaign to educate the next generation in the purity ideals fitting to "this age of light and water and soap."[6]

The image of reform as illuminating society while purifying or cleansing it was already an integral part of the temperance movement, which developed in the mid-nineteenth century in the U.S. and Britain and was taken up in Canada by such organizations as the Woman's Christian Temperance Union and the Dominion Alliance for the Total Suppression of the Liquor Traffic.[7] Many of the organizations involved in both temperance education and lobbying for prohibition took up social purity work as part of their task. In some respects, temperance and social purity acted as a single movement. However, some people involved in social purity work (notably doctors and lay sex educators) did not necessarily support prohibition – even though they usually advocated voluntary abstinence from alcohol – and undoubtedly there were many prohibitionists who were rather single-minded and did not share some of the concerns grouped under the label of "social purity." It is thus appropriate to undertake the more limited task of describing and analysing social purity work and ideas, remembering always its close connection to temperance – and to the other great single issue of moral reformers, Sunday observance – but without seeking to assimilate one cause into another.

Social purity was advocated by many of the same people responsible for spreading the "social gospel" in Canada; and since social gospel has been the subject of various studies[8] while social purity has been almost totally ignored by historians, a word about the relation between these two projects is in order. As defined by Allen, Cook, and others, "social gospel" refers to the attempts to humanize and/or Christianize the political economy of urban-industrial capitalism. Its prophets were generally moderately left of centre but included such mainstream figures as W.L. Mackenzie King, who collaborated with the Presbyterian Board of Social Service and Evangelism in his youth and was influenced by social gospel ideas in his popular 1919 book, *Industry and Humanity*.

There was an overlap in both personnel and ideas between social gospel and social purity, and therefore one can only offer a tentative clarification: while the focus of social gospel activity was the economy and the social relations arising from production, social purity focused on the sexual and moral aspects of social life. Prostitution in all its forms was the one "social problem" guaranteed to unify the diverse constituencies – feminists, right-wing evangelicals, doctors, social reformers – of the social purity coalition; and "sex hygiene," or purity education, was one of the main positive remedies promoted. While sexual concerns were important or even central, one must guard against seeking analytical clarity at the expense of historical accuracy: for many of the people who lived it, social purity was intertwined with socio-economic reform. Thus, the term "social purity movement" will be used sparingly; it would be misleading to imagine it as a distinct movement with its own headquarters and publications, when in fact it was in one sense an aspect of a wider movement that also included critical studies of industrial conditions and other issues not generally regarded as "moral."

Philanthropy and "The Social"

Sexual morality was the main target of the social purity movement, but the purity campaign has to be understood in the context of a larger project to solve the problems of poverty, crime, and vice. This larger project was primarily the task of philanthropy, with state activity often being confined to supplementing private initiatives or acting like a philanthropy.

There are various ways of characterizing philanthropy, and perhaps it is easiest to define it by contrast with what came before, namely charity. Charity, the traditional means of relieving poverty, was largely individual and impulsive, and its purpose was to relieve the immediate need of the recipient while earning virtue points for the giver. Organized charity or philanthropy sought to eliminate both the impulsive and the individual elements of giving. The London philanthropists of the 1860s who pioneered modern methods of philanthropy and social work constantly denounced the "indiscriminate alms-giving" of charity as unscientific and backward.[9] They believed that the problem with charity was not that it was never enough but, on the contrary, that there was too much of it and that the poor were becoming "pauperized" by dependence on abundant charity. A similar campaign (perhaps on a smaller scale) was carried on in the U.S.: a pioneer of organized philanthropy stated that "next to alcohol, the most pernicious fluid is indiscriminate soup."[10]

Philanthropists hence sought to rationalize and often curtail the material aid, focusing instead on training the poor in habits of thrift, punctuality, and hygiene – an economic subjectivity suited to a capitalist society. They also sought to eliminate pity from giving while maximizing rational calculation, so that, for instance, rather than give to old people, who were favoured by traditional charity, there was a new emphasis on children and, indirectly, on women, for with them one was making an investment in the future of the nation.[11]

Another way of contrasting charity and philanthropy is to differentiate poverty – the problem addressed by charity – and pauperism. In England, there was a strict legal definition of pauperism in the Poor Law: however, there was also a broader meaning of the term, indicating a larger social process specific to capitalism and affecting the working class in general, not just legal paupers. The vicar of London's parish of Stepney put it as follows in 1904: "It is not so much poverty that is increasing in the East [end] as pauperism, the want of industry, of thrift or self-reliance."[12] The term "pauperization" indicated a loss of initiative and dignity, not just physical want or legal dependence on the parish. That pauperism was moral as well as economic is evident from the fact that drinking, irregular work habits, sexual laxity, and infrequent bathing were discussed as often if not more often than low wages and poor housing.

If pauperism was more than economic, philanthropy was not merely an economic project to soften the hard edges of industrial capitalism. Its work took place in and largely shaped what Jacques Donzelot has called "the social."[13] Characteristic of this new social philosophy was an unabashed interventionism. In a liberal state, economic policy at least has to try to respect the individual autonomy of capital owners, but social policy is characterized by the opposite movement, i.e., one of expansionism even into the private sphere of family and sexual life. There is no question of letting social forces play themselves out – in modern societies there is no invisible social hand, and so some degree of engineering by visible hands in or out of the state is necessary. David Garland describes the main British social programs of the period under study (social work, eugenics, social security, and criminology) as "extending the power of government over life."[14]

While Donzelot and Garland see "the social" as a distinct realm with fairly clear if shifting boundaries separating it from both politics and economics, I would argue that "the social" is not so much a separate sphere but a new way of conceptualizing any and all problems of the collectivity. Municipal politics and industrial policy, to give two examples, were in our period seen increasingly under the aspect of the social.[15] Industry was seen as needing some form of regulation (maximum hours and minimum wages, for instance) not because of any contradictions within the economic system itself, but rather because extreme exploitation was defined as a *social* problem, involving the creation of paupers, the breakdown of the family, and a general crisis in the cohesion of the social formation.[16] Political questions, from war to immigration, also came to be regarded as more than political. The Boer War, apart from its strictly political aspects, generated a major social panic in Great Britain (which had echoes in Canada) about the poor quality of the soldiers and of the mothers who had produced them.[17] Hence, economics and politics were increasingly socialized, while social problems were persistently seen as "moral" even by modern scientific experts outside of the social purity movement.

The term "social" was usually an adjective, and the relevant noun that came to mind most readily was "problem." In the 1820s and 1830s, both French and English sources had used the term "the social question"; after mid-century, however, "the social" became fragmented into a multitude of "problems," among other reasons because the growth of specialized professions encouraged a fragmentation of jurisdictions within the social. Whether unitary or fragmented, however, the social domain was born problematic, as Donzelot's study indicates; and throughout the nineteenth century and into the first two decades of the twentieth, the answers to social problems were usually elaborated in the idiom of philanthropy. It thus followed that the first task of philanthropy was to enumerate and study, i.e., to know, "the social." In the last two chapters we will describe some of the methods used by the social purity and philanthropy activists to both study and solve not only particular urban problems but what they referred to as "*the* problem of *the* city." It will be seen there that the work of knowing the poor became a great deal more than a means to the end of remedying poverty: it became a science for its own sake – social science, a term that in the late nineteenth century included the present-day fields of sociology and social work.[18] This thirst for knowledge led social researchers to leave the library and enter into the neighbourhoods and homes of the poor (home visiting was a central practice in nineteenth-century philanthropy). This investigation began with the kitchens, clothes, and cupboards of the poor, but it did not end there: the prying gaze of philanthropy sought to penetrate the innermost selves of the poor, including their sexual desires, which were uniformly conceptualized as vices (incest, illegitimacy, prostitution).

Sexual desire was probed not only from the standpoint of morality but also from the standpoint, and in the context, of the new field of public health. Unlike other health matters, however, sex was difficult to quantify. This was a great disappointment to reformers like English public health pioneer James Kay, who said: "Criminal acts may be statistically classed . . . but the number of those affected with the moral leprosy of vice cannot be exhibited with mathematical precision. Sensuality has no record."[19] The absence of sensual records, however, did not deter investigators such as London's Rev. Mearns, who in the mid-1880s caused a public scandal by claiming that incest was common among the poor.[20] An important wing of the purity movement devoted itself to the production of books, pamphlets, and lectures with which people could probe both their own and other people's sexual habits in order to remoralize the individual and the nation. The title of what was probably the most popular sex education book in turn-of-the-century Canada, *Light on Dark Corners: Searchlight on Health*,[21] captures the distinctive emphasis on probing and rooting out vice with the powerful light of quasi-medical knowledge.

Although there was general agreement on the need to study the poor, preferably in their own homes, there were endless arguments about how to organize philanthropy, how to choose the proper targets, and how to improve its efficiency, as well as major arguments (especially in Britain) about whether the state or the private sector should be the main organizer of philanthropy. Amidst these debates, the status of philanthropy (whether private or public) as the main answer to the problem of the social was not questioned until the development of professional social work and systems of state welfare in the 1920s and 1930s – and even then, the legacy of philanthropy weighed so heavily on the new systems of relief that one could with some justice claim that philanthropy merely disguised itself as state-funded welfare and social work.[22]

The location of philanthropy in (or arising out of) the domain of the social does not imply that it was independent of politics and of the state or that it was unconnected to class formation and class struggle. The relations of gender, class, and race that both shaped moral reform and were shaped by it are, however, too complex to be captured by resorting to the hackneyed model of one class (or one gender) unilaterally repressing its class or gender enemy with Machiavellian tactics. The processes analysed in this book are best conceptualized under the rubric of "moral regulation."

Nation, State, and Morality

Insofar as there is a popular view of the social purity movement, this view is that once upon a pre-Freudian time there was a group of repressed clergymen and church ladies who tried to make everyone stop drinking, having sex, and gambling. The movement of 1885-1920 is seen as just another chapter in the history of Puritanism, and hence as a purely negative, prohibitory project.[23]

Like all popular myths, the myth of social purity as a force of negation does have a grain of truth. Such organizations as the Lord's Day Alliance were primarily concerned with preventing certain activities on Sundays, and it was only with the passage of time that reformers began to be more concerned about providing "suitable" Sunday activities such as picnics, supervised playgrounds for children, discussion groups for young people, and other activities classified as "rational recreation" (as opposed to commercialized amusements). But even the Lord's Day Alliance, and even the temperance movement, did not intend simply to stamp out one or more vices. They had a larger vision of how people ought to pass their time, how they ought to act, speak, think, and even feel. This vision – which I will here call "positive" not because it was necessarily good but to distinguish it from negativity, from mere prohibition – was often kept in the background as they pursued their efforts to prevent or negate evil, but it was always present and it became increasingly prominent after the turn of the century.

Those intent on banning the liquor traffic looked forward to the day when Canadians would not drink alcohol, but would drink great amounts of pure milk and clear country water. American temperance leader Frances Willard stated: "when you can get men to drink milk it means well for temperance, for the home, for purity," while her Canadian counterpart poetically evoked the "aquatic tendencies" of the women's temperance movement, adding that her home town of London, Ontario, was proud of its "abundant supply of pure, sparkling water – water that leaves no excuse for drinking anything else."[24] The beneficial social effects of pure drinks were trumpeted by experts at a Milwaukee conference attended by Canadian public health doctors, reported in the Toronto *Daily News* under the headline "Fewer Criminals with Pure Milk."[25] Toronto newspapers also featured advertisements for Purity Water, bottled water sold by appealing to consumers' wish to maximize their health. The ideal of purity was extended from liquids to solids in the following advertisement for the patriotic and pure Canada Bread:

> In kitchens flooded with pure air and sunshine, neat bakers, arrayed in clothes of immaculate white, deftly and carefully prepare the materials for the 'staff of Canadian life.' A visit here will show that cleanliness is indeed carried to extremes.[26]

Pure foods and drinks, most commonly embodied in milk and water, were simultaneously physically and symbolically pure. Pure milk – white like the ribbons worn by the WCTU women – and clean, clear water represented moral health, truth, and beauty, in contrast not only to alcohol but to the deceitful adulterated milk and impure water of the unsanitary cities.[27] The whiteness of milk was also sometimes linked to the snow central to Canadian mythology: Havergal principal Ellen Knox typically told her schoolgirls that Canada had "a glistening line of the future, pure and free as her own ice-clad peaks of the Rockies."[28] The combination of whiteness and coldness made snow an appropriate symbol not only of Canada but also of purity.

If even the self-described prohibition movement (which nevertheless preferred the less negative name "temperance") is at least partially an example of what theorists since Foucault are calling "the positivity of power," the social purity movement must also be interpreted as a great deal more than simply a campaign against prostitution, immoral amusements, and other public manifestations of vice. Social purity was a campaign to regulate morality, in particular sexual morality, in order to preserve and enhance a certain type of human life. It was not merely a campaign to punish and repress. This can be seen in the changing emphases of the federal government's Conservation Commission (whose journal was entitled *The Conservation of Life*). During and after the war, this Commission, which encompassed a variety of matters from the conservation of fisheries and forestry to public health, pure milk, and town planning, put more emphasis on conserving human bodies and less on trees and fur-bearing animals. Although it did not last long and the component parts were absorbed by more specialized government departments, its creation was part of an ongoing if not always successful attempt to unify all social problems into one macro-problem – conserving "life" – for which a macro-solution could be found. The Conservation Commission, dismissed by historian Paul Rutherford as "strange,"[29] can be properly understood by realizing that conservation of life was more than an attempt to unify various parts of the bureaucracy: it evoked Romantic vitalist philosophies as well as the Christian concept of "the Resurrection and the Life." These spiritual dimensions were emphasized by the ex-Minister of Labour and future Prime Minister W.L. Mackenzie King in his optimistic manifesto for Canadian reconstruction, *Industry and Humanity*. In this book, " the conservation of health and life" is said to be one of the three principles of reconstruction (the others were peace and work). Mackenzie King used the modern phrase "conservation of human resources" to name a priority of the Ministry of Labour, but this modern phrase incorporates Christian and Romantic meanings.[30]

The Great War caused a quantum leap in the concern about conserving human life. As Toronto's public health chief, Dr. Charles Hastings, put it in October of 1914,

National Conservation Commissions that have been engaged in the conservation of natural resources, such as forests, fisheries, mines etc., have in recent years embraced the conservation of human life and human efficiency.[31]

But as Hastings himself notes, even before the Great War caused a tangible crisis in human resources, men and women engaged in "nation-building" had stressed the need to conserve, preserve, and shape human life: to conserve its physical health, to preserve its moral purity, and to shape it according to the optimistic vision shared by all political parties of what Canada would be in the twentieth century. The

Methodist Church's sex educator for boys typically believed that one of Canada's untapped natural resources was its young people, and he saw his own educational work as furthering the production of "self": "Our young men themselves are producing a product, self, that will command in the market of the world a value – we are building this young manhood into some kind of product, that in later years we will have to offer in the markets of the world."[32]

This is not to say, I hasten to add, that the social purity movement was a stooge or puppet of the state; on the contrary, the various levels of government often lagged behind the initiatives of churches and professional groups. Dangerous as it always is to assume that the state is the only real agent of history, in the case of Canada at the turn of the century it would be ludicrous to assume that politicians or civil servants conspired to manipulate the powerful voluntary organizations with which this book is concerned. State officials and agencies did often work with or fund private agencies, and the phenomenon of co-optation was not unknown. One cannot assume, however, that the state was – or is at present – always the dominant partner. Indeed, there are very good reasons why liberal-democratic states, far from desiring to absorb all social policy activity, have a vested interest in fostering non-state organizations that will co-operate in certain aspects of social policy, particularly in areas such as regulating morality and gender and family relations. Except in situations such as war or internal rebellion, explicitly moral campaigns are difficult for liberal democratic states to undertake with any degree of success, since such states portray themselves as neutral arbiters of opinions circulating in civil society. Such states also have a structural commitment to non-interference in private beliefs and activities of a moral and/or cultural nature. It is far easier for the state to respond to popular outcries than it is to orchestrate such a campaign on its own – although the Canadian state at its various levels has been known to sow the seeds of popular panics in order to then cast itself in the apparently neutral role of responding to popular demands.[33]

Another related reason why the state was not, and in fact could not have been, the main protagonist in the social purity campaign is that social purity was only partially concerned with restricting behaviour. States may have a monopoly over the legitimate use of force and may therefore be in a privileged position to enforce rules about behaviour, but the state can only make its citizens *internalize* certain values if it has the full and active co-operation of the family and of voluntary organizations.[34] What we will see is that many voluntary organizations were far more concerned about nation-building and even about strengthening the state than the state itself; they often chastised it for not exercising enough power, particularly in the areas of social welfare, health, and immigration.

It may seem remarkable that private organizations had such trust in the state: the Canadian situation certainly contrasts with other more conflictive situations, such as the mutual suspicion of private charity and poor law authorities in England at this time. But, for reasons beyond the scope of the present work, by the 1880s both the federal and provincial states seem to have acquired an almost unshakeable legitimacy in the eyes of the educated Anglophone middle classes. Municipal government was often denounced as corrupt, but the higher levels were remarkably free from criticism, and even as citizens agitated for changes in the personnel of the state, the structures themselves went largely unquestioned.

One reason for this trust is that civil society was very sharply divided: the Methodists would far rather see the state take control of education than risk giving more power to their Catholic rivals, and mainstream Protestants preferred to have the provinces take over social work rather than see the Salvation Army flourish. Ethnic, religious, and class divisions were highly visible and conflictive, and in the face of this obvious disunity the state had little difficulty in portraying itself as neutral.

Furthermore, Canadian state formation (with the important exception of Quebec) has as one of its ideological pillars the establishment of Protestantism as a kind of joint-stock state religion. Bruce Curtis's perceptive analysis of the successful construction of a sense of citizenship suffused with Protestantism through Rev. Egerton Ryerson's 1840s reforms helps to explain why churches and other quasi-evangelical bodies regarded the state as a friend rather than a competitor.[35]

We see, then, that a large-scale effort to mould the moral values of the population was, given the particular character of the Canadian state, bound to rely greatly on the efforts of private or semi-public agencies, in part because whether moral reform movements are aimed at building the family, the church, or the nation, they emphasize training and even constructing the subjectivity of the members. As the Presbyterian press typically put it in 1908, "we want to build a nation, not gather together a mob."[36]

The building of a nation was rightly equated with the organization of assent, not just outward conformity to legal and administrative rules. This is one reason why the outright punishment of political or moral deviants came to be seen as a last resort and as an admission of failure. David Garland points out that the turn of the century witnessed a marked decline of eye-for-eye discourses on crime and their replacement by therapeutic and reformatory strategies.[37] While the criminal, the fallen, and the destitute were being increasingly seen as subjects of treatment, through the medicalization of crime, sexuality, and poverty,[38] non-criminal populations and in particular youth were being seen as requiring a process of character-building, the individual equivalent of the nation-building just cited. An individual without character, without the kind of self that W.L. Clark sought to build, was a miniature mob: disorganized, immoral, and unhealthy as well as an inefficient member of the collectivity. Character was not to be acquired bureaucratically, by learning information or following rules. What Clark called the production of self and others called character-building was an inner, subjective task. It involved learning to lead a morally and physically pure life, not only for the sake of individual health and salvation but for the sake of the nation. The social purity lecturer A.W. Beall was clear on this point, telling schoolchildren across Ontario that "it is up to you, to each of you, to become an A.1 father of A.1 children" and having them repeat: "JESUS CHRIST AND CANADA EXPECT ME TO BE AN A.1 BOY."[39]

As many writers have pointed out, the shaping of individual sexual morality is quite important in national and religious macro-projects.[40] This shaping of morality, in the context of a grand project that was both national and religious, is perhaps the core of the social purity movement. Placing moral reform in the specific context of nation-building and state formation at the turn of the century, we can see it as a particular national project rather than simply a manifestation of a trans-historical urge to suppress pleasure and sexuality. This national project was outlined by others from slightly different but complementary perspectives. For instance, Mackenzie King's book about industrial relations in the post-war era, which is suffused by a spiritualist optimism about the role of government in preserving the health of the national organism, echoes Clark and Beall without stressing the sexual aspect:

> Education in health and character is the best insurance against the hazards of industrial life . . . character is the determining factor in all things. An inner sustaining motive is more necessary than external support if, across the reaches of Time, the spirit of workers in Industry is not to flag.[41]

The "character" needed by the nation was a sexual as well as a national identity. In the literature exemplified in Canada by the "Self and Sex" series promoted by the WCTU and the Methodist Church, and by Beall's *The Living Temple*, clean bodies and clean minds are not just clean in the sense of having no dirt; they are portrayed as having been produced through the active and constant scouring that was a central metaphor of social purity.

That the relentless scouring of the soul and shaping of individual character would have an immediate impact on public and national affairs, nobody doubted. The housecleaning metaphors utilized by maternal feminists such as Nellie McClung did not only seek to legitimize women's entry into the public sphere by comparing politics to a house in need of spring cleaning; they also established a parallel between what was known as "political purity" and personal hygiene. Physical and sexual hygiene – which were to a large extent in women's sphere – were the microcosmic foundation of the larger project of building a "clean" nation. A speech at the National Council of Women's 1907 convention, for instance, introduced the topic of sex education as follows:

> It is with a great degree of hesitancy that I presume to introduce . . . the question we are now about to consider, and one of so great moment in our individual, our social and our national life, that of Purity. A question the underlying principles of which are the vital principles on which depends the successful building of the individual's or the nation's life.[42]

On his part, MP John Charlton, who in the 1880s and 1890s spearheaded many efforts to raise the age of consent, criminalize seduction, and promote sexual purity, introduced one of his many legislative efforts as follows: "No vice will more speedily sap the foundations of public morality and of national strength than licentiousness . . . ."[43]

The rhetoric of national decline and "weakening of the moral fiber" through excessive sexuality is so familiar (even in the present day) that few writers have taken the time to analyse its roots. It is important, however, to treat such statements not as vacuous rhetorical flourishes but as highly meaningful indicators signalling a belief in the nation's need for specifically *moral* subjects. The nation (as distinct from the state) is, in the discourse of national degeneration, seen as rather fragile and as subject to a quasi-physical process of decay that can only be halted if the individuals, the cells of the body politic, take control over their innermost essence or self. This is assumed to be morality, which a century ago included not only "the soul" but also what we now call the emotions, and the core of that is in turn sexual morality. Sexual desire is perceived as the most dangerous of forces, the worst threat to civilization, and hence as that which most needs taming. The specific sexual activities targeted for control changed over the years: in the mid-nineteenth century, masturbation, especially among boys, was the most talked about vice, while at the turn of the century prostitution would take the spotlight, to be replaced in the 1920s by fears about non-commoditized consensual sexual encounters among young people. But regardless of the specific sexual activity targeted, the loss of individual self-control over sexuality was perceived to have far-reaching consequences *even if nobody ever knew about it*. Again, it was not so much a matter of outward behaviour but a question of inner identity, of the subjectivity of citizens.

This subjectivity was not without content. The attempt to make young boys and girls learn self-control and develop character involved very specific ideas about the use to which such highly controlled units ought to be put, and about the class, gender, and racial composition of the nation being built.

The class basis of social purity is not a simplistic matter of middle-class reformers imposing their values on working-class communities. It is true that the vast majority of leaders of the movement were of the middle class, and in particular were members of what Robert Wiebe's classic study of progressivism in the U.S. called "the new middle classes," that is, professionals and managers (as opposed to capitalists).[44] But this subclass, precisely because it was new, was as concerned to make itself as to make others. Thus its activities cannot be wholly explained as directed at other classes or class fractions. What has been described as imposing values on another class is simultaneously a process of creating and reaffirming one's own class. Class formation is a dialectical process; it takes place in the bourgeoisie as much as in the working class, and often through the same practices.

The doctors, clergymen, and women employers of servants did not in any case expect immigrants and prostitutes to live and think exactly like upper-class Anglo-Saxon Canadians. They did want both immigrants and social deviants to embrace the culture and values of Anglo-Saxon, Protestant, middle-class urban Canadians, but this was to ensure that the power of the WASP bourgeoisie would appear as legitimate, not to democratize society and have everyone live in Rosedale- or Westmount-style homes. Both social purity and philanthropy sought to establish a non-antagonistic capitalist class structure, not to erase class differences.[45]

The gender organization of social purity is also a complex question that cannot be summarized by saying the movement was male-dominated. The movement sought to reform and organize gender, not merely utilize it. This gender reform meant that some women were given the possibility of acquiring a relatively powerful identity as rescuers, reformers, and even experts, while other women were reduced to being objects of philanthropic concern. Men were equally divided by the social construction of masculinity of the social purity movement: if many men, particularly "foreigners," were seen as the epitome of impurity, other men were provided with a potential new identity as reformed, moralized, and domesticated males.

Women were often marginalized, especially in church organizations (excepting perhaps the Salvation Army). The vision of Canadian womanhood promoted by the movement was one stressing maternal selflessness and passive purity, a vision clearly reinforcing patriarchal privilege.[46] Nevertheless, large numbers of women were active in this movement, and they cannot be dismissed by seeing them as victims of false consciousness. The "search for sexual order"[47] central to the movement was seen by women to be in women's best interests: males were viewed as the main culprits in sexual disorder (although some women blamed fallen women's wiles). Hence the protection of women against male harassment, sexual violence, and everyday disrespect was a legitimate feminist goal. Furthermore, the movement's upholding of a single standard of sexual morality ("the white life for two") did give a voice to married women's protest against philandering husbands.

The great paradox about femininity formation in/through moral reform campaigns was that certain middle-class women made careers out of studying "the problem" of the immigrant woman or the urban girl. These women doctors, social workers, deaconesses, and Salvation Army officers travelled freely around the city, protected by their uniform and their profession, and perhaps did not realize that their unprecedented freedom was built on the prior assumption that ordinary women were helpless objects in need of study and reform. The pure woman did not gain her purity exclusively through silence, chastity, and seclusion: she was partially public.

If the feminine identity established in the discourses and practices of moral reform was internally divided, this division was to some extent papered over by the traditional link between femininity and purity. This link made men's position in social purity problematic, as has been noted by social historians of evangelical Protestantism.

Ann Douglas's insightful study of changes in American Protestantism in the nineteenth century traces the development of a sentimental Christianity in the 1830s and 1840s that softened and feminized the face of Protestantism. Harsh Calvinist theology was displaced by an alliance between sentimental women writers (Harriet Beecher Stowe is only the best known of these) and ministers who, after church disestablishment, had to win over influential ladies to maintain their position. In the Gilded Age, mid-Victorian sentimentality began to be in turn displaced by what was known as "muscular" Christianity, a new perspective connected to social Darwinism. The scientific/muscular perspectives of the 1890s, however, supplemented rather than replaced the feminized religion constructed decades earlier.[48]

Although church organization in Canada differed considerably from that in the eastern U.S., Douglas's thesis about the feminization of theology helps to explain why Methodism lost much of its fire-and-brimstone language, embracing instead a more humanist perspective emphasizing education and nurturing. As nurturing and other domestic virtues increased in value, allowing women to serve in public roles through maternal feminism, social purity helped to reconcile the apparently passive virtue of purity with active masculinity. An effort was made by a section of the urban middle class to redefine masculinity as well as femininity as actively domestic. The challenge was to purge the new male bourgeoisie of the drinking and wenching habits of the aristocracy, while avoiding effete or ascetic disengagement from the claims of masculinity.

In the English context, Leonore Davidoff and Catherine Hall have analysed the Romantic attachment to suburban gardening as an attempt to cleanse the masculine soul from the grime of capitalist enterprise, and thus to help males to inhabit the domestic realm meaningfully.[49] The literature of Canadian social purity corroborates this. Through active gardening, physical exercise, and strenuous soul-searching, the new bourgeois male was envisaged as becoming pure without losing face or becoming weak. The popular American sex educator Sylvanus Stall, whose books were sold in Canada through the Methodist Church, addresses "young husbands" as follows:

> In woman, the love of home is usually more dominant than in man. By cultivating this in yourself you will produce a harmony of thought and purpose which will contribute greatly to the comfort and well-being of both. Adorn your home with your own hands. Beautify the lawn, the shrubbery, and all external surroundings.[50]

If domesticity could be reconciled with masculinity through the pale imitation of farming that was gardening, purity could also be defined so that it would not appear as exclusively female. Purity was not simply the absence of lust: it was an active, aggressive process of self-mastery that could be likened to a military campaign. It was furthermore connected to the unambiguously masculine pursuit of worldly success. Sylvanus Stall explained that purity was good not only for one's family but for one's business: he admits that some irreligious men are wealthy, but on the whole, pure thoughts are positively correlated with large bank accounts. Walking through the better part of any town, is it not obvious, he asks, that "the wealth of the nation" is "largely in the hands of Christian men and Christian women? These are the people who have the best credit, who can draw checks for the largest amounts."[51] The Canadian Salvation

Army often published stories about former male drunkards who, once saved from drink and sin, were able to impress bank managers enough to obtain loans with their new-found "character" as security.

Despite the obvious exaggeration in these stories, there was a grain of truth in the suggestion that male purity might reinforce the capitalist ethic, even in its apparently impure social Darwinist variety (as Paul Johnson's study of the differential fortunes of saved and non-saved male citizens of Rochester shows).[52] The discourse about the new reconstituted family, with a partially public mother and a partially domesticated father, was thus a discourse about class as much as about gender.

Finally, social purity had a clear racial and ethnic organization. The "whiteness" favoured by the movement was not merely spiritual but also designated (consciously or unconsciously) a skin colour. The racist fears about "the yellow peril" and about Anglo-Saxons being overrun by more fertile "races" (as they designated what are now called ethnic groups) pervaded Canadian politics and society throughout the period under study, and are receiving increasing attention from historians of immigration and of race relations. The specific contribution of the social purity movement to this general climate of racism is what needs to be highlighted here. This can be summarized by stating that the darker and hence lower races were assumed to be not in control of their sexual desires.[53] Lacking proper Christian and Anglo-Saxon training, they had not produced the right kind of self. "Racial purity" is a phrase that appears but seldom in the texts studied, but the concept underlies common phrases such as "national purity" or "national health." Moral reformers had a significant impact on immigration policies, both directly by lobbying for such innovations as the medical/moral inspection of all immigrants and indirectly by creating a climate of opinion in which certain groups were perceived as morally undesirable. The regulation of sexuality has always been linked to racial and population policies, and it is this link – rather than the far wider subject of racism in Canadian twentieth-century society – that will be analysed.

To conclude, then, the social purity movement was indeed concerned about urban vices, but its real aim was not so much to suppress as to re-create and re-moralize not only deviants from its norms but, increasingly, the population of Canada as a whole. This was a project the state could not possible have carried out; voluntary organizations played the starring role in the campaign to reconstruct the inner selves, and in particular the sexual/moral identity, of Canadians. This movement is by no means explained by being labelled as an agency of social control or a Puritan effort at censorship and repression: the movement was held together not only by its attacks on vice but by a common vision of the pure life that individuals, families, and the nation would lead in the near future. Therefore, despite the obviously repressive features of this movement, it is more appropriate to see its coercion as regulation and not as suppression or censorship: the term "regulation," which connotes preserving and shaping something and not merely suppressing it, more adequately captures the aims and the modes of operation of this movement.[54]

The entities being regulated were in the first instance the characters of individuals, with particular emphasis on sexual and hygienic habits; but the nation was also seen as held together by a common subjectivity, whose constant re-creation at the individual level ensured the continued survival of the collectivity. The collectivity thus organized had very specific class, gender, and racial/ethnic characteristics, generally supporting the domination of Anglo-Saxon middle-class males over all others but allowing women of the right class and ethnicity a substantial role, as long as they participated in the construction of women in general as beings who, despite their heroic and largely unaided deeds in maternity, were dependent on male protection. What this book seeks to reveal is how the practices that organized and consolidated these complex structures of social domination (along the axes of class, race, and gender) were both constituted by, and provided the operational basis for, the discourses of social purity and philanthropy generally.

2

The Work Of Allegories

Social purity activists relied in their work on statistics, on letters to politicians, and on other ways of organizing information and propaganda that are still familiar to us today. Because of their familiarity, the implicit politics underlying these apparently neutral techniques is often ignored. What strikes the contemporary reader of social purity documents as not modern, and therefore as value-laden and unscientific, is the extent to which social purity relied on powerful symbols woven together in bizarrely complex allegories. The discourse of this movement exhibits a kind of excess that has often been dismissed as the flowery rhetoric of the time, but that discourse needs to be seriously analysed. Such an analysis can help to explain the success of the movement by showing how certain images, words, or constellations of both resonated with pre-existing social cosmologies; it can also shed light on the practical organizational forms used by its activists.

The rhetorical "excess" is not so much a characteristic of individual symbols: light as a symbol of truth, for instance, is a recurring element in both Christian and secular Western culture from the New Testament through the Enlightenment to today's mass media. What appears to later epochs as overblown is the historically specific way in which these symbols were connected to social practices and to each other.

That the reformers studied here used an excessive grammar or a monstrous syntax is of course a judgement made from the perspective of our own prosaic and scientific style of writing about social problems; for the people for whom it was intended, the organization of symbols characteristic of social purity was invisible precisely because it was familiar. Resonating not only with the mythical content of Canadian Protestant culture but with the formal structures of turn-of-the-century social and religious discourse, the excessive metaphors we are about to dissect were neither rhetorical flourishes nor stumbling blocks in rational arguments, but were rather, to the audience, the inconspicuous vehicles in which truths about moral and social reform were conveyed to the public. As we shall see, these truths are best understood not as theoretical beliefs but as practical instructions on how the work of purity ought to be organized.

One characteristic of moral/social reform discourse was that the dichotomies of theory vs. practice, science vs. charity, were eliminated in favour of a holistic image of a knowledge that would be simultaneously scientific and charitable, true and useful. Medicine, as the useful science par excellence, provided the paradigm; the physician was perceived to combine the highest reaches of modern science with old-fashioned tender care of individual bodies and souls. Rather than explain this discursively (as I have just done), social purity activists made the same point by using metaphors. A Mrs. Spofford, active in the WCTU and in the National Council of Women, put it thus:

> Truth has ever been the most effective remedy for error, and if we would eradicate this loathsome social evil we must be willing that the searchlight of knowledge and truth be turned on at whatever cost before cleansing and healing will come to this running sore of the human family.[1]

Truth is here equated with light. But, unlike the torch of the Enlightenment or the Easter candles representing the light of Christ, the particular form of lighting advocated by Mrs. Spofford is both artificial and unidirectional. It is a "searchlight," held by someone in control in order to illuminate something else, namely "the social evil," which would hide away in the city's dark corners but for the intervention of the searchlight of surveillance (possibly embodied in the policeman's flashlight).

The light of truth, then, is not a candle, necessarily shedding light on the subject who wants to be enlightened as well as on whatever objects may be present. It is an intrusive form of lighting designed to help an observer see others but not him/herself. The authority figure implied by the text[2] is clearly a doctor, since the task at hand is "cleansing and healing." The disease is prostitution, described as a "running sore" not so much for the people involved but for "the human family" – a family apparently mothered by the National Council of Women.

The metaphor mixes two images – a collective body suffering from sores, and a searchlight – in such a way as to place prostitutes, women reformers, and male experts in a particular relationship to one another. The prostitute implied by the phrase "social evil" is the germ or virus causing the (respectable) human family to erupt in sores; the collective maternal narrator is presented as a "we" that "must be willing" to turn on the searchlight of truth and to call on authorities who can heal the sores in question. What is important here is not so much the clichéd identification of prostitution with diseases of the social body, or the equally trite identification of light with truth and knowledge, but rather the way in which certain historically specific groups are organized in relation to one another through the formal organization of images in a complex metaphor.

Another example of the use of light as a metaphor for both knowledge and healing is provided in a speech by the improbably named Reverend Virgin, an American moral reformer. Reiterating that social purity is not repressive but rather regulative, Rev. Virgin spoke as follows:

> The Purity Movement is not iconoclastic alone, leveling to dust all that it opposes; it is constructive. It gathers to itself the forces of the sunshine that falling upon the heap of compost stirs it to loathsome putrefaction till it is removed, [the sunshine that] shining upon the ice cliffs melts them to rivers that fertilize adjacent fields. . . .[3]

Here, the light of purity is not the urban searchlight but rather the rural sunshine. This light shines on social evil depicted as a farmer's heap of rotting organic matter – so intensely that it eventually turns it into beneficial compost stimulating new social growth. The rays of the sun then wander off to the northern ice cliffs (of the Canadian Arctic, perhaps), turning the sterile ice into life-giving river water to irrigate the farmers' fields previously fertilized by compost. The farmers' fields undoubtedly represent the geographical spaces of purity work; there is a clear intertextual connection with Christ's parables regarding the sowing of spiritual seeds in fertile fields.[4] The knowledge of purity is here brought by a sunlight that appears to destroy nature but in fact transubstantiates useless materials into eminently useful ones. The role of the moral reformer, then, is to shine relentlessly the light of truth on both the rotting souls of the vicious and the cold souls of the indifferent; and the eventual result is to combine the compost (that is, the rescued people) with the stream of a reformed, enthusiastic public opinion. Again, the way in which the images are mixed turns out to reveal some organizational prescriptions.

A different illustration of the activity of rescuing the vicious and fallen was provided by the Salvation Army. A large picture in their newspaper featured a group of nattily dressed men and women chatting or flirting on the edge of Niagara Falls. The powerful river and the falls, however, are teeming with a vast crowd of people plunging down into the abyss. The title (in lurid, horror-story capitals) is "The Mighty Niagara of Souls."[5]

The accompanying article (a plea for readers to get involved in the Army's evangelical and social work) begins by evoking the familiar Canadian scenario in travelogue style:

> Niagara! "Thunder of Waters," as the old Indians designated it. Everybody has heard of Niagara, but only those who have stood and gazed on the dashing, crashing, merciless volcano of water can form any real conception of the stupendous sight it presents.

As Barthes would point out, the fact that "Niagara Falls" was a cultural construct, and even in the 1890s had been shaped by the tourist industry to such a degree that people knew why it was picturesque whether they

Crowd of souls falling to their eternal damnation at the bottom of the Niagara gorge; from War Cry, *9 November 1895.* (Courtesy Salvation Army Heritage Centre)

had been there or not, is disguised by the naturalization of culture that characterizes myths in general.[6]

The river is then compared to the course of a human life: "Niagara – our life – at the first a little silver stream, then the smooth current of boyhood's river . . ." and so on. But this peaceful river/life suddenly turns into a murderous waterfall and an equally dangerous whirlpool:

> See the fond husband and breadwinner – now the dreaded drunkard or gambler – the sensualist, gripped with the iron grasp of his own lusts – the atheist . . . the lady of society, with her life of ease and plenty, whose only aim is to gratify her own pleasure, side by side with her 'fallen sister' . . . Millions are fast being hurried over the 'Niagara' of life into the whirlpool of eternity, and then where to?[7]

The reader is clearly meant to compare him/herself guiltily with the carefree picnickers standing a foot away from the Niagara of souls, heedless of the carnage going on behind their backs. Unlike texts clearly addressed to the fallen themselves, such as personal accounts of being saved followed by appeals for "you sinners" to do likewise, this representation addresses the respectable but lukewarm casual reader; the bystanders are clearly drawn, while the fallen people in the background are an indistinguishable mass. The emotional appeal of the text depends on utilizing a familiar Canadian scenario of leisure and pleasure, complete with questionable Indian etymologies and legends, and mixing it with a heterogeneous image of doom, i.e., crowds of souls falling into Hell.

The fire of Hell is here transformed into water, which allows the writer to mobilize the repertoire of images of rescue work (life rafts, beacons, and so on) so successfully deployed elsewhere.[9] Although no life rafts are portrayed, it is implied that the Army is involved in saving at least some souls from their watery grave: the horrified and guilty reader is told that "even the small amount of A FIVE DOLLAR BILL" would "keep a man from jail" or "avoid some despairing woman from a suicide's grave."

The analogy between social work and rescuing people from whirlpools and shipwrecks was a powerful one. But social purity did not stop at metaphors and metonymies. A technique that went beyond the use of rhetorical tropes was the production of various fund-raising commodities that were not only souvenirs of events or surfaces for messages, such as buttons and badges, but intrinsically meaningful objects whose very use-value embodied the work of purity. For instance, in the wake of General Booth's best-selling work on social and moral reform, *In Darkest England and the Way Out*, the English Salvation Army decided to simultaneously promote the book and market matches made in its own workshops. These were advertised in *The War Cry* as "Darkest England Matches."[10] The advertisement did not specify that one ought to reflect on the connection between lighting candles and fires and the purification of both "darkest England" and the individual match-user's soul; it did not need to. The Salvation Army elsewhere explained that the matches also symbolized purity in economic relations because they were non-phosphorous matches, produced without causing the dreaded jaw corrosion common among matchgirls. A lengthy article in *The Deliverer* – predictably entitled "Light in Darkest England" – gave a glowing account of the health of the women employed in making "Darkest England" matches. An accompanying illustration shows that the boxes featured the following messages: "Fair Wages for Fair Work" and (ironically in light of the Army's slogan "Blood and Fire") "Security from Fire."[11]

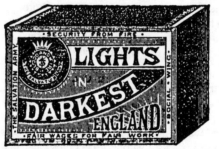

The Salvation Army's social work campaign began in England in 1890, under the slogan "Darkest England." (Ad for matches from War Cry, *courtesy Salvation Army Heritage Centre)*

Another purity product advertised by the WCTU publication *The Woman's Journal* carried a notice requesting members to buy a particular brand of soap, Happy Thought Soap.[12] The text did not explicitly say that the "beautiful thoughts" much promoted by WCTU educators[13] would be produced by using this soap, but the connection was obvious to the readers. What the text did say was that there was a pragmatic reason for this brand selection: the manufacturers were prepared to donate one cent per wrapper to the WCTU.

That the cleanliness of soap had not only Christian but also racial connotations is corroborated by another advertisement, for a soap by the name of Surprise, carried in *The Woman's Journal*. It featured a black man walking by a poster reading "Surprise makes everything white."[14]

The link between cleanliness and purity was hence perceived as actual as well as metaphorical. Another text on soap and water from the WCTU publication *What A Young Girl Ought to Know* (part of the "Self and Sex" series of sex hygiene books) shows this. The author, Dr. Mary Wood-Allen, addressing the problem of menstrual cramps and backaches, suggested the following cure: "Dishwashing is especially beneficial, as the hot water calls the blood to the hands and so helps to relieve the headache or backache." Then, not wanting to claim personal responsibility for discursive techniques in conflict with her training as a physician, she claims to be quoting someone else's religious interpretation of the meaning of dishwashing:

> This hot water represents truth, heated by Love. The soiled dishes represent myself, with my worn-out thoughts and desires. I plunge them in the loving truth and cleanse them thoroughly, then polish them with the towel of persistence and store them away in symmetrical order to await further use. So I myself am warmed and interested, and my work is well done.[15]

Here, the truth is represented not by light but by the water, which would, like truth, be rather cold if not warmed by Love. And the sinner's soul – ailing like the menstruating body of the teenage girl – is a dirty dish in need of purification through the combined efforts of heat, soap, and water, not to mention the "towel of persistence."

Taking these texts as a whole, it becomes clear that symbolism is too simple a concept to capture the complexity and the practical effects of social purity metaphors.[16] The individual metaphors or objects do more than symbolize a distinct spiritual or intellectual abstraction: they organize a universe in which water can represent a number of things (public opinion, the cleansing of the soul, even the descent into Hell) and in which the intellectual work of purity can be variously symbolized by a searchlight, the image of sunlight acting on compost, or a

"Darkest England" box of matches. The Salvation Army matches, as symbols, represent the illumination of social conditions and the spiritual fire of evangelism: but they produce actual as well as symbolic light and (to invert the relationship between rhetoric and reality once more) are a material reminder of the claim that one can produce commodities without injuring workers. The Happy Thought Soap, on its part, actually produces cleanliness, but it leads another life as a signifier of temperance and purity. These matches and bars of soap are both real and discursive entities, then; and the real effects they produce (a light, clean hands) turn with dizzying speed into signifiers of abstract entities.

The actual chain of representation may appear to be broken and confused because the discrete images, terms, and tangible objects are not arranged according to a one-to-one correspondence of signifier and signified. But the audiences knew precisely what was meant by the complex metaphors and chains of metonymies. The precision is found not in correspondences between particular representations and particular social realities; it is also not found in any simple behavioural relationship along the lines of reader X doing Y because of having read or seen a particular text. The precise logic and corresponding power of the vast whole represented here by a few examples lie rather in the character of the discourse as a whole. The structure of the discourse, that is, the complex relationships within each allegory and among different allegories/symbols, helped to lay out a framework for the work processes being promoted (becoming pure oneself, giving money so others can be saved, rescuing others). In short, what mattered was not the *what* but the *how*, the methods to be followed for purity work, which were learned not through abstract theoretical lessons but through parables, allegories, and poetic imagery.[17]

Purity work was like washing dishes, like cleaning sores, like striking matches, and like turning garbage into useful compost. The symbolic universe of social purity is not a static one in which one object or phrase stands for an abstraction, but rather a fluid one directed not at teaching people step by step but at producing in them, through inspiring imagery, the right type of consciousness as either rescuers or penitent fallen people. The discourse is both practice-oriented and concrete: once having been told that evangelism is like turning garbage into compost, the audience can be entrusted to know exactly how to put this in practice, whether or not they could produce an account of the abstract similarities between one level of social reality and another. A century later, we need to reflect on the analogies and metaphors and think abstractly about the possible common features that might have made washing dishes comparable to purity work; the intended audience, however, saw activities we would characterize as heterogeneous as identical in form if not in content. The particular things or acts mentioned are not as important as the practical relations that are established in the syntax of the allegories, which are carried into the work of social and moral reform as the subjectivity of the intended audience is transformed by their own receptivity to the images.

The discourse of purity, then, had real social power – not in the sense of creating social relations *ex nihilo*, as Gareth Stedman Jones and other users of discourse theory have assumed, but in the sense of organizing and mediating the social relations of both producers and consumers of the discourse.[18] Neither fallen women nor rescue workers were born, Athena-like, out of the heads of purity preachers. It is more accurate to state that the practices characteristic of purity activists were at once constituted by and mirrored in the grammar of the movement's allegories.

The social world organized by the tropes of purity was not populated by basically identical, empty individuals impartially interpellated by a ruling ideology that gave them thoughts and a poor excuse for subjectivity.[19] The sets of images we have discussed relied for their meaning and practical effects on a pre-existing organization of social groups, and hence of individual identities, according to various factors, notably class, gender, and race/ethnicity. This can be demonstrated through a randomly chosen example. Patriarchal gender relations were part of the spatial framework in a 1911 missionary gathering in which men dominated numerically and monopolized speech while women watched from the gallery.[20] Such a gathering undoubtedly spoke of people of colour in the third person; the position of speaking subject could only be held by a white Protestant. If that particular meeting had been regaled with the analogies quoted above, the listeners would not all have been expected to fall into a single subject position, but rather to distribute themselves in different positions according to their pre-constituted gender, class, and occupation. For instance, if any people of colour converted to Christianity had been present, such persons would have been expected to imagine themselves not as the physicians of society, but rather as simple spiritual nurses helping the white missionaries in their overseas tasks.

The language of missions and of purity work reflected pre-existing power relations (in turn always mediated by discursive relations) and relied on these for its assimilation by the audience. But while relying on common mythologies and discursive horizons to give their speeches meaning for the hearers, speakers at purity gatherings were also agents shaping and re-shaping social relations by means of organized systems of images and symbols. The discourse of social purity on the one hand relied for its meaning on the structural relations of class, gender, and race/ethnicity existing in turn-of-the-century Canada, but on the other hand actively contributed to shaping those relations in specific ways.

This is important because the deconstructive analysis of texts has often been undertaken in such a way as to delegitimize not only the oppressor but also the naive oppressed who continue to believe that "women" or "people of colour" can be described as a unified subject of history. This apolitical or even conservative use of deconstruction has often meant that class or gender analyses (particularly from a materialist perspective) have been counterposed to discourse analysis; but, as Chris Weedon and Mary Poovey have both argued in the course of reclaiming some elements of deconstruction theory for feminist projects, the critical skills of the deconstructionists can be used to unmask power as well as to decipher meaning. The decentring of the subject and the recognition of the power of discourse, while questioning triumphalist ideas about "the working class" and about "Woman," do not mean that actual women and/or workers can find no basis of unity, no common interests, or that their own discourses can be so cleverly deconstructed that no difference remains between hegemonic and counter-hegemonic discourses.[21] This shows the need to be steeped in the knowledge that history and sociology can provide, even as one undertakes deconstructive or other textual analyses. The meaning of texts is not contained within their boundaries; it can only be deciphered – and the power relations constituted by it exposed – through a thorough knowledge of the social context in which the texts were produced. In this case, the crucial social context was that established by the organizational networks responsible for moral (and social) reform; the next chapter will hence describe these institutions.

Moral And Social Reform

"The Gospel of the Toothbrush": Knowledge and Regeneration

Many writers today see the social purity movement as fundamentally contradictory. John McLaren, for instance, admits that it helped to advance the cause of social science, but he deplores the eruption of religious discourse into otherwise reputable "scientific" texts.[1] On his part, Reg Whitaker, whose analysis of the formation of the Canadian state from a Marxist perspective typically excludes sexual and moral regulation, states that the social gospel movement was sunk in "the confusion between social reformation (possibly eventuating in socialism) and moral reformation of the individual (most often taking the form of an idiosyncratic obsession with the prohibition of alcohol)."[2]

There are certainly good reasons for such an analysis. One of the genres favoured by Canadian social purity activists, the city social survey, can only be described as an amalgamation of moral judgements and sociological statistics, and this mix is found in many other texts. The mixture of evangelical purple prose and social science is extremely jarring to the reader of the late twentieth century, who tends to criticize their juxtaposition as a "confusion."

This analysis of turn-of-the-century reform efforts is based, however, on the arbitrary choice of our own standards of social science as the criteria to interpret all past discourses on social problems. Their paradigm of science was different, and it is therefore inappropriate to use our own standards to separate the scientific wheat from the moralistic chaff. Today, there is in fact a separation of moral and scientific discourses, but to read this separation back into 1910 is to commit the historiographical error of presentism.

For the reformers covered in this book, the discourses of morality and social science were not contradictory, or even separate, because moral reform and science were not conceived as separate practices. The regeneration of the individual through personal purity went hand in hand with science, both theoretical and applied. It is true that there was a certain tension between religious and secular reformers, or at least among some groups that identified themselves clearly as either one or the other;[3] however, this tension must not be elevated to the status of an absolute contradiction. For a few decades in the history of Anglo-Saxon Protestant social thought, there was a remarkable *lack of conflict* between religious and secular methodologies for changing individuals and society. As Ramsay Cook has documented, although a few old-fashioned clerics held on to an anti-scientific evangelical perspective, the intellectual leadership (for instance, the Methodist leader Rev. S.D. Chown) thought that the church could lead Canada in social science.[4] Methodist colleges pioneered the study of sociology as a university discipline, and the Toronto Methodist city mission named after Fred Victor Massey ran a series of weekly lectures on "Christianity and Social Problems" that featured several professors and two public health doctors as well as some clergymen and lay charity workers.[5]

Clergymen and charity workers, while not abandoning the language of evangelism, recognized that the church had a role in helping to organize a more equitable distribution of material resources and that this reorganization of economic life could not be brought about by old-fashioned charity but needed instead "scientific philanthropy" and sociology.[6] Kindergartens for poor children, labour exchanges for unemployed men, and other such schemes were thus seen not as replacing religion but rather as providing the material basis of a spiritual transformation among the working classes that would further the nations's moral and physical health.

The social reformers of the turn of the century constantly echoed (unwittingly) the French utopian philosopher Saint-Simon, who had stated that "the golden age" was in the future, not the past. A Nova Scotia woman declared in the opening speech at the 1896 meeting of the National Council of Women of Canada:

> This vast Dominion, stretching as it does from ocean to ocean, endowed by nature so lavishly . . . ; surely by every sign and token, whether of natural resource or racial heritage, the future of Canada will be, must be, the golden future of a great and mighty nation![7]

This patriotic optimism saw the problem of reconciling religion and science, individual regeneration and social reform, as one that might baffle the nations of tired Europe but that would be quickly overcome by "a great and mighty nation."

In the attempt to modernize religion and constitute an optimistic methodology of social reform, social workers were particularly keen on legitimizing their new profession, which had a tenuous status because it grew out of the unpaid work of church volunteers. "Social workers have not yet recognized that they are engaged in a task that requires as much scientific treatment as the problem of physical disease,"[8] a woman social worker chided her colleagues. The religious workers in turn admitted that scientific health education and social work had a place in evangelism, as the Methodist *Christian Guardian* recognized: "The gospel of the toothbrush, soap and water and fly-screens has a place in life."[9] The efforts of social workers to gain professional status certainly involved a number of key strategic moves into the state apparatus (as studies of Charlotte Whitton have shown[10]), but for this practical change to be legitimized, social work had to become a science as well as a profession – an applied but respected science. In this endeavour the churches played a key role; for instance, the fashion of doing in-depth quantitative studies of city life was popularized in Canada by the joint Methodist-Presbyterian surveys of cities done around 1910.[11]

The "personal purity" wing of social purity was also intent on acquiring scientific credentials. The Methodist Church's program for sex education of boys and girls did not rely on doctors, but both lecturers (Beatrice Brigden and W.L. Clark) tried to integrate scientific perspectives into their work and claimed that Christian child-rearing did not mean ignorance of sexuality but rather proper education.

As social purity activists sought to give their work scientific respectability, reformers in other areas (public health, urban reform) bridged the gap from their side by putting increasing emphasis on the moral regeneration of the city and its citizens. Early British reformers had believed that secular economic reforms, such as street paving and sewers, had a spiritual dimension, as Frank Mort points out in his discussion of "moral environmentalism."[12] The great Victorian statesman Edwin Chadwick had expressed an opinion common among his peers when he said: "The fever nests and seats of physical depravity are also the seats of moral depravity, disorder, and crime with which the police have the most to do."[13] Chadwick was echoed by NCWC leader Mrs. Drummond, when she argued in 1896 that to remove garbage and dirt was to attack vice at its source: "the connection between disease, dirt and degradation is closer than most people realize."[14] A prominent spokesman for the unity of social and moral reform, Toronto Controller J.O. McCarthy, put it this way:

A generation ago municipal departments were concerned with the plant, the material building, of the city . . . a new day is dawning, has dawned, and human beings, not bricks and mortar, are becoming the concern of City Fathers.[15]

Child saver J.J. Kelso, with his inimitable flair for visualizing easy solutions to large problems, wrote: "If there could be drastic measure passed requiring every house in which human beings dwell to front on a forty or sixty-foot street, or else be pulled down, how long would drunkenness, vice and ignorance exist?"[16] And along similar lines, those medical experts who worried about the "feeble-minded" always highlighted the *moral* decay that such "degenerates" symbolized, not just their own suffering or the economic burden to the taxpayer.

Both religious and secular reformers, then, shared a belief that social and moral reform were inseparable, even if there was a degree of specialization among the agencies involved in this ambitious project to transform Canadian society. Clean water and milk were necessary if working-class mothers were going to raise their children as Christian Canadians; on the other hand, no amount of physical cleanliness would by itself suffice to bring about moral reform. The Methodist city missionary S.W. Dean may have been one-sided in his views of vice and poverty, but most social reformers would have partially agreed with him when he said: "Some may be convinced that 'the sty makes the pig.' There can be no question but that the pig makes the sty, and to prevent sty conditions the porcine nature must be transformed."[17]

In the project to bring together personal regeneration and scientific urban reform, there was a crucial go-between that linked the two poles of reform both symbolically and practically: medicine. Doctors became increasingly important as leaders of both social purity and urban reform generally (with a consequent decline of clergymen), and when they spoke about immorality, their judgements had all the authority of science merely by virtue of their professional status. Doctors, while primarily in the secular realm, had by the early twentieth century managed to claim jurisdiction over many ethical issues, particularly those relating to sexuality, and thus they were in a perfect position to speak the mixed religious-scientific language of social purity. Dr. Gordon Bates, Canada's leading expert in venereal disease control, explained that "social hygiene" was not simply a euphemism for curing and preventing venereal disease but was rather a term signifying a larger vision. These diseases, he stated, are only a symptom of a "social disorder": "I would suggest that 'social hygiene' simply means social health or the establishment of normal relations between all individuals in society . . . ." To really cure venereal disease one had to provide not only sex education but education "in citizenship."[18]

One particular embodiment of the new synthesis of science, social reform, and morality was Dr. Margaret Patterson. Like many of the first generation of Ontario women medical graduates, her first practice was as a medical missionary in India. After spending six years there, she came back to Canada and proceeded to civilize the urban jungle. From 1922 to 1934 she was the first magistrate of the Women's Court in Toronto. For twelve years she served as convenor of the NCWC's Committee on Equal Moral Standards; she was also a member of the Canadian Purity Education Association. In addition, she served on various committees of the Protestant social reform organization, the Moral and Social Reform Council of Canada (MSRCC, later re-named Social Service Council of Canada), including those on criminology and on the family. She was regarded as an expert on prostitution and other forms of vice/crime, and was at the same time very influential in sex hygiene work, lecturing across the country on behalf of the YWCA and the NCWC and establishing a "Department of Moral Health" in the YWCA.[19] Even before becoming a magistrate, she heartily advocated long reformatory sentences (rather than fines) for women convicted of prostitution. Using medical language to slide from the categories of criminal justice to those of morality, she exhorted the Social Service Council's 1914 Congress:

> When will we have a proper system of treating both these morally, and usually physically sick, men and women, and a *moral hospital* to which they will all be sent on indeterminate sentence? When will these people be regarded as patients, and treated in a way that will lead to their moral recovery?[20]

Then she ominously added: "Cases of natural viciousness in either sex should be given surgical treatment. It is the only kind or safe method."

In Dr. Patterson's speech, law-and-order aims (harsh punishments, including compulsory sterilization, for those convicted of sexual and moral offences) are justified by appeals to both religion and science, or more accurately, to the peculiar unity of religion and science implicit in the term "moral hospital." In the language of evangelism, rescue homes had already been described as moral convalescent homes: but the women in them were there voluntarily, and their conversion to Protestantism, though much encouraged by the rescue workers, could not be completely forced – and could certainly not be brought about through surgical intervention. Patterson takes the idea of a rescue home, combines it with the modern lay hospital, and adds the coercive force of the correctional system: the result is a Kafkaesque "moral hospital" in which those deemed to be "naturally vicious" will be operated upon to rid them of viciousness. The combination of religion, medicine, and criminology was in this case a great deal more coercive than any of the three elements taken separately; to describe it as science marred by moralism would be to miss the point.[21]

Although Patterson's "moral hospital" was not necessarily the dream institution of other Canadian reformers, it is nevertheless true that, for the movement as a whole, the synthesis of morality and science, of evangelism and sociology, was a much more powerful ideological system than either of the two components would have been on their own. And in this synthesis, the doctor – who already had a dual image as both a scientist and a charity visitor, a person of learning and one of practical reforms – played an important role both in practice and as a symbol of reformers as a group.

In this context it is worthwhile to examine more closely one of the organizations in which Dr. Patterson was involved: the Canadian Purity Education Association. Although the name suggests a nation-wide popular movement, in fact the organization was Toronto-based and constituted almost solely by doctors. The most renowned member was undoubtedly Dr. Peter Bryce, secretary of Ontario's Board of Health from 1882 to 1904 and then Chief Medical Officer of the federal Department of Immigration. Dr. Bryce was one of the few people who was involved in purity work primarily through state organizations, but it must be noted that both of the agencies for which he worked had developed to some extent as a response to the lobbying efforts of reformers outside the state.[22] One of Bryce's contributions was to argue against the predominant view of the link between race and moral/physical health: arguing against those who would curtail south-ern European immigration, he said immigrants hailing from British slums were the ones threatening Canadian national health and purity.[23]

The less renowned members of the CPEA were primarily women doctors. Dr. Susan Fotheringham worked at Women's College for four years before going in 1918 to the same Women's Christian Medical College in Ludhiana, India, in which Margaret Patterson had also worked, and died shortly after arriving in India.[24] Dr. Laura Hamilton, also associated with Women's College Hospital before the war, was a volunteer at the Methodist Fred Victor Mission; unlike most doctors involved in public purity education, Hamilton went on to open her own general practice. Hamilton, like Patterson, combined medicine and criminology: she was a city probation investigator. She did not herself go to India but was a member of the Indian college's Canadian auxiliary, which raised the funds to send white women doctors (mostly Toronto graduates) and to provide scholarships for Indian medical and nursing students to eventually staff the college.[25] Another female physician, Dr. Ellen Burt Sherratt, was active in the Social Service Council of Canada along with Patterson. And finally, there was Dr. Jenny Gray Wildman, who was on faculty at the Ontario Medical College for Women from 1892 to 1906. She is an important figure in the history of Canadian women doctors because in 1898 she and two other women doctors founded a dispensary for poor women at the Toronto City Mission on Sackville Street, which quickly moved to the Medical College for Women and later evolved into Women's College Hospital. In the 1920s she continued to be involved in free clinics for the poor; and she, too, was involved in the auxiliary for Ludhiana Medical College.[26]

Even without sources such as letters and diaries, it is clear that the Canadian Purity Education Association was both tapping into and helping to form a network of women doctors with common interests not only in medicine but in philanthropy, both in Toronto slums and in India. These doctors were all organization women, many of them lecturing frequently through the Federation of Women's Institutes and being involved in various national as well as local committees. Further biographical research could shed light on how they experienced the connections between their status as females in a male-dominated profession and their non-medical work in philanthropy and criminal justice.

Nevertheless, as if to warn us against the dangers of seeing the social purity movement as a monolith, the man who was in 1914 president of the CPEA turns out to be rather different from the purity activists we have encountered so far. He was Dr. Albert Watson, who was on the staff of three Toronto hospitals and member of the Methodist Department of Evangelism and Social Service as well as a leader of Methodist mission work. But he seemed to be more interested in mysticism and psychical research than in purity. His obituary in the *Canadian Medical Association Journal* noted that he held seances in his home; and the titles of some of his many works include *Love and the Universe, The Immortals and other Poems*, and *Mediums and Mystics*.[27] Dr. Watson was clearly closer to the cosmic consciousness of Dr. Richard Maurice Bucke[28] than to the orthodox religiosity of most of the purity movement. His presidency of the CPEA may be an indication that the Whitmanite and spiritualist current of Ontario social thought (represented, for instance, by Flora MacDonald Denison in her post-suffrage phase) was not completely isolated or separate from the social purity movement.

The Canadian Purity Education Association, which was active only around 1906-14 and was certainly not a major organization,[29] nevertheless shows the attempt by Toronto-based doctors (mostly women) to take some control over the work of purity education. Its president, Dr. Watson, gave a report on its work to the Methodist Board of Temperance and Moral Reform in 1912. The Board's minutes state that "it was agreed that we cooperate with this society in the spread of purity literature and the education of the people along the line of sex problems and the proper training of children."[30] But in this and subsequent years the Board continued to pursue its own work and did not seem to be enthusiastic about collaborating with doctors. The CPEA may have been a failed attempt by doctors to take control over the synthesis of religion and science signified by the term "purity education." Or, if we do not assume conspiratorial intentions, the CPEA may have vanished from history precisely because the purity work done by churches and lay charity workers already included a scientific perspective.

Be that as it may, it is remarkable that there never was a Canadian equivalent to the British and American associations for moral and social hygiene of the 1910s, organizations that were physician-led and used a "purer" scientific discourse. There is in Canada very little evidence of conflict between doctors and church workers. Gradually, doctors (and other professionals, such as professors of social work and sociology) came to be seen as more legitimate authorities on social problems than ministers, but this was a slow process without much evidence of struggle. The synthesis of medicine, morality, and social reform was a powerful one, and the various wings of the movement all had a stake in preventing its fragmentation.

The Organization of Purity

The modest practical effect of the Canadian Purity Education Association points to a larger pattern: in Canada, purity work was largely conducted not through specially designed groups but through already existing organizations devoted to moral, social, religious, and/or gender reform work. The character of the organization largely determined how purity was interpreted in both theory and practice. A survey of these organizations' work will show both the breadth and depth of purity work in Canada, and reveal the similarities and differences in the interpretations that different organizations gave to the general belief that purity was important.

One very important commonality among the organizations is that they were overwhelmingly voluntary bodies existing outside the state. After 1918, there was an increasing tendency for state organizations, especially those in the fields of child welfare, social work, and health, to undertake moral reformation schemes, many of which had their roots in the purity movement. Before World War One, however, social work and child welfare were almost completely in private hands even though the state, especially the provinces, often funded their work; and the health system's moral-policing bodies (notably those dealing with venereal disease and the feeble-minded) were in their infancy where they existed at all. The few militant purity advocates within the state apparatus, such as MP John Charlton or Ontario's Superintendent of the Feeble-Minded, Dr. Helen MacMurchy, saw themselves as waging an uphill battle to convince a reluctant state to take strong measures against vice and degeneracy. Their perception was shared by moral reformers outside the state, who felt that even after successfully obtaining legislation (the Lord's Day Act of 1906, anti-procuring measures in 1913), the enforcement of these measures by judges and policemen left much to be desired.

There were some exceptions, of course, such as Toronto's vigilant morality police officers, whose pioneering work against gambling, houses of ill fame, and Sunday commerce was emulated elsewhere in Canada on a smaller scale. There was also a fleeting effort in 1912 – apparently suggested by BS. Steadwell, head of the more centralized American purity movement – to lobby the Ontario government for a "new provincial bureau of purity" with a "provincial police for the regulating and abolishing of social vice." Such an effort, linked to the purity movement's perception of municipal politics (and hence municipal police forces) as potentially corrupt, was probably little more than an attempt to shame the always reluctant municipalities to do more against prostitution.[31] But as a rule, the leaders in purity work came from outside the state and worked through the extensive network of private philanthropic agencies whose contribution to Canadian social life has often been unrecognized by historians focusing on the growth of the state.

These private bodies interacted heavily with the state, however. They organized their work with a view to influencing state legislation and policy, as well as setting up pilot projects in public education and rescue work that might then be taken over, or at least funded, by the state. The state in turn responded to the pressure from these organizations and from public opinion as moulded by the moral reformers by taking moral initiatives with greater or lesser enthusiasm. The private bodies were much more powerful than their successors of today: in the absence of large government bureaucracies and associations of professionals, churches and women's groups commanded a great deal of respect and were in many ways treated as experts, not as opinionated interest groups.

Methodists and Presbyterians

Moral reform work drew churches into close collaboration with the state. This move was not without controversy, since a stream in Christianity preaches unconcern with worldly policy problems. The Methodists, whose theology was more liberal and whose leaders since Egerton Ryerson had been crucially implicated in Canadian state formation,[32] did not experience as many anxieties about this, but the more old-fashioned Presbyterians clearly had qualms. The Presbyterians had participated eagerly in prohibition efforts and were the main force behind the Lord's Day Alliance, which sought a total ban on Sunday shopping and commercial leisure activities; however, lobbying for repressive legislation was different from engaging in social work that drew the saved and the unsaved together in practical work. Constructive collaboration with the state was defended by Rev. G.C. Pidgeon, head of moral and social reform work, in an interesting analogy in which the state is portrayed as the masculine practical force while the church, referred to as "she," is seen as providing the spiritual leadership. "The state is not immoral," argued Rev. Pidgeon, claiming that because the Canadian state embraced Christian principles "it is absurd to treat it as wholly evil."[33]

The Methodists were the leaders in both theoretical and practical purity work. Their Department of Temperance and Moral Reform was set up in 1902, and although at first it merely continued the temperance and prohibition work that had existed since Canadian Methodist unification in 1885, by 1908 it was promoting civics education for children, the suppression of gambling and obscene literature, the need to enforce the abortion law, and various other causes.[34] The Department had a smallish budget, a fraction of the amount devoted to missions; but it was headed by the extremely influential Rev. Samuel Dwight Chown, who in 1910 became General Superintendent of the Methodist Church. At first two field secretaries travelled around the provinces to spark interest in this new branch of work; in the 1910s there were three field secretaries, plus two lay purity educators who also travelled extensively. The Department lobbied the federal government to raise the age of consent, ban liquor, criminalize adultery, pass tougher obscenity legislation, and provide more modern care for criminals and the feeble-minded. It also issued pamphlets on such topics as the dangers of white slavery in Canada; and, after 1910, it linked sexual with national purity in advocating stricter control over immigrants;

> While many of our non-Anglosaxon population are amongst the best of the people from their native lands . . . it is lamentable that such large numbers have come to Canada during the last decade bringing a laxity of morals, an ignorance, a superstition and an absence of high ideals of personal character or of national life. . . . [They] may constitute a danger to themselves and a menace to our national life.[35]

In the absence of city-wide or congregation studies, it is difficult to evaluate the impact of the Department at the grassroots level. One innovative aspect of its work, the two lay purity educators, was influential with ordinary Canadians, as we shall shortly see. There is also little doubt that much of the legislation about prostitution, procuring, importing opium, and banning "obscene" texts and plays that was passed in the decades from 1890 to 1920 owed its existence to the efforts of Chown and his colleagues, who claimed to speak directly for about 18 per cent of Canada's population and indirectly for the two-thirds of Canadians who were Protestants.[36]

A final area of influence was the contribution of Chown and others to shaping the intellectual elite of Canada; in 1907-08, the Methodist Board of Temperance and Moral Reform began to give lectures on "sociology" at Victoria College in Toronto and in Winnipeg's Wesley College. In the absence of university departments of sociology, this teaching – which combined both practical and theoretical concerns, the split between social work schools and sociology departments not having yet occurred – was crucial in beginning to define the scientific study of social problems. Ramsay Cook's study shows that Chown was responsible for introducing the ideas of Toynbee and others to Canada in such a way as to reconcile religion and social science: in Chown's own words, "the perfect sociology, perfectly applied, will realize the Kingdom of God on Earth."[37]

The Presbyterians were less interested in sociology and social work. Their main purity activist, Rev. John G. Shearer, appears to have been a man of limited intellect and narrow views. From 1899 to 1906 he was the indefatigable general secretary of the Lord's Day Alliance, and after the Alliance's success in obtaining the federal Lord's Day Act he was asked to organize a Presbyterian counterpart to the Methodist Department of Temperance and Moral Reform. He headed this department from 1907 to 1915. In 1909 he became one of the founders of the Moral and Social Reform Council of Canada (MSRCC) and headed that Council's subcommittee, the National Committee for the Suppression of the White Slave Traffic; from 1915 on he devoted all his considerable energies to the MSRCC, renamed Social Service Council of Canada in an effort to appeal to lay social workers and reformers. In 1918 he became the editor of that Council's magazine, *Social Welfare*, Canada's leading social work publication of the 1920s. He died in 1925 and the Social Service Council, which had relied on Shearer's personal energy to a large extent, in turn declined.[38]

A self-described Puritan of the twentieth century, Shearer comes closer than any other figure studied here to the stereotype of the moral reformer keen on prohibiting pleasures and uninterested in people's

Rev. John G. Shearer led the campaign for the 1906 Lord's Day Act and subsequently headed the Presbyterian Church's moral reform department. (Courtesy Thomas Fisher Rare Book Library)

welfare. The records of the Lord's Day Alliance show that it was an organization less concerned with building character than with stamping out vice and establishing what they called "the English Sunday" as an invented Canadian tradition. Viciously attacking Orthodox Jews and Seventh Day Adventists, who had complained that their freedom of religion was being infringed by the Sunday-observance laws, the Alliance said that the keeping of Saturday rather than Sunday was "alien to Canada" and that Jews and others ought to be grateful for being in Canada at all: "Is it too much to ask, therefore, that having sought our land FOR THEIR OWN GOOD, they should conform to our laws, and recognize the civil customs prevailing in the life of our own people?"[39] The 1911 annual report of the organization echoed this anti-Semitic definition of "our own people" and constructed English/Scottish Protestant customs as native to Canada: "a number of Jews in Toronto, at Englehart, and other places, who have found asylums and home comforts in Canada when driven by persecution from other lands, do not scruple to break our laws while enjoying the protection they afford them."[40]

While the Methodists tried desperately to be modern and enlightened and to give positive images of the pure life, for Shearer purity was largely a matter of negation.

> We may not want to copy the Puritans in every particular, but, in their respect for righteousness, law, order, religion, and the Lord's Day, we could stand a good deal more Puritanism than we are getting . . . . Let [our] Puritanism be that of the twentieth century – wise, tolerant, gracious, and inflexible . . . let us go ahead in the present crusade unterrified by all sneering cries of 'puritanical legislation' raised by cavilling newspapers that would cater to an evil-minded crowd.[41]

Under Shearer, Presbyterian reform did not even put much emphasis on the established evangelical practice of rescue work. A home for fallen, abandoned, and/or delinquent girls was set up jointly by Presbyterians and Methodists in Truro, N.S., but this was a privately operated reformatory, not a voluntary rescue home in the evangelical-feminist tradition. Although paying some lip service to the principles of voluntary reformation, Shearer was a firm believer in prisons as the place for prostitutes and other sinners, as he said when questioned during the Winnipeg Royal Commission on vice: "I would think this, that they [prostitutes] could be convicted and detained in prison unless they show a disposition to lead better lives. If they did instruction should be provided for them."[42]

Shearer was responsible for a combined sex-and-race panic in the city of Winnipeg in 1910 – or more accurately, a panic in Toronto about vice in Winnipeg. After a month's tour of western Canada in the company of purity activists and two American detectives, Shearer returned to his Toronto base and gave sensationalist news to the papers: "Social Evil Runs Riot in Winnipeg" was the *Globe* headline.[43] Shearer claimed that the chief of police had personally organized a vice district in Winnipeg by suggesting to the most prominent madam that she and her colleagues relocate their scattered businesses to one fairly isolated downtown district; he also claimed that the brothels were illegal liquor dens and that the $100 quarterly fines were simply licensing by another name. These allegations were proven to be largely true by a subsequent royal commission. Shearer, however, had also made allegations of graft in the police department, and these were unsubstantiated. The honour of the police, mayor, police commission, and other authorities was successfully defended throughout the Royal Commission hearings in the winter of 1910-11; and in the subsequent civic election the mayor was re-elected by a comfortable margin.[44] The racial aspects of the moral panic, however, went unchallenged. Shearer had claimed that "most of the dens of vice are owned by Chinese and Japanese. No doubt many of the girl inmates are owned by them also." He further claimed that Native people sold "their" women to white men.[45]

Shearer, who was extremely uncomfortable when put in the position of having to substantiate his charges of graft before a judge, seems to have been chastened by the Winnipeg experience, and subsequently he avoided going to the press with such stories. Speaking at a 1911 WCTU convention in Calgary, Shearer apparently said that "more could often be accomplished by quiet persuasion applied to governments than by public protests. He promised to take up the matter of the Calgary brothels with the Alberta government."[46] And indeed, Shearer's work through the Moral and Social Reform Council of Canada consisted largely of lobbying the government for tougher anti-vice legislation, organizing conferences, and quietly pressuring both state and non-state bodies of experts and law enforcers, through personal contact and letters and through the Council's magazine, *Social Welfare*. He may indeed have been correct in his estimation that such methods were more successful; he was never again subjected to judicial questioning about potentially libelous claims.

Shearer's successor as head of moral and social reform work for the Presbyterian Church, Rev. George Pidgeon, appears to have been less fond of thunderous conservative rhetoric and more sympathetic to the social gospel. While continuing Shearer's zealous pursuit of tougher laws, he stressed the need for education, and, unlike Shearer, he discussed the evils caused by private property and by women's subordinate position. In an account of why his department was organized, entitled "Moral and Social Reform," Pidgeon's list of "difficulties in the way" began with the traditional "lust for sin and greed for gain." But he quickly moved on to denounce "the materialistic basis of our criminal laws," which cared more about property than moral welfare, "particularly of women" – and, following the feminist argument, he went on to compare the low sentences given to seducers and rapists to those given for minor property crimes.[47]

It is clear, then, that even among the most theologically and politically conservative moral reform organizations, there was no unity of views: attacks on male sexual violence and quasi-socialist attacks on the evils of production for greed existed comfortably side by side with virulent racism and extreme sexual and social conservatism. It is perhaps therefore appropriate to describe some of the work of the most radical of the moral reform organizations, the WCTU.

The Woman's Christian Temperance Union

The American WCTU had begun in Ohio in the 1850s, as groups of evangelical women stood and prayed outside or even inside barrooms in an effort to shame men into avoiding bars and turn them into responsible, domesticated husbands. The initial goal of "temperance" was to be achieved through moral suasion. Quite soon, however, and in Canada from the beginning of WCTU work in the 1870s, state-legislated prohibition became the preferred path to purity. The WCTU in Canada was largely a small-town organization, particularly in the West. While drawing on women who already worked in Protestant churches to maintain the cross-gender social bonds of congregations, its exclusively female membership gave many Protestant women their first glimpse of autonomous organization.[48.]

Although temperance was the original focus of the WCTU, the Canadian organization devoted much of its time and educational resources to other aspects of reform, particularly anti-smoking and social purity work; from 1886, the newspaper of the Ontario WCTU was subtitled "Devoted to the Advocacy of Temperance and Moral Reform." Its emblem consisted of a Bible, a picture of a bourgeois family with six children reading around a fireplace, and the slogan "For God and Home and Native Land."[49] WCTU members usually wore a knot of white ribbon on their dress, in order both to recognize each other and to symbolize the militant purity that was the positive vision underlying their prohibition work. A poem entitled "The

White Ribbon" made these connections using the Canadian archetype of snow:

> Pure and unsullied as new driven snow,
> Fair with the whiteness of the lily, gleams
> O'er all the earth like sunshine's rarest beams,
> The spotless honour of our little bow. . . .
> Go, ribbon white! entwine the world around,
> Carry thy message over land and sea.
> Save from the drink all those within its snares,
> Guide each aright who now the emblem bears.[50]

Both provincial and Dominion WCTUs set up specific departments of Social Purity. These were not the top priority for most women, as pleading reports from their superintendents make clear, but they performed an important educational role in telling women how they should talk to their children about sexuality, reproduction, and family life. It is significant that the Purity departments were renamed "Moral Education and Mothers' Meetings," since the mothers' meetings became one of the two main practices of the department, the other one being school lectures on purity by the Ontario WCTU's purity agent, Arthur W. Beall.[51] That these talks were not merely condemnations of vice but had a positive character is clear from a report from the local WCTU president in Oshawa: "Miss Murray's address on a 'White Life' was of a highly interesting character. She held the audience spellbound as she lifted their thoughts upward, and in simple language pictured the beautiful purity in which God intended men and women to live."[52]

Just as anti-alcohol agitation gave respectable women an opportunity to condemn male domestic violence and financial irresponsibility indirectly, so the agitation for purity had a certain anti-male character. Commenting on the joking way in which MPs had debated a proposal to raise the age of consent for girls, WCTU women took the opportunity to uphold purity and denounce the all-male character of Parliament in the same breath. The debates in the House, they said, "show only too plainly our legislators make the laws for the protection for their own sex."[53] The WCTU consistently agitated for the "equal standard" (the opposite of the double standard), against tolerated prostitution, in favour of a higher age of consent, and in favour of women's suffrage.

The WCTU also pursued work against "obscene" literature through its department of Purity in Literature, Art and Fashion,[54] while the related department of Health and Heredity was largely responsible for popularizing eugenic ideas among ordinary Canadian women, in the guise of what Frances Willard called "the religion of the body."[55]

Eugenic education, however, was only one of the department of Health and Heredity's priorities. Others included promoting physical education in schools, dress reform, and "food reform." The latter two issues, which have been unjustly neglected by social historians, referred to efforts to establish "rational" (as opposed to fashionable) dress among middle-class women and to introduce what we would now call health food into middle-class homes. Wearing tight corsets and eating too much meat or overly spiced food were denounced as contributing to the degeneration of the (Anglo-Saxon) race, while tobacco and caffeine were seen as corrupting soul and body, just like alcohol. The WCTU sought not only to ban one particular substance from Canadian life but totally to reform both the spiritual and physical lives of its people.

Throughout, a language of social motherhood was used to justify these reform efforts. For instance, the superintendent of the Moral Education department stated in 1910 that the three mottoes of the department were: (1) "A white life for two" (that is, the single standard of sexual morality); (2) "Every child has the right to be well born"; and (3) "Save the children and you mold the nation."[56] The meaning of the last two slogans was explained elsewhere by Sara R. Wright, president of the Dominion WCTU. Quoting a U.S. doctor who reported to President Theodore Roosevelt on the dangers of tobacco and alcohol, she said:

> Dr. MacNichol further added with startling emphasis: 'A degeneracy appalling in magnitude threatens to destroy this Republic. Let this degeneracy continue at the same rate for 100 years and there will not be a native-born child five years old in the United States.' We Canadians can claim no exemption from the same cause: every alcohol-tainted child is not only deprived of its rightful heritage of being well-born, but becomes a real menace to the development of the highest and best in our national life.[57]

While pursuing this eugenic line of reasoning, the WCTU women did not see themselves as mere servants of the race; rather, they legitimized their feminist valuation of women's reproductive work by linking women's actual experience of child-bearing and child-rearing to racist and imperialist discourses on race.

The racism of the WCTU, even if derived largely from male sources on eugenics and racial degeneration, was not an external factor contaminating their feminism; racism was integral to their view of feminism, of woman's mission as "mother of the race." Reproduction and nurturing constituted the link between women and the race; since women's nurturing role was the keystone of their feminism, and this nurturing was perceived as involving the reproduction not of human beings in general but of their race in particular, racism and feminism were integral parts of a single whole.[58]

Having specified the racially specific form of their feminism, it is important to note that the language and practices of the WCTU were more feminist than anything found in other organizations of the time. The WCTU also played the central role in mobilizing support for women's suffrage, not only so that women could vote for prohibition but as a right that women (of the right race and religion) ought to enjoy. In 1912-14, the pages of the *White Ribbon Bulletin* were full of positively ecstatic descriptions of the courageous English suffragettes, and there was no editorial attempt to distance the Canadian WCTU from violent English tactics. Women's entry into non-traditional professions was also much praised.

In general, the WCTU women confined its work to other women of the same ethnicity and religion: they did not undertake much philanthropic work, at least not as WCTU members.[59] They were thus more like a contemporary women's group than like a nineteenth-century charity, with mothers' meetings as the equivalent of consciousness raising. They did carry out some work among children and younger women, particularly after suffrage and prohibition had both been won. For instance, they were instrumental in the Travellers' Aid work that sought to guide young women coming into the city, keep them from white slavers, and ensure that they did not engage in morally deviant conduct.[60] But young women were the particular preserve of the more philanthropic YWCA: the WCTU was distinguished by the fact that it was set up by Anglo-Saxon Protestant (and largely middle-class) women to uphold their own interests and seek relevant changes in Canadian society.

National Council of Women

The National Council of Women of Canada was similar in its make-up and general aims, but it was less feminist (they endorsed suffrage only very late, in 1910) and it was also not exclusively Anglo-Saxon and Protestant. Founded in 1894 by Lady Aberdeen, an English aristocrat who had headed the Women's Industrial Council (a British middle-class women's bureau of social research and advocacy group for women workers) before coming to Canada as the wife of the Governor General, it was from the beginning close to the federal state. One sign of this was Lady Aberdeen's fairly successful efforts to include substantial numbers of Francophone Catholic women and a handful of Jewish women in the NCW. Its non-denominational character caused some friction, however, since both the YWCA and the WCTU refused to join officially due to the NCW's custom of silent prayer (instead of the Protestant prayer favoured by the more evangelical groups); further-more, Lady Aberdeen was criticized for serving alcoholic drinks at official functions.[61] Its less religious character, however, did not mean that it was in any way less concerned about purity; rather, the slightly more secular orientation meant that it tended to emphasize coercive state measures over face-to-face philanthropic work in the evangelical tradition. It was a powerful force in favour of tough enforcement of obscenity law;[62] and it played a key role in beginning to agitate about the dangers that "feeble-minded" women of child-bearing age posed to the public. It also joined with churches and others in lobbying the state for a higher age of consent for girls, stronger anti-procuring laws, special women's and children's courts, and institutions for the feeble-minded.

Basically a coalition of already existing groups, the NCW had less of a local base than the WCTU; there were local Councils of Women in major cities, but the NCW probably had little effect among rural and small-town women. The Local Councils pursued a variety of activities in accordance with the general aims of the national organization, and in this work they were encouraged by Lady Aberdeen to investigate matters properly, collect statistics, and learn to make reports. One instance of this was the Toronto Local Council's participation in the Social Survey of 1915, which attempted to map out vice in Toronto and seek scientific/moral remedies.[63] The NCW's organizational form was different from the WCTU in being less geared to self-help among women and more concerned about getting the ear of the state. For instance, its Standing Committee on Objectionable Printed Matter managed to obtain the post office's list of prohibited publications even though it was confidential. As a result, the Victoria Local Council got to work and quickly discovered that some prohibited books were for sale in the city bookstores, while the Toronto Council made a tour of shop windows and decided that objectionable postcards ought to be censored as well as books and films: "A censor for postcards is suggested, and it is recommended that journals be invited to refuse publicity or give prominence to scandals, murders, indecent happen-ings and certain medical advertisements [for abortifacients and v.d. remedies]."[64]

Nevertheless, the NCW, like the Methodist Church, tried to give its purity work a positive character. On the topic of obscenity, much areas for services, and allowed people to wander in and out of these halls rather than insist that people purposefully set out for church dressed in Sunday clothes.

The stories published in *The War Cry* about people who fell into alcoholism and suicidal thoughts due to grinding poverty, only to be given a warm bed and an instant community in the Army when they converted, ring true to the experiences of the poor even though – or perhaps because – they are full of clichés and melodramatic conventions. Domestic violence, drinking, unemployment, and crime were, after all, real experiences of the poor, not just figments of social workers' imaginations. Although the Army insisted on conversion as the all-purpose solution, it gave some poor people a new family that cared for their material needs even if it demanded that they engage in evangelistic work. Furthermore, the Army was extremely authoritarian, but it was meritocratic, and most of its leaders both in Canada and in Britain do not appear to have come from the social and economic elite that dominated mainstream Protestantism.

One reason for the Army's popularity was its effective use of working-class forms of entertainment and communication. The rousing songs accompanied by trombones and tambourines were much closer to working-class tastes than the ponderous organ-accompanied hymns of respectable Methodists; the sharp uniforms of the officers appealed to people's sense of ritual and spectacle, while conveniently erasing the distinction between those who could afford many good clothes and those who had only one old outfit; and the lively melodramatic stories, engravings, and poems of Army publications were similar to the penny dreadfuls and ballads about famous criminals enjoyed by the poor. The Army had a very keen eye for popular journalism, as was noted by Evangeline Booth's biographer: "The Salvation Army has taken the good in life and made it as sensational as the evil. It has made the spiritual as sensational as the material. The melodrama had been devoted to downfall. It now included uplift."[73]

The Army's success thus hinged on its individual work, primarily with working-class or lower-middle-class people. The recruits were often young, single, and rootless, and the Army gave them a home, a job, security, a purpose in life, and a spiritual strength that was not to be found in the ordinary lives of the urban poor. In this sense, the Army was not far from its competitors, the socialist parties, who denounced the Army at great lengths partly because in some ways they were competing for the same social terrain.[74] (It is perhaps worth noting that it was the socialists who adopted Salvation

emphasis was put on the need to provide pure books rather than simply banning impure ones:

> I believe that the prohibition of these papers and books would be a very good thing, but I believe that substitution is better than prohibition or even suppression. (Applause.) We want to substitute for all this pernicious stuff – we want to substitute that which is bright, healthful, and pleasant.[65]

The London, Ontario, Local Council had librarians not only remove certain books from shelves but also encourage patrons "to read less fiction and to substitute books of a more educational character." The Committee on Objectionable Printed Matter said approvingly that "London also approves of the advisability of making this committee one for the encouragement of good literature, rather than confining it to a suppression of bad."[66]

The NCW's encouragement of pure literature and pure thoughts, however, was somewhat academic, since unlike the WCTU it did not sponsor mothers' meetings or do other grassroots work. Yet, it was precisely the lack of a single issue or particular geographical or religious base that made it important, and as a powerful national coalition the NCW helped to bring Canadian women's groups closer to the international women's movement. It fostered research and political skills among its members; and it included traditional charity and church workers but also appealed to the secularly oriented doctors and social workers, and hence formed an important organizational link between the nineteenth and the twentieth centuries. Through the practices now known as networking, the National Council of Women constituted "the women of Canada" on a national rather than strictly religious, ethnic, or local basis, and although the WCTU also performed this function (and undoubtedly was much more effective at the local level), the somewhat broader basis of the NCW made it crucial in the constitution of a feminine/maternal presence in the project of building a "pure" nation.[67]

The YWCA

The roster of national women's organizations in this period was completed by the Young Women's Christian Association. Like the WCTU and the NCW, it was not primarily aimed at relieving the poverty or changing the habits of the very poor but was rather aimed at women who were already respectable, in this case, young working women and, to a lesser extent, college women.[68] There was, however, a class difference between the women who ran the YWCA and those who used its boarding homes and recreational facilities, a difference compounded by the generational gap, which led the lady reformers to treat adult working women as girls, as daughters in need of guidance. The "daughters" had to be certified pure; Adelaide Hoodless, president of the Hamilton YWCA, explained this in 1896:

> The present design is not to provide a refuge for fallen women. The work of reclaiming the unfortunate is one of the noblest that can engage the attention of the philanthropists; but it is not the work of which the ladies who now ask attention to their plans have undertaken. Their scheme is, and necessarily must be, wholly distinct from any work of reclamation. *The two cannot be united*. For if fallen women were admitted to the rooms of the Young Women's Christian Association, respectable young women would be driven away.[69]

The respectable boarders were nevertheless subject to a thorough system of surveillance, as though their purity and probity were always in question. One of them complained to the Board of the Toronto YWCA Boarding Home:

> Ladies, I regret to have to trouble you . . . I came here with the expectation of finding a kind and Christian home but at present it cannot take that name. It is a libel on the word Christian . . . as it is we who pay our [$3 per week] are treated as though we were taken of [sic] the streets and should be thankful for even a crumb of bread. I am not one who has just left my mother's knee but have taught school for five years. . . . I never was treated by servants as I am by those who call themselves Ladies.[70]

The boarding homes were designed to meet the practical need for cheap housing for urban working women; but they were also envisioned as all-female spaces supervised by certified Christian matrons, promoting proper domestic habits and purity.

The YWCA's work among college students, from 1886 onward, was primarily evangelistic, aimed at combatting the secularist and free-thinking dangers of a college education. It also trained women for possible paid work as YWCA secretaries or as foreign or domestic missionaries. In the mixed and secularist atmosphere of the campuses, it created all-female spaces where femaleness was defined through evangelical Protestantism.

It is clear that the mainstream women's organizations (WCTU, NCW, YWCA) were generally aimed at preserving the purity and respectability of middle-class or respectable working-class womanhood. The WCTU,

for instance, believed it was more important that the social elite example by having alcohol-free parties than that alcoholics be p ally helped. Believing in the filter-down-through-the-classes the moral values, their efforts in respect to the poor were largely co to seeking prohibitive legislation to remove bars and liquor sho

The Salvation Army

This orientation, based partly on a genuine need for middle women to get together with women like themselves and agitate fo own needs and beliefs, and partly on a distaste for personally de with the poor and fallen, meant there was an opening f organization that would not shirk face-to-face contact with crim prostitutes, and alcoholics, and that would devote itself to intera with them rather than creating and re-creating the social bon respectability. This organization was the British Salvation A brought to Canada by English immigrants in the mid-1880s. Canadian Salvation Army's work will be analysed in some deta Chapter 6; but a few comments to contrast it with the other orga tions involved in purity work are in order here.

Other organizations (notably the Methodist Church, of which Salvation Army was a kind of schism) were often dismayed by Army's aggressive outdoor evangelism, by the freedom with w their women officers walked through slums (often with loud b bands), and by their generally "vulgar" methods and rejection of l theology and traditional rituals.[71] But at the same time, the A obtained a grudging admiration: it was recognized that the Army fi a major gap in the spectrum of moral and social reform work. Th typically described in the obituary for General Booth published in WCTU's national magazine:

> [T]he women of that Army, heroic 'slum angels' have penetra the dens and vile places of the vast centres of humanity, and today continuing this great effort in raising a degraded womanh into better life and nobler ideals. . . . Wherever the emblem of Salvation Army has been planted the outcast has been reclaim the drunkard has been set free, and degraded men and wom elevated to higher conditions.[72]

The Army broke with many of the customs that had ensured that churches remained middle-class despite their lip service to the idea gathering in the "unchurched masses." For instance, they had no p rents and did not even have church buildings: they rented halls in p

Army hymns and put socialist lyrics to them, rather than the other way around.) Be that as it may, while socialists sought to organize the wretched of the earth on a collective basis, seeing individual growth and fulfilment as something for after the revolution, the Salvation Army stressed the immediate personal (especially psychological) needs of its clientele and thought that "social regeneration" would follow more or less automatically "when men shall have so learned to live, that the vicious, the criminal, the depraved and the dangerous part of the community shall have been brought into a state of comfort, decency, and usefulness."[75]

Having sketched out the main organizations involved in purity and moral reform work, let us now turn to a more specific discussion of the purity-education work carried out by some of Canada's first sex educators.

"Light On Dark Corners": Purity Education In Canada

The work of the purity movement on sex education has been generally dismissed as unscientific, anti-sexual, repressive, and plain silly. Michael Bliss's article, virtually the only relevant Canadian source, although showing that the ideas of the church-sponsored educators were not substantially different from those of the medical profession, treats purity education as somewhat of a historical joke. Assuming Freud to be the beginning of real sexual science, he uses Freud's repression hypothesis to judge the work of his predecessors, stating for instance that the work of the WCTU's Purity Department was "specifically designed to promote the doctrine of sexual repression in all its manifestations."[76]

The bad press of purity education, also known as "sex hygiene," can be traced back to educators who, in the 1910s and 1920s, claimed to be pioneering a secular and scientific view of sex and sex education. In England, Havelock Ellis, and in the U.S., Columbia Teachers' College professor Maurice Bigelow, presented themselves as "modern" by decrying purity educators as old-fashioned: in building up their own constituency they presented a distorted view of their competitors.[77] Bigelow made a distinction between purity education, which he regarded as anti-sexual, and modern sex education. His criteria, however, do not stand up to scrutiny. He stated, for instance, that purity education was pessimistic, even "depressing," when in fact many purity educators were cheerful in the extreme and preferred glorifying virtuous sex to condemning vice, while the eugenic views of the modern sex educators were in some ways more anti-sexual and "depressing" than anything in the nineteenth century.

Bigelow's agenda included the delegitimization not only of evangelical neo-Puritans but also of the feminist purity activists (notably Christabel Pankhurst in England) who had discussed the social evil and venereal disease as part of their campaign to claim women's rights. Pankhurst's admittedly alarmist views about males as the source of venereal disease and her perhaps unfortunate slogan of "Votes for Women and Chastity for Men" became Bigelow's straw-persons as he preached a modern, "post-feminist" view of sex education:

> Such depressing interpretations of life are bound to come from the radical type of 'purity' preaching based on the sexual mistakes of the past and on the lives of animals. A similar pessimistic view regarding the function of eating might be based on mistakes of drunkards and gluttons and on the habits of the porcine family.[78]

As in the case of Havelock Ellis, the superior tone adopted by Bigelow toward purity educators was intertwined with a masculinist and heterosexist attempt to ridicule the feminist aspect of social purity work.[79]

One of Bigelow's criticisms of "sex hygiene" was that it allegedly singled out sex without examining sexuality as a whole in its sociological and ethical aspects. But for the purity educators sexuality was not an isolated activity that ought to be curtailed for the sake of virtue, but rather a central aspect of human life that ought to be revered and treated in all intellectual and moral seriousness. From Elizabeth Blackwell in the 1870s to the English scientists J.A. Thomson and Patrick Geddes in the 1910s, they were agreed that sexual feelings are "normal and necessary," and that they ought not to be suppressed or denied but rather channelled and guided: they "need to be firmly controlled, indeed, but not silenced; for in them, or intertwined with them, lie all the elements which have made life fullest and most beautiful . . . ."[80]

Purity educators certainly denounced sexual excess; but they also denounced prudishness and warned parents that the road to sexual hell was paved with well-meaning attempts to keep children "innocent." The basic opposition was not that between innocence and experience, but rather that between right knowledge (acquired from well-informed mothers and from experts) and wrong knowledge acquired from peers and from "bad books." This was illustrated in the frontispiece of the much-reprinted American book *Light on Dark Corners: Searchlight on Health*, which portrayed a young couple facing a fork on the road. One path was labelled "sex hygiene" and climbed up on steps marked "Education, Love, Modesty, Temperance, Health, Ambition, Sanity, Normalcy," and so on, to a sunlit hilltop with a gorgeous house behind which the sun of "Happiness" was setting. The other road, labelled not sexual experience but "False Modesty," plunged down into a dark sea of "Ignorance, Lust, Obscenity, Disease, Defective Children, Lunacy, Poverty, Coarseness, and Senility."

The refrain that "intelligent purity is supremely better than blind innocence"[82] was repeated ad nauseam by the WCTU, the NCW, and the Methodist Department of Temperance and Moral Reform. Attacking prudish parents as irresponsible, the promoters of sex education did not see their task as suppressing but as bringing to light sexual questions – in order to forestall vulgar sexual knowledge, but also with the more positive aim of constructing a healthy sexual subjectivity among young Canadians.

Before we examine the work of three important Canadian pioneers of sex education, it might be useful to discuss one of the main bones of contention among purity educators, namely their views of the differences between male and female sexuality. The masculinist wing of purity education was well represented by Dr. Sylvanus Stall, whose books on young men for the "Self and Sex" series have been cited earlier. Stall's description of fertilization, for instance, already portrays the egg (and by implication, the woman who produces it) as purely passive; discounting the fact that the sperm is thousands of times smaller, he portrays the sperm as powerful, active, male. His conclusion is that "in the very fibre of her structure she is quiet, while he is more active." This sociological reasoning then makes him conclude that women ought to stay in the home, for after all "man is life's centrifugal force. . . . Woman might be said to be, both in the family and in society, the centripetal force."[83] Throughout, men and women are portrayed as having opposite and complementary natures, men being heroically active and women being stoically passive and confined to the family sphere; this view of society is then read back into his account of physiology.

Elizabeth Blackwell's feminist views of society lead her to describe physiology and reproduction very differently. Denying that women are passionless, she argues that women are on the contrary very passionate, even physically so, and that the apparent smallness of the clitoris is deceptive because there is much "erectile tissue" below the body's surface. She holds that male and female reproductive and sexual organs are exactly parallel – except for the fact that males exhibit "a striking deficiency" (the lack of a womb).[84]

This gynocentric physiology is complemented by her claim that women, not men, are the true agents of history, because they bring their superior spiritual and intellectual faculties to the work of civilization, whereas men are all too often ruled by the lower passions. Her rejection of the Victorian theory of female passionlessness is thus undertaken not from the "modern" perspective of a Margaret Sanger or a Havelock Ellis (who tried to bridge the gender gap by claiming that female desire was much the same as men's) but rather from the maternal feminist position that women are highly passionate but that their passion is qualitatively different from that of men.

Another curious feminist text on sexuality, Dr. Alice Stockham's *Karezza: Ethics of Marriage* (highly recommended by the WCTU's Purity Superintendent in 1897), anticipated Shere Hite's research in denouncing male selfishness in sex and the "ordinary hasty spasmodic method of cohabitation . . . in which the wife is passive."[85] Stockham's text advocates practising *coitus interruptus* unless conception is desired, gives glowing descriptions of what later came to be called foreplay, and states that women ought to have the final say in deciding how often to have sex. In line with the purity mentality, she believed women would prefer to have sex only every few weeks or even months, and she waxed eloquent about the spiritual component of sexual desire; but she strongly recommended that women, not men, control and define sexual intercourse, and in this sense her work can hardly be dismissed as puritanical or repressive.[86]

These debates on gender were never clearly articulated in the Canadian context, but they are present as a subtext. The women of the WCTU and the Methodist Church's Beatrice Brigden put forward a subtly feminist approach to sex hygiene, whereas men like W.L. Clark and A.W. Beall were more influenced by Sylvanus Stall. Since A.W. Beall was the first Canadian to conduct sex hygiene classes in schools (as fas as we know), he shall be considered first.

Arthur W. Beall, whose origins are obscure, was hired in 1905 by the Ontario WCTU as its "purity agent" for schoolchildren. (The WCTU had gained ample access to Ontario schools through its "scientific temperance" campaign, which was supported by the Ontario Department of Education.) His lectures appear to have been rather old-fashioned for their time, being clearly influenced by J.H. Kellogg's writings of the 1880s and focusing a great deal on the need to stop boys from masturbating.[87]

In 1911, the WCTU was able to transfer Beall to the Ontario Department of Education; at the same time, the Purity department was re-named Moral Education and Mothers' Meetings.[88] It is unclear whether the WCTU was unhappy with Beall's negative view of sex or his exclusive emphasis on male sexuality, or whether they were simply trying to save money; be that as it may, Beall continued to work in Ontario schools until the mid-1930s.

In 1933 Beall published his standard lectures, with a preface by a major-general. There are two basic themes in them: one is the old purity idea that the body is "a living temple" owned by God, not by the individual "tenant" who happens to live in it, and so it ought to be kept clean. The other theme is that to indulge in sexual vice, tobacco, or drink is to be "unpatriotic." Beall joined other purity activists in stressing the national importance of sex hygiene. He defined his goal as teaching children to be "A1 women and men, A1 engineers of the train called Canada," and at the end of his lectures gave children cards with the following printed inscription: "It is up to me, who make my home in a Living Temple so beautiful, so glorious, so noble, so wonderful, to be an A1 Clean Tenant . . . and live an A1 Life for Jesus Christ and Home and Canada."[89]

Beall familiarized schoolchildren with the idea that the new nation of Canada needed not only natural but also ethical/sexual resources, drawing a direct parallel between the value of natural resources and that of subjective human resources. "From Windsor to Cornwall, and from Port Colborne to Cochrane and Keewatin, Ontario yields a myriad variety of products, natural and manufactured. . . . [But] how much do you suppose is the value of a boy or a girl to Canada in hard cash?" The answer was forthcoming in large capitals letters, presumably inscribed by Beall on the blackboard:

CANADA'S MOST VALUABLE PRODUCTS
EVERY BOY AND GIRL HERE TODAY
IS WORTH TO CANADA AT LEAST
$50,000

Beall's nationalism was unusually blunt, not to say vulgar; but in a more refined or spiritual form, a strong Canadian nationalism was also present in the work of the Methodist Church's two roving sex educators. The Methodist Department of Temperance and Moral Reform hired William L. Clark in 1910 specifically to give lectures on sex hygiene to boys and men using the network and the format established by temperance preaching. Clark, a layman, was influenced not so much by J.H. Kellogg and the anti-masturbation writers but by modern American sex educators. Dr. Winfield Scott Hall contributed a preface to Clark's published lectures, giving the work a veneer of science.[90] Beall's theme of pure subjectivity as a national resource is echoed by Clark, who states: "Our young men themselves are producing a product, self, that will command in the market of the world a value according to the power they possess and use."

The patriotic theme was complemented by Clark's resolute positioning of sex hygiene in the constructive and optimistic pole of Methodist sexual politics. Implicitly criticizing rescue work and other practices highlighting the tragedies of the fallen, he emphasized that his own work was not with the vicious but rather with average, healthy children: "My work is not with the sin-cursed portion of this world. It deals with the beautiful, ever-bubbling stream of young men and women, to which you belong, which starts from the pure spring of youth."[91] This approach was in keeping with the Methodist reluctance to set out in rescue boats upon the ocean of sin (a type of work, and an allegory, which they tended to leave to the Salvation Army), and with their preference for the far vaster field of normal people, especially children and youth. This approach to sexuality was in keeping with the general tenor of Protestant moral reform, the positivity of the social gospel, highlighted by the leading Canadian missionary educator, Rev. W.T. Gunn: "Our Gospel must be positive as well as negative. We must learn that, if it is divine to heal the sick, it is divine also to keep people healthy, that if it is Christian to denounce bad amusements it is also Christian to provide helpful recreation."[92] What this meant was that even among the normal and healthy, purity and sexual normalcy would not arise spontaneously out of innocence. Rather, they had to be positively produced through exhausting labours: Clark claims to have written 3,649 letters and addressed 800 meetings in a year alone, reaching, he estimated, 100,000.[93]

Clark's work with boys and men was complemented by the work of Beatrice Brigden with girls and women, which lasted from 1913 to 1920 and is an important episode in the history of Canadian non-school education. Brigden, born in 1888, grew up on a Manitoba farm; her father was a temperance activist and her mother a Quaker pacifist.[94] She studied English and sociology in Brandon and in 1911 obtained a degree in elocution from the Toronto Conservatory. Having already been active in missionary and Sunday school work in Manitoba, she visited the Methodist Fred Victor Mission while in Toronto, and this acquaintance with slum conditions was deepened by doing temporary factory work.

Her combination of public-speaking training with Methodist social work made her an obvious candidate for the job of purity agent for girls and women. Hired in December of 1913, she was sent to the home of American purity leader B.S. Steadwell for a few weeks of intensive reading and training in "the sex question." From the beginning, Brigden distanced herself from the likes of Rev. Shearer by expressing a disinterest in the "sordid history of the social evil" and a marked interest in the "psychology of sex" as taught by Dr. Winfield Scott Hall and other American educators.[95]

Linked to this more "modern" approach was her incipient feminism. Contrary to B.S. Steadwell's advice that visiting Jane

Addams's Chicago settlement on the way back to Toronto would be a waste of time, she wrote to her employer, Dr. T. Albert Moore, expressing a strong interest in Addams. Her letter is worth quoting at some length, since it gives us a rare glimpse of the thoughts of a Canadian feminist purity activist.

> I admit a little partiality to women workers among women, and in my reading and observation much as I have admired the many splendid men in the work there has often come to me the picture of a man and a woman working side by side, the man nearly always overshadowing her best efforts, then one day they come to the end of the road, but she slips on alone up the little path he failed to see, sometimes she goes quite a way.... The path I suppose is womanly sympathy and her guide possibly her capacity to love, and I am convinced that I am only one of the host of women who follow her, because she understands *best*.[96]

From February of 1914 onward, Brigden engaged in an exhausting schedule of lectures throughout Manitoba and Saskatchewan. Although unlike Beall and Clark she never published her lectures, from her correspondence and the flyers advertising the lectures it would appear that she stayed away from diatribes against masturbation and sexual vice, giving instead cheerful messages about the positive aspects of purity. She, like American educational theorists of this time, was a strong believer in segregating adolescents from both young girls and women, and her favourite work seems to have been with this group. A typical series of fifteen lectures in one town (over the course of a week) included "Pansy Blossoms," for girls six to eleven, which was probably a basic talk on how flowers reproduce and on the wonders of God's creation; "Life's Story," for mothers, which was probably similar to the WCTU training sessions for mothers to talk about sex to their daughters; "The Marriage Tie Among the Birds," for young women; "Pure, White and Crystalline," for girls twelve and over, and finally, a general town meeting entitled "The Menace." This may have referred to venereal disease or perhaps to white slavery; it is the only lecture out of fifteen that comes close to the thunderous denunciations of conservative purity activists like Rev. Shearer.

As time went on Brigden was influenced by the growth of prairie socialism, and when the Methodist Church saw its careful coalition between right- and left-wing social reformers collapse in the wake of the Winnipeg General Strike of 1919, Brigden chose to go with the labour church movement headed by the Methodist preacher turned Communist, A.E. Smith of Brandon, Manitoba.[97] Her letter of resignation first expresses her bitterness at the subordinate position of women in the church: "I am obliged to earn my own living and if possible provide for my old age. Being just a woman I am fully aware that the church will not interest herself in such practical matters."[98] Then it goes on to state that she likes the labour church movement, and that "my enthusiasm for the orthodox church has been greatly modified" as a result of the Methodist hierarchy's condemnation of this movement, a condemnation she describes as "the peevish and anemic utterances of old age." (This was in reference to the comments of the General Superintendent, Rev. S.D. Chown.) Without directly mentioning the Winnipeg Strike or the subsequent cowardly attitude of the top Methodist leaders toward the state prosecution of some of their ministers (notably J.S. Woodsworth and A.E. Smith), she concludes that "my sympathies are strongly inclined to movements that seem just however unpopular they may be."

Brigden then worked with A.E. Smith for several years, and in the 1930s she became a leading prairie activist in the Women's Labour Leagues.[99] Her feminist and labour activism was in some ways a break with her earlier purity work, but there was also a remarkable degree of continuity. Her enthusiasm for Jane Addams, her interest in sex psychology, her concern to raise women's consciousness and to address social injustices generally were indications of lifelong beliefs, even if these were transposed from a religious to a secular socialist framework during the great crisis of 1919. Her feminist and socially radical views were already present, however undeveloped, in her purity work; and it is noteworthy that her supervisor, T. Albert Moore, stated that he was fully aware of the fact that some congregations found her too radical and yet chose not to reprimand or fire her. The broad-church character of Canadian Methodism was of course somewhat deceptive, since when the state took the offensive in persecuting "reds" the church apparatus went with the state and not with its own populist wing. Nonetheless, one cannot conclude that Brigden's experience of purity education in a Methodist context was wholly negative or contributed nothing to her later feminist and socialist work.

The work of sex educators raised some important jurisdictional questions. Should such education be undertaken by parents on their own, by parents trained in WCTU Mothers' Meetings, by school teachers, by special lecturers, by clergymen, or by doctors? Should it take place in the home, in the school, in the church hall, or in the doctor's office? We have seen that many purity books were written by doctors, but those hired to teach sex hygiene were more likely to be church people than medically trained personnel. Little research has been done on the history of Canadian sex education, and thus no clear picture emerges of the extent to which various school boards or departments of education followed Ontario's lead in hiring A.W. Beall. It should furthermore be noted that after Beall's retirement in the mid-1930s there was no sex education in Ontario schools until after World War Two, which suggests that the decline of social purity in the 1920s did not result in the establishment of scientific sex education but rather simply in a vacuum.[100]

While Methodists preferred to combine purity education with consolidating their church, and the Presbyterians appear to have avoided it altogether, the women's organizations took an early and strong stand in favour of sex education in the schools. The WCTU and the NCW reiterated this demand at many points, although always carefully stating that they did not want to supplant parental authority. The Superintendent of Purity for the Dominion WCTU typically stated in 1900:

> Nothing can take the place of home teaching, but failing this, we must aim at having purity taught in the schools. Our teachers know the need there is for such instruction, and many of them will gladly avail themselves of any aids we can give them. The leaflet 'Teachers' Opportunity' is suitable to hand to a teacher whose sympathy we desire to enlist, and Dr. Wood-Allen's series (which should be in every WCTU library) will equip them for their work.[101]

This report cleverly turns around mothers' fears of being replaced by teachers by suggesting that mothers educate their children's teachers before the teachers instruct their pupils. Needless to say the conflict between mothers and teachers was not solved this easily.

The NCW's Committee on Citizenship requested all through the war years that sex hygiene be taught in schools, but local Councils of Women across the country reported no successes. Seeking to institutionalize the feminist critique of the "double standard of morals," the NCW suggested that this feminist message, which they envisioned as taught by special lecturers (undoubtedly chosen with the Council's advice), would simultaneously help the war effort: "such moral education would be patriotic work of the highest type. It cannot be left to parents nor to ordinary teachers."[102]

At about the same time, the WCTU, possibly also disappointed at teachers' lack of enthusiasm for sex hygiene, stated it was no longer advocating that sex hygiene be part of the regular curriculum; rather, a "lady doctor" should be brought in to speak to the girls and a male doctor to the boys. This expert effort, however, should be accompanied by renewed efforts to train mothers to speak to their children about sex, so that the doctors' lectures would be reinforced and supplemented by home teaching.[103]

It appears that few school boards actually implemented a program of sex hygiene education, at least before 1920. The WCTU's Mothers' Meetings and school lectures and the Methodist Church's travelling sex educators seem to have been the primary vehicle through which ordinary Canadians were exposed to both old-fashioned ideas about the evils of spending semen and to "modern" ideas about the proper training of adolescents. The work of the early purity educators cannot, in conclusion, be dismissed as simply repressive or unscientific. It must instead be seen as a very mixed bag in which fear of sex was juxtaposed with cheerful optimism about the joys of at least some forms of sex. Perhaps more importantly, through purity education sexuality became a discursive site in which to elaborate diverse political and social ideas, ranging from extreme Canadian nationalism to feminism (and, exceptionally, socialism). The social and political meanings and implications of purity work were perhaps most clear in the anti-prostitution work of the purity movement, which is the topic of the next chapter, but it is important to note that even the apparently more private sphere of sex hygiene work was intertwined with public concerns about the race, about gender, and about the nation.

4

The White Slavery Panic

The "Social Evil" as Symbol

Insofar as there was a single issue that typified or symbolized the whole work of social purity, it was prostitution, referred to as the "social evil." This was not a mere euphemism: for many Canadians prostitution was really *the* social evil, the most important of a long list of social problems ascribed to modern urban life. As the previous chapter makes clear, it was not the sole focus of the purity movement, as drink was for the temperance movement; but prostitution was *the social* evil (in contrast to masturbation, the "solitary evil") and the fight against it was an ongoing campaign that was guaranteed to unify an otherwise diverse movement.

There was nevertheless a great diversity in the solutions proposed. Some reformers sought harsh criminal measures against prostitutes themselves; feminists sought to expose and shame the men who used prostitutes; doctors declared prostitution to be an indicator of mental illness (among women only); and so on, until most activists had taken a practical and/or theoretical position on what was universally acknowledged to be the *great* problem of prostitution.

Why was prostitution central to moral reform? To answer this question one must go somewhat beyond the text of the documentary sources and reflect on the unstated assumptions and mythical images on which these texts are grounded.

The first reason is that, unlike most other sexual activities, prostitution is notoriously public. It often takes place in spaces defined legally as public, such as parks and streets; but even when the sexual acts are conducted in the privacy of a bedroom, the preceding negotiation involves a transaction that is public in the sense that any sale of a service is public. Since sexuality has been constructed as belonging exclusively within the familial sphere, both the state and private citizens feel entitled to comment on, judge, and police the participants in prostitution (as well as other extra-familial sexual activities).

Stigmatization and policing have not affected all participants in "public sex" equally, however. In the case of heterosexual prostitution, the woman's activity is seen as making her a different type of woman – a prostitute – while male customers are not perceived as essentially defined by their purchase of sex. Prostitution is thus identified with the woman who sells the service, not so much the man who buys it. A prostitute is a prostitute at all times (as the repeated efforts by both authorities and moral vigilantes to curtail prostitutes' freedom to walk the streets, go shopping, and so on, demonstrate); to be a prostitute is not merely to hold a particular job but to have a whole identity.[1] The British Contagious Diseases Acts of the 1860s presupposed that any policeman could spot prostitutes without necessarily witnessing activities such as soliciting; Canadian criminal law made being a "street-walker" a status crime. Paralleling legal discourse, Canadian reformers believed that they could distinguish "fallen" from what they called "unfallen" girls at a glance. What the glances observed were not empirical facts about the woman's work but rather signs – clothes, demeanour – taken as outward symptoms of inner moral corruption or vice.

Vice was (and still is) a larger category than crime, since it includes solitary, secret, and decriminalized vices. The second reason for the key symbolic role of prostitution was that it occupied a central place in the turn-of-the-century cosmology of vice, as the female vice par excellence and hence as constitutive of femininity. Working-class males were seen as potential alcoholics and criminals and acquired masculine virtue by being sober and honest; females of the working class were by contrast evaluated according to their perceived distance from the paradigmatic female working-class vice, prostitution. Some women drank or robbed, and some men undoubtedly fell into sexual vice rather than drink or theft, but at the level of myth and allegory there was a strict gendering of vice, observable in novels about working-class life.[2]

Third, prostitution was central in social purity thought and practice because it mobilized the powerful symbolism of the whore of Babylon in the campaign to clean and purify the city and especially the slums. From biblical prophecies to today's mass-media exposés of vice, the theme of the vicious woman as symbolizing or representing the fallen city has been a powerful one. The fear of becoming a fallen city (through harbouring fallen women) was implicitly mobilized in Toronto's campaign against Sunday streetcars, a campaign supported by labour initially but increasingly defined by social purity. Without referring to prostitution directly, the leading reformer and ex-mayor, W.H. Howland, invoked this spectre in 1893 by warning that "if Toronto gets Sunday cars she will be proclaimed far and wide *a city that has fallen* and her moral and financial standing will be gone."[3]

In the time period under study there were two contrasting but complementary symbolic representations of the city. One was Coketown, hard-working, ugly, and functional; the other one was Babylon, the night-time city of lights and temptations, the city of leisure – and of sex. The former was clearly masculine while the latter was feminine. (Toronto police court reporters sometimes referred to prostitutes appearing in court as "Babylonians.")[4] Coketown and Babylon were of course the same physical place, but the symbolic split between them was rooted in the concrete experience of urban life insofar as it reflected the lived experience of the split between labour and leisure, day and night, duty and pleasure. The gendering of night/pleasure as female had practical as well as discursive consequences: a woman walking alone at night in the city ran the risk of being arrested as a prostitute if, in the words of the streetwalker section of the Criminal Code, she could not produce "a satisfactory account of herself."[5] The combination of "night" and "city" sufficed to make a woman guilty of vice unless she could prove otherwise by a counter-narrative.

To summarize, then, prostitution makes sex public and challenges the private/public split, highlighting women's active role in both sexuality and commerce. Prostitution also played an historically specific role in the gendering of vice and the differential moral regulation of men and women. And as the social evil, it played a key role in organizing urban space by gender, class, and moral status. For these reasons, it was an ideal theme for a movement primarily concerned with the regulation of morality, class, sex, and gender in the new urban environment. Indeed, if prostitution had not existed, the social purity movement would have had to invent it – which helps us to understand why white slavery, which was never proven to exist on a large scale, was so successfully invented.

Regulatory Dilemmas

For turn-of-the-century Canadians, the debates on public policy regarding prostitution constituted a key terrain within and through which the social was discussed and regulated: municipal reform, new ideas about sexuality and gender roles, class differences in culture, and ethnic/racial tensions did not only help to shape the prostitution debate but were also shaped by it. This section, which does not attempt to cover Canada but instead contrasts the cities of Toronto and Winnipeg, will analyse the policing of prostitution to show the ways in which gender, sexuality, class, and race were regulated through prostitution policy.

In the late Victorian period, there were two basic systems used in Europe and North America to regulate prostitution. Unhappiness with one often led to a partial adoption of its opposite, which in turn generated unexpected problems and led for calls for a return to the previous status quo. One was the continental system, and its opposite was what we shall call, for lack of a better word, the English system.

The continental system involved the formal recognition by the authorities of *tolerated houses* (brothels), often in *segregated districts*. This system, known as "toleration" and/or "segregation," was usually linked to the compulsory registration and medical examination of the women who worked in brothels. It was justified as a way to contain "vice" in a designated area of the city, hence purifying the rest of the city, and it was also argued that this system contributed to checking venereal diseases. It was undoubtedly true that the continental system had certain health advantages, but it resulted in a tyrannical surveillance of prostitutes, who were often not allowed to go out and who could not easily obtain other jobs if they wanted to. More significant from the point of view of administrators was the fact that the attempt to register all prostitutes and exercise police and medical surveillance over all brothels was never a success, even in the administrative paradise of Paris. Large numbers of women continued to work on their own in the streets, and these "insubordinated" women (as the French police called them) constituted a constant headache for the authorities as well as for citizens inclined to moral reform.[6]

In Victorian Britain there was great resistance to introducing any of the features of the continental system of regulation, at least officially. The evangelical revival spirit that swept England at periodic intervals in the second half of the nineteenth century was staunchly opposed to any formal state recognition of vice such as prevailed in Paris. These moralists did not imagine that lack of an official policy of toleration meant that no brothels existed; rather, they knew that "dens of vice" existed, but they preferred to make these dens into potential objects of moral reform and conversion rather than state administration. Clergymen and nonconformist ministers, together with ardent Christian feminists such as the famed Josephine Butler, undertook evangelical missions to persuade both prostitutes and their customers to leave their lives of sin. Police measures to regulate prostitution did nothing but disrupt the work of moral reform and make prostitutes suspicious of reformers, these people argued.[7]

Even in England, there was a temporarily successful attempt to introduce at least parts of the continental system, through the Contagious Diseases Acts of the mid-1860s. The Acts were opposed by a coalition of evangelicals, working-class men concerned about the harassment of working-class women by police, and feminists. This coalition lasted for about a dozen years and helped to shape both future state policy on moral regulation and feminist attitudes toward the state. After the repeal of the Acts in 1883, the English system remained in force. Even during World War One, when the health of the troops provided a perfect argument to re-introduce the surveillance of women under the guise of health regulations, the British government was reluctant to institute any compulsory measures to regulate prostitution for fear of attacks from feminists and evangelicals.[8]

Nevertheless, the English system did not involve perfect freedom for prostitutes to ply their trade. Women were arrested under vagrancy statutes and subject to police harassment and, perhaps most importantly, were subjected to the weight of social stigma, which as Walkowitz argues increased greatly through the Contagious Diseases Acts but did not disappear once the Acts were repealed. And after 1885, they were also subject to new criminal penalties, devised allegedly to punish procurers and pimps but often used to restrict the freedom of young women themselves.[9]

Canada inherited the English approach to prostitution, at least in laws and official declarations. Policing practices, as we shall see, often took a distinctly Parisian cast, especially in the West and in Montreal. But the official discourse meant that when cities experimented with a form of toleration/segregation, they claimed they were not doing it, as Winnipeg Chief of Police McRae tried to say to the 1910 royal commission on the policing of prostitution in Winnipeg.[10] Furthermore, when harsh penalties were introduced into the Criminal Code in the years from 1890 to 1914, protestations were made that moral reform and "preventive work" were far preferable to criminal sanctions, and great care was spent on ensuring that the new laws appeared to be protecting "girls," not punishing them.

In contrast to England, Canada never had a strong feminist-evangelical voice comparable to that of Josephine Butler and her co-workers in the Ladies' National Association. Thus, although Canada shared with England the distaste for any official recognition of vice in the shape of formal red-light districts, the feminist concern for the double standard of morality (and the double standard of law enforcement) was not as prominent. Law-and-order measures against prostitutes, not so much against prostitution in general, were somewhat harsher in Canada than in England throughout the period under study, and feminist protests against this were sporadic and muted. John McLaren has pointed out that "Canadian legislation made the very status of being a streetwalker or prostitute a crime,"[11] which made it possible for police to arrest women even if they were not doing anything. (Under English law, women had to both be streetwalkers *and* be behaving in a "riotous" or "indecent" manner or "annoying" men.)

Interestingly, the Contagious Diseases Acts were imported into Canada, but it would appear that the Canadian government was a reluctant partner: the 1864 English Act was imported to British North America in 1865, but only for a five-year period, and in any case it was not enforced.[12]

The policing of prostitution was one of the concerns that led Toronto (famous for its strict blue laws) to take the lead among Canadian cities in setting up a morality division, headed by the ardent moral reformer Inspector David Archibald. This squad seems to have been fairly effective in keeping brothels down to a minimum, and, unlike most other police bodies, it arrested male customers as well as female inmates.[13] Prostitution was by no means the only concern of the morality squad: it also dealt with domestic disputes (though men were almost never charged as a result) and with offences as diverse as witchcraft and gross indecency. Sunday observance was an important area of the squad's activity: for instance, in one particularly fruitful year, 306 charges were laid under the Lord's Day Act.[14]

The result of this vigorous police activity was that relatively few Torontonians resorted to brothels, and there was never a red-light district as in other Canadian cities (although some streets had several houses of assignation or even brothels).[15] The police authorities congratulated themselves on their success in every annual report; nevertheless, one critical observer noted that as a result of the suppression of brothels, "loose women have scattered themselves about." This observer, the moral watchdog C.S. Clark, proclaimed that

> In the course of a ramble over the island on a Saturday night, I came across several couples *en flagrante delicto* [sic]. Houses of ill fame in Toronto? Certainly not. The whole city is an immense house of ill-fame, the roof of which is the blue canopy of heaven during the summer months.[16]

Clark's claim that Toronto did not need brothels because it was all "an immense house of ill-fame" was an idiosyncratic view of the city, not borne out even by police statistics. Armed with new Criminal Code provisions on keeping common bawdy houses, the morality squad did manage to find a small but persistent number of bawdy houses. (One prominent purity activist, Rev. R.B. St. Clair, claimed in 1911 that

100 brothels existed in Toronto and that children in the poor area of St. Patrick's Square knew where they were.)[17] The nature of these houses remains unclear. McLaren's study of arrests shows that in many instances the same women were charged both as keepers and as working prostitutes, which suggests that the police may have charged individual women in their own homes under the guise of closing down brothels.[18] But be that as it may, from 1900 to 1914, slightly over 2,000 charges of keeping houses of ill-fame or disorderly houses were laid (many of these were probably repeat charges against the same person, however). Almost two-thirds of these were women, disproving the myth that it was evil Chinese or other male exploiters who owned brothels. Further proof that the protection of women was not most prominent in the minds of the police was that only a handful of procuring charges were laid, and these were laid against women as easily as against men.[19]

Clark's other point, the deliberate inclusion of couples engaged in consensual embraces in parks under the label of prostitution, was by contrast widely accepted by moral reformers, especially in the early 1910s, when concern for the moral standing of young single white-collar women reached new heights. In 1913, Toronto's leading moral reformers joined together to investigate "social vice" in the city, and their 1915 report does not recognize a distinction between prostitution and going out on dates. The investigators found very few bawdy houses and no evidence at all of coerced prostitution, but this did not lead them to conclude that all was well. On the contrary, they created a moral panic about the women who were not prostitutes but went out with men to parks or ice cream parlours and on occasion had sex with their male dates.

> One of the very serious – if not from a social standpoint most serious – of the many phases of the social evil in Toronto is the large number of what may perhaps be described as 'occasional prostitutes'. . . . Some are married women who 'sport' with or without their husbands' knowledge or connivance; some are girls living at home, sometimes in quite respectable homes. . . . With some [the reason] is, as they declare, 'for fun' or 'for a good time'. . . .[20]

Toronto's moral reformers were undoubtedly following the lead of the more famous Minneapolis Vice Commission, which in 1911 had proclaimed "Young Girls on Our Streets" to be a major social problem.[21] In Toronto as well as in various American cities, inquiries originating out of a desire to document the existence of a white slave traffic quietly became inquiries not about male procurers (who could scarcely be found) but about the morals of young working-class women.

The new cities of the Prairies presented a very different moral picture. Railway-building was causing towns to appear overnight, often without planning or without any of the municipal institutions common in eastern Canada. The railways were also responsible for bringing large numbers of young single men in search of work. People were quite aware of the different gender ratios in different parts of the country; for instance, a large headline in the *Mail and Empire* declared that "MORE MEN THAN WOMEN RESIDENT IN CANADA BUT IN TORONTO THERE ARE NOT ENOUGH MEN TO GO AROUND – IN THE WEST, OF COURSE, THE WOMEN ARE LARGELY IN THE MINORITY."[22] These facts, while obviously not necessary causes of either prostitution in general or any particular form of it, were seen by municipal authorities in the West as justifying a different arrangement than would be appropriate in Toronto. Winnipeg's Chief of Police, C. McRae, said that Winnipeg had "a very great many young unmarried men," which "increases the difficulty of settling the question of social vice." He also expressed the view typical among policemen (with the possible exception of Toronto's morality squad) that it was impossible to abolish the social evil completely, contrary to what moral reformers said. "Never. . . . There is no city I know which is free from it. It is like the poor, evil is always with us."[23]

McRae's resigned views were not shared by the Winnipeg social purity movement, composed of the WCTU, a citizens' committee known as the Civic Social Purity Committee, and the local Moral and Social Reform League (a branch of the Moral and Social Reform Council of Canada). The Civic Social Purity Committee apparently never had more than 150 people, but the Moral and Social Reform League was a fairly powerful coalition of many groups, including the Trades and Labour Council.[24] These groups lobbied the municipal authorities until, in 1909, the Winnipeg City Council told the Chief of Police to take any measures necessary to stop offensive public displays. This order was understood by all concerned – aldermen, police commissioners, and the police itself – to mean that the police ought to confine brothels to a small and inconspicuous area of the city. It was, however, equally universally understand that no "official" order to either set up or recognize a red-light district could ever be made. (A small red-light district had existed earlier, on Thomas Street, but was closed down in one massive raid in 1904.) McRae hence contacted a real estate agent by the name of Beaman, who quickly found houses on Rachel and McFarlane streets and sold them at inflated prices to women keepers contacted by the leading madam of the city, Minnie Woods, who had been contacted by McRae and told to speak to Beaman. Thus, a new red-light district was created, and since the women who bought the houses had paid far above market value,[25] they were reluctant to move even when Dr. Shearer's tour of vice in the West put the red-light district in jeopardy.

Mayor Evans's testimony stated, in an argument reminiscent of the Paris system, that one of the reasons for wanting to segregate vice was to check the spread of venereal disease. It would have been politically difficult for a Canadian municipality officially to set up compulsory examinations of prostitutes, but some of the madams testified that they were "advised" (obviously by the morality squad, though the women never admitted this) their "girls" should have a doctor examine them every two weeks and give the healthy ones certificates.

From the testimony of both madams and officials, it is clear that the Winnipeg red-light distriet provided prostitutes with a ghettoized but relatively secure workplace with its own kind of culture. The stereo-type of the lonely woman under a lamppost, who might be rescued and put into a "Home" if approached by a reformer, was completely contradicted by evidence about how the real homes of prostitutes and madams were run. Indeed, as a Salvation Army officer intent on rescue work admitted, "my wife and my workers found it very difficult to get these girls away under any circumstances, because they were sur-rounded with luxury and thought they were having a good time."[26]

If the moral reform movement had little power to convince women to give up their finery and become "honest," it did hold considerable influence over public discourse. This is evident in disingenuous denials that there was an official policy of tolera-tion/segregation, such as Mayor Evans's reply to a question by Rev. J.C. Walker, "Has the mayor denied that there has been a segregated district of vice in this city?"

> No. . . . I may have stated that there has been no official policy of segregation, which is true. That there are houses together which are supposed to be houses of ill repute is a fact which I have never denied.[27]

The lack of congruence between official policy and fact was not peculiar to Winnipeg. In mining and lumber towns as well as in cities such as Edmonton, brothels were a "fact" and were only suppressed during periodic moral panics. In Edmonton, for instance, there was a campaign by the YWCA in 1909-11 to rescue girls form the alleged traps set by white slavers, and in 1911 thirty-seven under-age girls were turned over to the Children's Aid Society after being arrested for prostitution. But even after this panic, brothels continued to exist, apparently in larger numbers than in Winnipeg, and in 1914 there was an inquiry into police collusion with prostitutes similar to the Robson Commission of 1910.[28]

Prostitution in the West was shaped not only by demographic and municipal particularities, but also by the sharp racial conflicts between Native peoples and white settlers and between Asians and whites, conflicts that interacted with the gender divisions in each racial group to create severe problems for women of colour. Canadian churches ritually denounced the "traffic" in Indian women that allegedly went on near white male settlements in the West, but it is impossible to tell whether these allegations referred to voluntary prostitution by Indian women or to cases of coercion by either white or Indian men. For instance, in 1886 a missionary on the Blood Indian reserve near Fort Macleod claimed that Indian women were being sold to white men as concubines, and these women were subsequently abandoned to become prostitutes when the men got tired of them. The Macleod *Gazette* denied the missionary's charges in an interesting article reprinted as an appendix by Gray:

> We do not argue that there are not many cases where white men do keep Indian women. We may show our depravity when we say we do not see anything wrong in this. In the great majority of cases the primitive bonds of matrimony were entered into long before the civilizing influence of white women was felt.[29]

The role of Native women in the prostitution business in the West would need to be studied in much more detail before statements such as the article quoted here can be properly interpreted.[30] It is clear, however, that the "civilizing influence" of white women settlers brought about a lower status for Native women and encouraged their ghettoization in prostitution.

In Vancouver and Victoria, there was much discussion about the role of Chinese men in the organization of prostitution. The images of white girls entrapped by Chinese men conjured up by Dr. Shearer and later by a famous early feminist, police magistrate Emily Murphy,[31] took attention away from the real problems of intra-racial gender domination and of cross-gender racial domination. A brief discussion of the work of Protestant middle-class women in helping/reforming Chinese prostitute and non-prostitute women in British Columbia might shed some light on the complex interaction of gender and racial relations of power and on the way in which these relations were perceived.

Partly as a result of the Canadian government's escalating head taxes and other measures to curtail Chinese immigration, it became increasingly difficult for Chinese people to immigrate to Canada as families. The presence of large numbers of single men, or married men who had to leave their wives at home because of Canadian immigration restrictions, encouraged the semi-clandestine importation of Chinese women to be prostitutes or concubines to the male Chinese community. Tamara Adilman claims that between 100-200 women were imported from China to Canada to serve as prostitutes and sold to brothelkeepers (and possibly others in need of female labour) for between $500 and $2,000.[32] It is doubtful that the official figures can differentiate between prostitutes or working women destined to other jobs, but it does appear that some Chinese merchants did import women for the purpose of providing sexual services to both the male Chinese community and to white men in search of "the exotic." The head tax imposed on Chinese immigrants clearly helped to support the system of forced prostitution, since independent women were unable to emigrate,[33] and those who were brought by merchants would be considered as merchandise because a substantial tax had been paid on their behalf.

The fact that there was economic and sexual exploitation in the Chinese community gave rise to a variety of interpretations on the part of educated Anglo-Saxon Protestants. Some said this showed the inherent viciousness of "orientals" and argued for a policy of total exclusion. Others – in the Methodist Church and in women's organizations – worried about populations of single men and called on the government to allow those Chinese labourers already in Canada to bring their wives into the country. A few were so "radical" as to advocate the Christianization and assimilation of Chinese immigrants.[34] One group practising the latter approach was the Women's Missionary Society of the Methodist Church, which from the late 1880s on ran a rescue home for Chinese women in Victoria. Karen Van Dieren's research into this institution shows that although the original intent was to rescue women from forced prostitution, little success was achieved in this, and the home quickly became a general social work centre. Domestic servants in trouble with their employers and abused wives seemed to be more frequent inmates in the home than prostitutes; and the education of Asian children in the principles of Protestant Canada played a larger role as time went on. The home was also used as a place for Japanese immigrant women (who, unlike the Chinese, were not excluded from Canada). Ironically, the home was eventually closed down in 1942 and turned into a servicemen's recreation centre: the children boarding and studying in it were deported to Saskatchewan as part of the Canadian government's anti-Japanese campaign.[35]

The little evidence that exists of work with prostitutes shows that the women running the home had mixed feelings: on the one hand, they attempted to welcome Chinese prostitute women as "sisters," but on the other hand they had very specific expectations that these women would show Christian repentance and would transform themselves into penitent but saved pious women. They also insisted on teaching them to sing hymns, drink English tea, and learn Canadian ways of housework with a view to getting jobs as domestic servants. Some Chinese women did indeed convert both to Protestantism and Canadian ways; but many more found the home not to their liking. The women running the home stated:

> A Chinese woman sought refuge with us. We made her welcome and tried to induce her to stay, but after three days, she preferred to return to the dark life which had already claimed six years of her existence.
>
> ... We had charge of a Chinese woman for nearly three weeks, but she is unimproved in her life, and she is an inveterate gambler and prostitute.[36]

The work of the rescue home, widely publicized through the reports of the Women's Missionary Society of the Methodist Church, probably helped to shape the attitudes of many ordinary Canadians, including many feminists, to both Chinese men and Chinese women.[37] This practical work, which was certainly suffused with ethnocentric values, nevertheless helped to make the progressive wing of the Methodist Church question some of the most fantastical claims made during the white slavery panic.

The policing of prostitution was thus caught up in a web of interests – around municipal government, around morality, gender, class, and race – that made it impossible for authorities to settle on any policy and be consistent in its enforcement. Perhaps the only thing that can be said with certainty is that, whatever the rhetoric on gender might have been, the authorities were never especially interested in suppressing male exploitation of women, whether in or out of prostitution. During a sample four-month period in 1911 that saw four or five cases of voluntary elopement of couples harshly prosecuted in Toronto courts and sensationally reported in the newspapers, the only case of male sexual abuse given prominence was one of a Chinese man allegedly guilty of sexual overtures to girls at the Canadian National Exhibition.[38] That it was his race and not his abuse of gender/age power that was deemed newsworthy is clear by comparing that news item to a story concerning two indecent assaults by an English-speaking and probably middle-class male. One J.C. Williams, charged with indecent assault on two girls, aged eleven and thirteen, "was acquitted by the jury at the direction of the judge, without leaving their seats":

A mass of evidence was brought forward to show that the accused had borne a previous exemplary character and that the two girls had very questionable reputations. . . . His Honor declared it would be very unsafe to convict a man on the uncorroborated testimony of two girls who, if their reputation was deserved, were neither innocent nor reliable.[39]

The way in which the rape of these girls was treated in the courts lends support to the hypothesis that the moral panic about white slavery that swept Canada at this time was not primarily a response to violence against women.

White Slavers: Deconstructing a Moral Panic

In 1909, the annual report of a leading Canadian social reform organization declared that "the most startling and painful feature of the year's work" was the "discoveries made in regard to the existence of the white slave trade. . . . when we first sounded the alarm in regard to this traffic many would not believe that such a diabolical evil really existed in Canada, but we have been able to establish . . . the fact that it is carried out in Canada."[40] In 1911 the same organization reiterated that

This awful traffic in procuring the daughters of our goodly homes for the vile and shameless social evil is carried on in this Dominion. As we pursue our labours, evidence accrues more and more that there are pimps and panderers who are vigilantly and tirelessly seeking to enslave the beautiful girls who dwell beneath the blue skies of Canada.[41]

It would be easy simply to dismiss these statements as the fantasies of repressed clergymen and/or techniques in a Machiavellian plan to heighten the power of both moral reformers and state authorities. The rhetoric of "beautiful girls dwelling under blue skies" being pursued by "pimps and panderers" certainly lends itself to ridicule. The fact remains, however, that many people believed white slavery was a serious social problem. If we do not want to argue that a large part of the population of Canada was completely duped by a small group of puritanical conspirators, then an analysis of how and why this particular moral panic *worked* is necessary.[42] In today's Canada we no longer worry about white slavers, but large-scale panics have been organized around the issues of abortion, pornography, and AIDS. The particular issues around which panics coalesce change over time, and therefore the content of the white slavery panic is historically specific: but the structure of the panic and its methods have a broader relevance. Thus, the analysis will focus as much on the forms used to mobilize people as on the content. It will also avoid the temptation of quickly proceeding to find the "real" problem lying hidden under the deceptive surface of the panic. White slavery, like all other moral panics, can easily be dismissed as merely a cover for the real issue by interpreters who have decided beforehand what the real issue always is: for instance, one might want to prove that under the rhetoric of white slavery lay real shifting class relations in an urbanizing Canada, or, alternatively, that the panic was merely a patriarchal ploy to frighten women into staying in the domestic realm. Such unidimensional approaches do not help us to understand the complex ways in which a moral issue that appears to be singular serves as the site for social debate on a number of important and interrelated issues; and they certainly do nothing to further our understanding of what I call the back-and-forth "slippage" among categories such as class, gender, sexuality, and race.[43]

Let us then begin with an analysis of the founding event in the white-slavery panic: the 1885 exposé by the English muckraking journalist W.T. Stead entitled "The Maiden Tribute of Modern Babylon," published in Stead's *Pall Mall Gazette* in July of that year.

The first paragraph of the "Maiden Tribute" evoked the plight of Athenians forced to send seven youths and seven maidens to the Cretan labyrinth inhabited by the Minotaur. This pagan rite, Stead argues (erasing the boys from the account), was being re-enacted in "the maze of London brotheldom." The classical analogy was treated quite loosely, as Athens is replaced by Babylon, the latter city being renowned for its wickedness in Protestant lore. Stead then described his attempts to prove that girls were being sold into prostitution, in a kind of travel piece that introduced readers to the night-time vices of a city inhabited by day by business and politics: "It seemed a strange, inverted world, that in which I lived those terrible weeks. . . . London beneath the gas glare of its innumerable lamps became . . . a resurrected and magnified City of the Plain, with all the vices of Gomorrah."[44]

Stead had some difficulties buying girls, and to help him he enlisted the reluctant help of Rebecca Jarrett, a reformed procuress recommended to him by Josephine Butler (who, like other feminists, was uneasy about Stead's experimentation with live women).[45] Jarrett then apparently convinced a Mrs. Armstrong to sell her thirteen-year-old daughter Eliza to her for a few pounds. Following Stead's orders, she had Eliza examined by a doctor to prove her virginity – in a peculiar re-enactment of the state action that enraged feminists during the fight against the Diseases Acts – and brought Eliza to her "owner." Stead then took the woman and the girl to a real-life brothel. In it, Stead claims to have given Eliza chloroform so that she would become unconscious, but the girl resisted and refused to sniff the soaked handkerchief Stead gave her; thus, she was awake when, in the middle of the night, Stead walked into the room shared by Jarrett and Eliza. The "virtuous" forced medical examination and forced administering of "knock-out drops" were followed by what can only be described as a "virtuous" rape scene. No sexual intercourse took place, but Stead's sudden entry into the girl's room probably made her feel violated or at the very least frightened. The journalistic gaze having penetrated the bewildered girl, Stead turned around and walked out of the room.

After this, rather than returning the girl to her family and neighbourhood, Stead chose once again to enact the white slavers' alleged tricks: he sent her off to France accompanied by Jarrett, who was herself forced to act the part of a real, unreformed procuress. There she was put in a Salvation Army home to be "rescued" by being taught how to do domestic labour. In the meantime, however, Stead's revelations having been published, the parents of the girl contacted the police and had Scotland Yard trace the girl and her procuress-cum-chaperone. They were brought back to England, and Stead was charged with abduction (ironically, one of the offences against womanhood and purity listed in the 1885 Bill).

In his trial, Stead claimed that no abduction had taken place because there was no intention of harming the girl. "I bought Eliza Armstrong to save Eliza Armstrong," he claimed.[46] During his speech, he managed to shift all blame for Eliza's suffering on (a) her own mother, who had already been constructed as the true villain of the piece in the "Maiden Tribute,"[47] and (b) Rebecca Jarret, whose already low public credibility was further undermined by Stead's dark hints that his "agents" had not followed orders.

Although the original articles and the subsequent speeches made by Stead depicted women as the immediate villains, the articles and accompanying editorials did not neglect the more familiar scenario of "daughter of the working class being exploited by aristocratic rake." This scenario, which receded into the background during the trial due to Stead's attempts to save his own skin by blaming women, was originally intended to rally the (male) working class in defence of the Criminal Law Amendment Bill. The editorial accompanying the first instalment went so far as to suggest, using the best of radical rhetoric, that the poor and downtrodden would rise up against the rich when they found out about procuring practices.

[U]nless the levying of the maiden tribute in London is shorn of its worst abuses – at present, as I shall show, flourishingly unchecked –

resentment, which might be appeased by reform, may hereafter be the virus of a social revolution. It is the one explosive which is strong enough to wreck the Throne.[48]

Stead's radical discourse was, however, seriously undermined by his callous behaviour toward working-class families in general and the Armstrongs in particular. During Stead's trial, large numbers of people (possibly the Armstrongs' neighbours) gathered outside the court to protest Stead's abduction. The Salvation Army, which defended Stead, interestingly neglected Stead's radical language in favour of the language of respectability. Catherine Booth, wife of General Booth, wrote a letter of support, which stated that the prosecution of Stead was being denounced by "the middle and better working classes":

> The adverse aspect of the crowd outside the court is no criterion whatever of the attitude of the people, for our agents in disguise mingled freely among them, and found that they were low, drunken characters, and largely connected with the interests of brotheldom.[49]

Therefore, a scandal that had origins in an attempt to blame the rich for exploiting the daughters of the poor had become a complex construct in which mother-blaming, misogyny, and contempt for the "rough" poor coexisted with the original elements. The discourses of the scandal contained the germ of practices, notably the harassment of working-class women, which followed the passage of the 1885 Criminal Amendment Act.

Ripples of the Stead scandal reached Canada just at the time when social purity activity was being organized – the Methodist sects united in one church in 1885, the same year the Dominion WCTU was established; the Salvation Army had been established in Canada in 1884. The Knights of Labor, and Phillips Thompson in particular, took up Stead's revelation as a class issue, decrying the exploitation of the daughters of the working class by the dissolute rich.[50] Canada was, however, much more affected by the second wave of the white slavery panic, that which took place in 1909-14. This period witnessed large-scale immigration, increasingly from non-British and non-Protestant countries, as well as rapid urbanization, and both of these phenomena provided the context to fuel white-slavery fears.

At this time, there was agitation in England for further amendments to the Criminal Code regarding age of consent, seduction, and procuring.[51] In the U.S., a similar campaign culminated in the Mann Act of 1910, which prohibited interstate traffic in women and has often been used to harass and detain unmarried couples travelling together.

American cities were also at this time in the grip of a crusade to eliminate corruption in municipal government; the municipal reformers often claimed that politicians benefited financially from tolerating or even owning brothels.[52] Canadian moral reformers seized the international conjuncture and tried to put Canada on the vice map of the world.

The Canadian reformers' first obstacle was to convince people that Canada was not as healthy and pure a nation as was generally believed (and as they had claimed on other occasions). One technique was to suggest that even if white slavery was invisible in Canada itself, Canadian girls were being procured across the border to fill the brothels of American or other foreign cities. "Everyone knows," Dr. Shearer said, "that for many years a constant stream of Canadian girls have crossed the border to earn their living as writers, nurses, teachers, stenographers. . . . Stories of their success are widely known. This makes the work of the procurer easier."[53] What "everyone knows" was repeated by the Methodist sex educator W.L. Clark to adolescent boys: "Does she [your sister] know the dangers of bad men and bad women who travel the country . . . for the sole purpose of stealing pure girls to be sold in the horrible market. . . . Visit some of the foreign countries and you will find there American and Canadian girls. . . ."[54]

This claim acted as the thin edge of the wedge. Once convinced that Canadian girls might indeed be working in the notorious brothels of Buenos Aires, Johannesburg, or Chicago, churchgoers and readers were told that not all was well at home. The superintendent of social work and missions for the Presbyterian Church, Rev. Pidgeon, chastised his workers for not producing evidence of the vice that he was sure lurked in every Canadian city.[55] And the National Council of Women took up the campaign, inviting the English head of the international anti-white slavery committee to address their 1912 annual meeting and forming a Committee on the Equal Moral Standard and Traffic in Women. This committee reported that "we rejoice in the fact that there is a general movement throughout Canada to suppress the business of social vice, including the white slave traffic, for purity is the very foundation of national life."[56] Repeating the supposed facts that "everyone knows," this committee said: "In Canada, no less an authority than the secretaries of the moral reform associations of the churches tell us that 1,500 girls from Canada go yearly into the traffic," and added that some of these ended up in Chicago.[57] The committee's report also repeated verbatim the claim made by Shearer that "in the cities [of the West] most of the dens of vice are owned by Chinese and Japanese. No doubt many of the girl inmates are owned by them also."[58]

Although the NCW committee was clearly in the business of reproducing the racist and sensationalist "facts" produced by Shearer and

company, there was within the NCW, and within other women's organizations such as the WCTU, a range of views on the question of
prostitution. The NCW women generally stressed that men were largely
responsible for the existence of social vice and drew attention to the
hypocritical practice of punishing only the females:

> One of our great weaknesses has been that we have construed this
> social evil as a female proposition; and our criminality has been the
> persecution of the woman, while permitting the easy escape of the
> man.... Some of us think the social evil is a masculine proposition;
> certainly we shall never accomplish much until we lay upon the man
> the heavier end of this burden of guilt.[59]

Some women raised the same points made by the Canadian left
about economic exploitation as the root of women's vulnerability, as
is seen in an interesting exchange between the English white slavery
crusader A. Coote and Toronto feminist Flora MacDonald Denison at
the 1912 annual meeting of the NCW. Denison, the minutes record,
"thought that the cause of prostitution was largely an economic
one.... She advocated technical training as a partial remedy." Coote
"did not agree with Mrs. Denison that the greatest reason of prostitution
was an economic one.... Instead of taking the girl to a rescue home
or a clergyman we should take her to the doctor. The feeble-minded of
our land are supplying sixty percent of the illegitimate children."[60]

Coote's belief that feeble-minded women became prostitutes and
had illegitimate and defective children was certainly shared by some
of the members of the NCW Committee on the Equal Moral Standard
and Traffic in Women. It also resonated with the ideas of the Committee on Feeble-minded Women, which had pioneered eugenic thought
in Canada and consistently called for either institutionalization or
sterilization of women of child-bearing age who fell under the vague
category of feeble-mindedness. Denison's approach to the question of
prostitution – and indeed, her view of women's rights – was not shared
by the conservative leadership of the NCW, which dominated the
committees mentioned.[62]

Despite some internal dissension, then, the NCW on the whole
supported the male church leaders in their definition of the problem of
white slavery. Like the WCTU, they occasionally mentioned that "white
slavery" was the wrong term because women of colour were often more
exploited in prostitution than white women; both women's organizations had subcommittees that deliberately avoided the word "white"
and used the race-neutral term "traffic in women." But they did not
openly and consistently challenge the racist undertones of the moral

panic. To do so would have necessitated revising their views about men of colour.[62]

The NCW participated with church organizations in the 1912 organization of a National Committee for the Suppression of the White Slave Traffic as a subcommittee of the Moral and Social Reform Council of Canada – an administrative location that put the issue of white slavery firmly under the control of Rev. Shearer and other conservative clergy. This committee was active for a few years in seeking tougher laws and law enforcement; in 1917 it de-emphasized white slavery to take up the new burning issues of venereal disease and control of the feeble-minded.[63]

What was the secret of the moral reformers' success? Since virtually no evidence was found of a traffic in Canadian women either within or without Canada's borders, how was this successful campaign organized?[64] And what purposes did it serve, both for those who organized it and for those who passively acquiesced in it?

The answer to these questions lies in the way the construct of "white slavery" was elaborated, as symbol or emblem of everything that was dangerous to single women in the new urban environment – and everything that was dangerous *about* such women. Feminists and anti-feminists, socialists and conservatives, extreme racists and moderate assimilationists were all able to join the campaign by conveniently stressing one or another of the variegated analyses and images of white slavery produced in the literature. The flexibility of "white slavery" as a construct, and its consequent ability to act as a condenser of anxieties about shifting race, sex, and gender relations and about urbanization can be best seen by a couple of detailed analyses of white-slavery narratives.

One common feature of these narratives was what one might call the pseudo-eyewitness account. This was a second- or third-hand story told by someone *as if* he/she had been there. In journalistic style, there is an emphasis on reporting details that give the account verisimilitude and also act as triggers for mythical beliefs supplied by the audience. Let us look at a story told at the 1914 annual meeting of the Social Service Council of Canada by Rev. T. Hunter Boyd, the Presbyterian Church's Canadian immigration agent in Glasgow (who also represented the Canadian National Committee for the Suppression of the White Slave Traffic on the international bureau under Coote's leadership).

"A young girl of British parentage in service in Montreal was inveigled by another girl . . . into a room occupied by two Italians. . . . She was held in bondage vile for a period of several weeks." She was then transported to British Columbia, where she was put in a brothel. The keeper, however, noticed that "the girl was not one of the usual sort" and helped her to escape. "The Italian white slaver was arrested, tried and convicted," Boyd added, while the "girl" was put in a "redemptive home."[65]

The plot of this story begins, like the "Maiden Tribute," with one woman defiling another. This is followed by the appeal to views of Italians as overly sexual and hence immoral; by the melodramatic train trip across the continent; and finally, the rescue, which takes place only when she is recognized as *not like other women*. The resolution involves the punishment of the Italian but also the reform of the girl herself, who, although portrayed as innocent, requires a period of purification. Forced prostitution is thus denounced without challenging the belief that there are many women who deserve their fate, and that most men (notably Anglo-Saxons) are "normal."

Another pseudo-eyewitness account, in the volume *War on the White Slave Trade*, gives a different cast of characters. This account was authored (or perhaps quoted, one cannot tell) by Rev. R.B. St. Clair, head of the interdenominational clergymen's association of Ontario. Under the heading of "White Slave Traffic in Toronto," Rev. St. Clair begins by evoking the journalistic cliché of a young woman in a new clerical occupation: "A young lady employed at the glove counter in one of the large department stores in this city was recently requested by a male customer to consent to take a drive with him after store hours."[66] The clerk, having undoubtedly been well brought up by her mother, "indignantly refused." This apparent happy ending, however, was the beginning of her downfall. A woman customer "dressed in deep mourning" congratulated the clerk for her virtue – only to offer her, as a kind of prize, a ticket to a "Massey Hall entertainment" for that evening. The clerk accepted.

By this time the reader, familiar with white slavery narratives, suspects that neither the philanthropically built Massey Hall nor the "widow" are what they seem. One of the recurring elements of these narratives, shared with other social enigma genres such as Gothic novels, is that social appearances are always mysterious or deceptive. Rev. St. Clair's next paragraph describes the beginning of a fall that has been constructed by the narrative form as inevitable; "On the way to the Hall, the 'widow' produced a box of dainty chocolates, offering the girl some. The young lady ate several of them." The reader would here fear the chocolates contained knock-out drops. But just as the young lady is about to succumb to the dragon-like procuress, the white knight of purity appears on the horizon, in the shape of a "Methodist deaconess." She tells the clerk the truth about both the apparently mournful widow and the apparently sweet chocolates, in the nick of time. Rev. St. Clair concludes: "Had she been in the care of the woman in black she would have been hustled into a closed cab, and within a very short time would have been another recruit to the already large army of white slaves."

This story and the many other similar ones were designed to tell young women that ordinary precautions are not enough in the mysterious city.[67] A widow may turn out to be a procuress; the blandest of entertainments in a respectable hall may be but the stepping stone to prostitution; the girlish pleasure of eating chocolates may result in being drugged. Things are not what they seem, and motherly advice is not enough. Rev. Shearer warned, in a sermon reported in the newspapers, that 60,000 girls across North America "sink into the underworld" every year, and he drew public attention to the 25,000 girls in Toronto who worked for their living and boarded, and were hence outside the protection and control of the patriarchal family.[68] In confronting a problem of such vast proportions, only the *ex machina* intervention of a white knight (usually a male, but occasionally a female philanthropist) can protect the working girl.

Even the Knights of Labor, who did more to organize women workers than any other group, were affected by the protectionist, chivalric mentality fostered by sensationalist accounts of white slavery and seduction. In 1885-86, in the wake of the "Maiden Tribute" revelations and a Hamilton, Ontario, story of working girl's seduction and eventual infanticide the Knights lobbied (successfully) for anti-seduction legislation. Karen Dubinsky's account of the origins of the 1886 seduction clause shows that W.T. Stead's white knight approach was quite influential in shaping not only the language but also the political response of the Knights to the problems of workplace sexual harassment and general sexual exploitation of working-class women.[69]

White slavery narratives established a catalogue of dangerous places that included not only the proverbial "chop suey palaces" and music halls but practically every public place in the city. They also elaborated a list of dangerous people, which began with Italians, Chinese, blacks, and Jews but did not neglect the respectable-looking English-speaking matron.[70] Following this to its logical conclusion, aspersions could also be cast on the genuineness of philanthropic workers, a possibility contemplated in a federal government pamphlet issued at the request of the White Slave Traffic Committee and titled "Warnings to Girls."

Do not loiter in public places, and remember that there are women as well as men in strange cities, or travelling by train, who are watching for chances to decoy the innocent. They have many traps set, such as pretending to be in a faint, or wishing to be taken home; claiming to know you, or to represent some society for the protection of strangers, etc.[71]

This warning curiously undermined the work of the organizations that had caused it to be printed. Having questioned not only informal female support networks but also private philanthropies, the pamphlet firmly directed travelling young women to men in uniform and state officials:

Take no notice of any printed matter given on the train unless endorsed by the company or conductor. Do not ask the way from any but officials. . . . When you are in trouble be careful to whom you tell it.

The mapping of dangerous people and places was so comprehensive that the solution recommended in the last of the "Warnings" appears quite plausible: "When in danger, mentally pray to God for deliverance."

The white slavery narrative acted as a funnel for a variety of social fears. The melodramatic/journalistic form, the stock characters, and the descriptions of the seamy side of urban life for the voyeuristic pleasure of a middle-class churchgoing audience were literary elements constituting a very successful genre, pioneered by W.T Stead and continuing in today's news accounts of crime and vice in the city.[72] The narrative, however, did not stand on its own as a purely literary text. Just as Stead's "Maiden Tribute" interspersed description with lobbying, the stories of "real cases" were accompanied by analyses of the causes of the social evil and recommendations for action.

Moral reform organizations constantly produced accounts of the causes of the social evil, most often not in a sustained argument but rather in the form of a list of causes. The same causes appeared in different lists, in haphazard rank order. A typical list (of causes of the white slave traffic) was produced by the Methodist moral-reform organization:

(1) Lack of character, because of parental inefficiency in training and counsel.
(2) Attending theatres and amusements which pander to passion. Seeking pleasures at dance halls, and thinking they shall have lots of fun. By occasionally visiting Chinese restaurants . . . .
(3) Too much liberty at nights on the streets.
(4) Insufficient wages in stores and factories.
(5) Inordinate love of fine clothing and an unreasonable desire for an easy life.[73]

Who is then to blame for the social evil? Parents are responsible;

but girls themselves are also to be blamed for "thinking they shall have lots of fun" in Chinese restaurants and on the streets. Employers who pay low wages are chastised, but at the end, as a kind of conclusion, women are blamed for their laziness, vanity, and love of finery.[74]

Every year this organization produced a similar list. The one for 1915 was somewhat different in highlighting basic Methodist doctrine on sin and only then moving into sociological discourse:

1. The sin and depravity of the human heart.
2. The double standard of morality.
3. Insufficient wages for women workers.
4. Lack of proper home training and control.
5. Indecent forms of amusement.
6. Neglect by the authorities to provide care and control for the feeble-minded. It is well known that fully one-half of all prostitutes are mentally defective.[75]

This list blames the authorities more and the women less; but the feminist view listed in cause #2 is not regarded as disturbing other explanations. On the surface of it there is a striking contradiction between point #1 and point #6, that is, between the fundamentalist vs. the medical explanation of female vice; but, as argued earlier, moral reformers adhered to many heterogeneous explanations simultaneously and did not regard them as being in conflict.

By establishing the appearance of consistency between various frameworks through the simple technique of writing down different explanations as so many numbered causes, social purity discourse minimized conflicts among member organizations. The technique also had the theoretical effect of creating what David Garland calls "horizontal linkages," through which social problems are connected in an unspecified manner.[76] In this case, these linkages allowed the conceptualization of white slavery as a kind of collective noun under which all manner of social problems huddled. This is a feature of moral panics in general: an entity (mugging, drugs, white slavery) that appears to be quite concrete and empirically visible turns out to be a complex and multi-layered emblem representing moral, social, economic, and political regulatory crises in a condensed form.

Practical Consequences: Punishment and Rescue

Analyses of the causes of the social evil were followed by practical recommendations, generally under three headings: (1) legislative and police efforts; (2) rescue work among fallen women; (3) "preventive" or educational work. The tripartite solution was widely adhered to and allowed reformers to seek harsh law-and-order measures while making a space for voluntary philanthropy. The mayor of Winnipeg explained to the 1911 Robson Commission that "what the police can do is only a small part of what can be done. . . . There must be rescue and reformation work which is equally active and efficient, and, above all, there must be educative and moral agencies as well."[77] Despite the consensus on the limits of policing and the need for education, some organizations pursued law enforcement with great vigour, notably the National Committee for the Suppression of the White Slave Traffic, co-chaired by the ubiquitous Rev. Shearer. Women's groups, by contrast, tended to focus on education (notably the WCTU) or on rescue work (women's missionary societies and the Salvation Army).

The law-enforcement strategy consisted of lobbying for changes to the Criminal Code paralleling English and American anti-procuring laws, while the educative strategy consisted in publicizing the accounts analysed above in the press and in various gatherings. The strategy that requires some explanation, because of its historical specificity, is rescue work among fallen women.

Rescue work had been undertaken since the 1850s, and although privately controlled it received municipal and later provincial support in many instances.[78] The refuges or asylums for fallen women were sometimes used as shelters by abused or homeless women. The mixing of innocence and vice was denounced by Ontario's watchdog over charities, Inspector J.S. Langmuir, who complained that the voluntary admission procedures of Magdalen asylums (as rescue homes were officially designated) hampered the state's objective of criminalizing "habitual offenders against public morals."[79] Langmuir's ambitious plans for the state notwithstanding, private organizations continued to run asylums for women well into the twentieth century; when the courts began to sentence women to serve time in these homes the philanthropists were not replaced by state corrections officials but simply assumed quasi-public powers.

While private philanthropic workers assumed quasi-police powers, the public police also came to see itself as exercising benevolent functions. Toronto Mayor W.H. Howland explained to the Royal Commission on Capital and Labour that his city's morality squad did not merely prosecute vice but also sought to reform prostitutes: "I may say that I always send an officer before [a raid], telling them that if they will take up decent work, or if they will go to any home, we will get homes for them."[80] Howland does not explain to what extent the "homes" available for women were coercive, and does not specify how officers distinguished between rescue cases and punishment cases. That he had his own moral criteria with which to make this distinction

The Salvation Army led the way in the work of "rescuing" prostitutes; from War Cry, *2 March 1895.* (Courtesy Salvation Army Heritage Centre)

is shown by his explanation that some "unfortunate girls" fall into temptation due to hardship,"but it is rooted laziness which is the greatest difficulty with those who are really prostitutes."

The moral reformer D.A. Watt, while denouncing the draconian powers of the police over women of the Contagious Diseases Acts, followed Howland in classifying Criminal Code measures against prostitution not under "punishment" but under "prevention," explaining: "Of all preventable [*sic*] agencies nothing can equal a decent, reputable and moral Criminal Code, not so much in its punitive character as in its deterrent, and especially in its educative character."[81]

Moral reformers, then, stressed the educational and reformative powers of the law and argued that tough law enforcement, rather than hindering the voluntary work of reform, facilitated such moral transformation. The Salvation Army was particularly forceful in suggesting to judges and lawyers that there was no contradiction in the state using religious bodies as amateur prison guards. This was not due to simple opportunism – although the official status acquired by the Army within the penal system was greatly prized by their leaders – but to a sincere belief that the secular punishment of offenders was far inferior to evangelical methods. Those convicted of drunkenness or morals offences, if they were put under the Army's care by force, would soon voluntarily convert and reform. This belief fitted in quite well with the regulatory dilemmas of a liberal democratic state faced with moral panics; as Garland has put it, "the ideology of liberalism, and its strict division between public and private spheres, specified that such questions of morality and welfare were private matters unsuitable for state concerns."[82] The Army stated that, regardless of the merits of prison rehabilitation, in the case of fallen women "no mere reformation will do . . . God must make a thorough change in their hearts before they can ever hope to regain their character and womanhood again."[83]

Rescue work had begun in the mid-Victorian era, when prostitutes were perceived as temptress Eves. When the image of prostitution changed in the mid-1880s, the new child-like white slave did not supplant the harlot but was added to the repertoire of clichés. The Salvation Army, which embraced rescue work much more warmly than its more respectable counterparts, made little distinction between willing prostitutes and white slaves in its practical work, describing all the inmates of its Toronto rescue home as "troops of girls . . . earning the wages of sin."[84] Whatever their route into prostitution, they all needed to be saved (it should be recalled that even W.T. Stead's non-defiled girl victim was sent off to a Salvation Army home in France to regain her character through domestic work). The Army did not merely wait for fallen women to come to its door but promoted neighbourhood surveillance: "Write to us, giving the name and address of anyone who seems in danger of going astray."[85]

Once in the rescue home, the women and girls – who might number between four or five and twenty – were subjected not only to evangelical training but to lessons in domestic work and sewing, all with a view to their future employment as servants. This was also the case in the Victor Home run by the Methodists in Toronto. The little information available on this latter home also suggests that no distinctions were made between willing prostitutes and victims of white slavers, or indeed between prostitutes and non-prostitutes: the women were considered to be "fallen" by virtue of the fact that they were in a Rescue Home, and "rehabilitated" by doing commercial laundry work.[86] A

Victor Home social worker stated contentedly: "It is something worth while to make it possible for them to win back a large measure of the respectability which sin has forfeited."[87]

Thus, despite the white-slavery narrative construction of some women as innocent victims, the innocence only lasted as long as the narrative. The practices of rescue work continued to treat all women in rescue homes as requiring conversion and reform, regardless of their guilt or innocence. The workers admitted that there were degrees of vice, but were not willing to admit that any of their girls were truly "unfallen." They generally portrayed the women simultaneously as "sinned against" *and* as a "menace to society."[88]

The other branch of anti-prostitution work, prevention or education, was also characterized by a tendency to suspect everyone of sin, which in practice meant the reformers' reach included as many as possible. The work of Beatrice Brigden and other sex-hygiene educators addressed not the deviant women but the non-deviant adolescent population. The WCTU, on its part, decided that rescue work was not a priority and concentrated on educating middle-class mothers in child-rearing. They also sought to have the government ban obscene literature while encouraging temperance and sex-hygiene education in the school system. Through their work with middle-class Protestant Canadians, they hoped to consolidate "home and native land" in the face of an uncertain future.[89]

The fears that underlay the white slavery panic – young women moving to cities and taking up new occupations, urban anonymity, immigration, the breakdown of traditional networks of support and social control – were the fears of a large sector of the Canadian population. Anglo-Saxon middle-class Protestants were somewhat uncertain about their ability to manage the drastic changes in social, economic, and cultural relations taking place in turn-of-the-century Canada in such a way as to preserve their newly won economic superiority and cultural hegemony. They also worried about changing gender and generational relations; the panic allowed them to admit that the city was dangerous to young women without attacking the patriarchal and class relations that produced such dangers. Their unconscious anxiety about the possible sexual desires of people of more "passionate" races was also given recognition in white-slavery narratives. Although not orchestrated consciously by the ruling group, the moral panic about white slavery, in some respects an import from Britain and the U.S., also served an historically specific purpose as a site on which Canadian dilemmas in social and moral regulation were indirectly discussed.

5

Racial Purity, Sexual Purity, and Immigration Policy

"The Purity of Our National Lifeblood": Race and Morality in Turn-of-the-Century Thought

The clean souls and bodies prized by social purity were not only symbolically but literally white. The profound racism of Anglo-Saxon Canadians at the turn of the century had many different roots, some in common with the U.S. and some specific to Canada; racist ideas and strategies permeated the economics, politics, and social policy of early twentieth-century Canada. There is a growing literature on immigration history, but it has generally neglected to examine the sexual/moral components of Canadian racism.

Sexual morality was an important component of what was known as "character," in turn an important part of the project of building a nation that was moral as well as prosperous. As the Presbyterian social reform leader Rev. George Pidgeon said on the occasion of the fortieth anniversary of Confederation, Canada can be "proud of [the] growth of natural resources, of [its] place in the Empire . . . [but it] must not forget that the source of national wealth and power lies in the character of its people."[1] White people were seen as having more character, as a group, than Native people or people of colour; and among whites, people of British descent were regarded as having the most character.

Character was both presupposed by and acquired through activities such as clearing prairies and building transcontinental railways; but it was also centrally related to the ability to control one's sexual needs and wants. That the civilization Europeans believed they had brought to North America was built on sexual self-denial was taken almost for granted by most educated, middle-class Canadian Protestants during this period. In the words of Charlotte Whitton (who spent the first four years of her working life under Dr. Shearer in the Moral and Social Reform Council), the ruling group saw "the regulation and control of instinct and emotion as the basis of civilization."[2] The Anglo-Saxon "race" was regarded as much more capable of controlling their instincts than other races; the Anglo-Canadian educated elite accepted without a thought John Stuart Mill's statement that "both in a good and a bad sense, the English are farther from a state of nature than any other modern people. They are, more than any other people, a product of civilization and discipline. . . . In England, rule has to a great degree substituted itself for nature."[3]

This "rule" or "regulation and control of instinct" was crucial for gender formation, for class order, and for racial and ethnic organization. If blacks and East Indians were undesirable immigrants, it was not because they had no capital and no schooling (many British immigrants were poor and unskilled), but rather because they were "savages," that is, people who could not control their sexual desires and were thus unlikely to lead orderly and civilized lives, saving for rainy days and postponing gratification.[4] Any moral regulation brought to bear on these people would have to be external and coercive. This caused no moral or theoretical problems in Africa or India, where British rule was unabashedly undemocratic. It was, however, a problematic choice for Canada, both for pragmatic reasons and because of the inherent contradictions facing liberal democracies undertaking coercive measures to uphold moral or social values. (Liberal democracies have a structural commitment to a "private" sphere and to juridical equality among all citizens; as I have argued elsewhere, this helps to explain the key role of extra-state voluntary organizations in moral reform campaigns in liberal democratic states.[5])

In the Canadian context, internalized control was seen as the best foundation for a social order envisioned as built primarily through consensus and genuine, internalized respect for authority, and only exceptionally through coercion and force. As the political economist James Mavor put it, the essence of "the social question" was to ensure "spontaneous regulation" among "the mass of the people," and only the failure of self-regulation would make "compulsory action" necessary.[6] The British system was held up as embodying both respect for authority and (somewhat paradoxically) self-control, self-regulation.[7] The Moral and Social Reform Council of Canada was "persuaded that in a new country, whose stream of national blood contains strains from almost every nationality and race in the world, it is of vital importance that the traditional British respect for law, order, and authority should be maintained at all costs." Britishness, a peculiar mixture of social order and individual freedom, functioned as a sign of both sexual and civic self-policing.

The sovereign individuals agreeing to respect authority composed the nation; but this nation was not so much a mechanical addition of individuals as an organic whole, whose bloodstream – identified with "the race" – had to be guarded against contamination by external poisons.[8]

This national "blood" had metonymic associations with other bodily fluids. This can be seen in the following text, by Rev. S.D. Chown, head of the Methodist Church and key social purity activist:

> The immigration question is the most vital one in Canada today, as it has to do with the purity of our national life-blood. . . . It is foolish to dribble away the vitality of our own country in a vain endeavour to assimilate the world's non-adjustable, profligate, and indolent social parasites. . . . It is most vital to our nation's life that we should ever remember that quality is of greater value than quantity and that character lies at the basis of national stability and progress.[9]

The national blood is here unconsciously linked to the semen individual men and boys were constantly admonished not to "dribble away." The taboo on masturbation is thus combined with unconscious fears of miscegenation, as the link between individual character and nation-building is mobilized in the service of an exclusionary and racist immigration policy. Chown does not have to state that the "parasites" he has in mind are of Asian, black, or Jewish origin; his audience would have supplied those images from the repertoire available to them.

The links between sexual excess, mental and moral degeneration, and the decline of the nation were made repeatedly. It was not a view to be argued for but rather a premise the moral reformers took for granted and elaborated with images, prejudged examples, and rhetorical figures of speech. In a meeting of the Canadian Council on the Immigration of Women, a report authored by Dr. C.K. Clarke (Canada's most famous psychiatrist) shows how racism was constructed by a medical authority – and quickly transposed into the religious key by a clergyman who was present. Clarke's opinion about plans to bring to Canada Jewish children caught in the Ukraine famine was very negative. Since Jews were known to often be educated professionals, Clarke had to resort to complicated discursive twists to support his frankly fascist views:

> It must be remembered that the Jewish children of this type [immigrants] belong to a *very neurotic race*, and while many of them are of unusual ability, yet a certain proportion prove to be mental defectives or are already showing evidence of mental disease. . . . [They] should be kept for several days under inspection, *and the weaklings weeded out remorselessly.*[10]

On hearing this, Rev. Chisholm, who made his living welcoming immigrants and attempting to direct them to Presbyterian churches, added almost automatically that "Jews have much to do with commercialized vice" (prostitution). The minutes do not record any dissent from the chain of associations being assumed here: Jews – neurosis – disease – vice – prostitution. As Barbara Roberts has shown, the eugenic ideas prevalent among Canada's doctors gave racist immigration policies a scientific veneer: the inquiry into medical inspection of immigrants (which resulted in social purity activist Dr. Peter Bryce being named as head of the federal medical immigration inspection) concluded that "racial criteria were even more important than medical ones" and that "immigrants from northern stock could be rehabilitated and remain healthy in good clean Canadian conditions."[11]

Although many reformers agreed that British people and their descendants were by nature morally superior, Clarke's extreme eugenicist views – shared by important government officials in the 1910s and 1920s – were not the main framework through which moral reformers organized their racism.[12] Unlike the doctors and bureaucrats who came increasingly to monopolize social issues, the evangelical reformers tended to put more emphasis on the role of centuries of parliamentary rule, civilized sexual habits, and Protestantism in producing what they thought was the highest "race." "Race" was not for them a strictly biological concept; it was organized through traditions as well as through genes. This belief was necessary in their evangelical efforts, since if character were completely biologically determined there would be little point in converting Chinese Canadians or Native people to Protestant habits of life. Although they certainly did not think that a Christian Chinese person was the equal of a Christian of British descent, the more hopeful among them thought that in a few generations the objectionable culture of non-British immigrants might disappear, even if the physical ethnic types remained.

The appeal to British traditions put Canadian reformers in a difficult position, since at the same time that they were trying to infuse "foreigners" with the moral values of Tennyson and Ruskin they were also beginning to assert the autonomy of Canada within the Empire, an assertion that necessitated finding specifically Canadian cultural traits. This contradiction was suppressed through an interesting discourse on "nativism" and "traditions" that erased not only Native peoples but also French Canadians through the claim that the (Anglo) Canadian nation's life "extends over milleniums [sic]."[13]

"Nativism" was perhaps also a disingenuous term in the eastern U.S.; but it was downright fantastical in western Canada, which until quite late in the nineteenth century was not even administratively white. Probably because of the precariousness of white/European western Canadian life, the efforts to invent a "native" Anglo-Canadian tradition were most vigorous there.[14] By 1914 this invented tradition was so well accepted that a Methodist newspaper could defend the exclusion of Asian immigrants (in the *Komagata Maru* incident) on the basis of the "evident" statement that white Europeans were native to British Columbia: "it is evident that each race is better off on its own natural environment . . . the unrestrained mixing of the races on this coast would lead to economic disaster and ethical demoralisation."[15]

The races, needless to say, only began to be mixed when the whites came. And contrary to the racist fears of whites being swamped by other races, the population of B.C. was in fact becoming increasingly white during the period under study: in 1880-81 almost half of B.C.'s 50,000 inhabitants were Indian, but by 1901 the Indian population remained at about 25,000 while the total population increased dramatically to 180,000. The much-feared Chinese, on their part, made up slightly less than 10 per cent of the B.C. population in 1880-81 (before the great railway boom), more than 10 per cent of the B.C. population in 1901, but less than 6 per cent by 1921: their numbers, like those of the Native people, had remained fairly stable, but the white population grew tremendously.[16]

As Howard Palmer has pointed out in his study of racism in Alberta, white Canadians of European descent did not generally study demographic trends or react to people of colour and/or immigrants out of economic rationality; their actions were the product of a complex set of cultural constructs.[17] One of the most important among these has been studied in other contexts but hardly at all for Canada, that is, the idea that "the race" was in imminent peril of "degeneration."[18] Let us look a little more closely at the connection between sexual and racial degeneration.

From 1911 to 1916, Dr. C.K. Clarke claimed, studies conducted in the psychiatric clinic for poor people at Toronto General Hospital showed that immigrants were overrepresented among the feeble-minded. The vague category of feeble-mindedness had been in turn linked to sexual deviance, by American claims that prostitutes were often feeble-minded, and by Dr. Helen MacMurchy's sensationalistic reports as Ontario's Inspector of the Feeble-minded in the 1910s – reports in which "illegitimate mothers," as she called them, were circularly deemed to be feeble-minded because they had a child out of wedlock. The connections linking deviant sexuality, immigrants, and national degeneration were thus firmly established.[19]

Degeneration, however, was not a single process; and immigrants and people of colour were not seen as a homogeneous mass equally responsible for degeneration in general. There were fine gradations in both the problem and the agencies causing it. "Degeneration," a term popularized by the French medical writer B.A. Morel, meant originally the physiological process of nervous system degeneration, an individual condition like multiple sclerosis (degeneration of muscle tissue). Very quickly, however, European medical and social writers used the concept to refer both to moral and psychological flaws that might encourage nervous-tissue degeneration, and to a wider social process of decay. As George Moss and Robert Nye have argued for Germany and France respectively, anxieties about urban crime and about political upheavals were welded to fears about the mad and the racially "other."[20] Max Nordau's influential work *Degeneration* (translated into English in 1895) extended the concept even further: "Degenerates are not always criminals, prostitutes, anarchists, and pronounced lunatics; they are often authors and artists."[21] Nordau claimed that the fin-de-siècle decadence seen in such writers as Nietzsche and Oscar Wilde was rooted in physiological nervous-system decay and would in turn lead to harmful evolutionary consequences, such as "hereditary hysteria," if allowed to flourish. The artists and writers despised by Nordau were characterized as emotional, melancholic, and generally feminized; Nordau's plan for regeneration thus involved both the purification and the masculinization of "the race."

Like Nordau, W.L. Mackenzie King held Lamarckian rather than Darwinian views of evolution, believing that acquired traits could be passed on to future generations. It was therefore important to pass special legislation to control the work of women of child-bearing age, for the nervous strain of the new white-collar occupations might form traits that would then be inherited by the offspring:

> What physical and mental overstrain, and underpay and underfeeding are doing for the race in occasioning infant mortality, a low birthrate, and *race degeneration*, in increasing nervous disorders and furthering a general predisposition to disease, is appalling.[22]

The meaning of "race" in this passage, and many other similar ones, is ambiguous. On the one hand it referred to the Anglo-Saxon race; but there was also an implication that the fate of the whole human race hinged on the preservation of the racial health and political dominance of Anglo-Saxons. In this way, "the human race" was also intended, in a secondary way. The phrase "race suicide," popularized by Theodore Roosevelt, meant both the numerical decline of the Anglo-Saxon race with respect to other more fertile groups, *and* the decline of humanity as a whole. The slippery term "race" allowed Anglo-Saxons to think of themselves as both a specific race and as the vanguard of the human race as a whole. the ambiguity of the term hence allowed white Anglo-Saxon supremacy to be justified without argument or evidence: it was obvious that as Anglo-Saxons progressed or declined, so would the world.

Anglo-Saxons could see themselves as a specific race only in contrast to others. These others were not all identical: there was an elaborate classification system that ranked national and ethnic groups according to a combination of geographical, physiological, and moral criteria. Generally speaking, northerners were to be preferred to southerners (and the role of old European ideas about the sexually passionate nature of southerners and easterners cannot be underestimated in this context); lighter-skinned people were to be preferred to dark-skinned people; and Protestants were far preferable to Catholics, with Christians in general being preferable to non-Christians. These general principles of classification, including the idea of "character" as sexual self-control, then gave rise to a taxonomy that bore little relation to the self-representation of the peoples in question.

The principles of immigration taxonomies were rarely articulated explicitly. For instance, in what was probably the major work on the topic, J.S. Woodsworth's *Strangers Within Our Gates* (1909), the chain of racial being is laid out not through a reasoned discussion but through the simple process of organizing the chapters on each immigrant group in a descending metaphysical order. That this was the "correct" order of precedence would not be questioned by the intended readership. The first group is "Immigrants from Great Britain"; then, those from the U.S., followed by the Scandinavians. The Germans are then discussed, followed by the French (Germans were more likely to be Protestant and hence higher in Woodsworth's scale). Then the book moves on to the "non-preferred" categories: Austria-Hungary; the Balkan states; the Jews, portrayed as though they were a single geographical group; the Italians; a peculiar conglomerate known as "the Levantine races," which includes Greeks, Turks, Armenians, Syrians, and Persians; and finally, the most alien of all, "the Orientals" and the "Negro and the [East] Indian."[23]

This taxonomy, which was not Woodsworth's invention but was part of the dominant culture of the time, is perhaps best illuminated by looking at the fate of the most despised groups, namely Asians and blacks. With respect to Asians, the terms "Chinese" and "Oriental," which were used interchangeably, did not refer so much to geography or physical appearance as to the mythical image of the "Oriental" derived from European and American views of China.[24] Central to this myth was the view that the Orientals were not savages (since Marco Polo, Europeans had had a certain awe of China) but were, on the contrary, so civilized that they had degenerated. Theodore Roosevelt's evocation of "the over-civilized man, who has lost the great fighting, masterful virtues" was probably a reference to the Chinese; and the Canadian Royal Commission on Chinese and Japanese immigration of 1902 took it for granted that immigrants from these two countries could not possibly ever be granted citizenship status because of the vices inherent in "an ancient and effete civilization."[25] The young women from university branches of the Dominion YWCA typically heard a lecture on "Japan and its Degeneration" in 1910.[26] In discussions of the opium trade, suggestions were made that Chinese sexual vice was not characterized by impulsive aggression but rather by a loss of manhood and consequent need for drugs to induce sexual desire.

This view of the Chinese as hopelessly degenerate, as a nation in evolutionary and moral decline, was the justification for the policy of not allowing Chinese labourers to set up permanent families and communities in Canada. (It also helped to justify the total exclusion of Chinese immigrants in 1923.) The Royal Commission on Chinese Immigration of 1885 held the generally accepted view that the Chinese were a "non-assimilable race," and Sir John A. Macdonald, who overrode the objections of the British Columbia government and allowed Chinese contractors to bring in labourers to build the railway, assured the anti-Chinese immigration forces that there need be "no fear of a permanent degradation of the country by a mongrel race."[27]

Given this official discourse, it is not surprising that grassroots racism against the Chinese flourished in subsequent decades.[28] Chinese stores in Calgary were wrecked by a racist mob in 1892 with the acquiescence of the local police force; in 1907, an anti-Chinese riot in Lethbridge resulted in restaurants being attacked and their owners being roughed up; and Vancouver's Asiatic Exclusion League incited a major riot in 1907 without suffering any legal consequences.[29]

The moral/sexual overtones of anti-Asian racism were made quite explicit by moral reformers. In 1910, the staff inspector in charge of Toronto's morality division accused the Chinese of enticing white girls into vice:

> Immorality among young girls is increasing, caused by too much liberty to roam the streets, and the consequent results therefrom. The lure of the Chinaman is also developing among this class of girls, to their utter demoralization in many instances.[30]

The theme of "the lure of the Chinaman" was explored at length by the well-known conservative feminist Emily Murphy. In 1922 Murphy published as a book a series of articles that had appeared in Maclean's on the drug trade in Canada. This book, *The Black Candle*, shows that social-purity ideas about vice and sexuality were suffused by racism – and vice versa, ideas about race were partly shaped by ideas about the sexual practices of different groups. Murphy raised the spectre of white women being lured through drugs and taken into opium dens; although sexual practices are only hinted at, there are enough hints to indicate that the fear of miscegenation was a profound one in Murphy's mind.

Interestingly, Murphy's sensationalist photographs of drugged individuals included a photo of a *black* man apparently in bed with a white woman. Canadians were at this time exposed to American panics about the sexual influence of black men over white women, and Murphy's picture has to be interpreted in the context of the significant rise of Ku Klux Klan activity in Saskatchewan and Alberta. Black men, who were generally portrayed as oversexed and hence as probable rapists, became the target of a combined sex-and-race panic in Alberta in 1910-11, when a group of black Oklahoma farmers sought to emigrate to Alberta (ironically, to escape Klan persecution in their own country). Although white farmers were being courted as immigrants at this time, the black farmers were strongly discouraged; the federal government even sent a black doctor to Oklahoma to warn potential immigrants that they might die of cold in northern climes. Women's organizations added their own gender-specific racism to the discussion, as seen in a petition by the International Order of Daughters of the Empire:

> We do not wish that the fair name of western Canada should be sullied with the shadow of lynch law, but we have no guarantee that our women will be safer in their scattered homesteads than white women in other countries with a Negro population.[31]

As William Calderwood has shown, Protestant ministers were quite active in the Saskatchewan KKK in its heyday and this activity was not seen as untoward by their congregations; rather, it shows the continuity between mainstream or "ordinary" racism and the activities of racist groups perceived as marginal to Canadian history.[32]

But if race (as a socially constructed category, not as experience or as anthropological fact) was a crucial variable in the attempt to stem sexual and social degeneration, it was not the only one. British urban working-class immigrants came increasingly under scrutiny. Some Canadians (such as Charlotte Whitton and Peter Bryce, head of the medical inspection of immigrants) went so far as to deny that the urban poor of Britain were more desirable as immigrants than the ethnically inferior but healthier farmers of central Europe. Others preferred to take an environmentalist approach and argue that the degeneration taking place at the heart of the Empire could be reversed after immigration to Canada, at least in the following generation. Moral reformers usually preferred this latter view, as expounded by the Missionary Society of the Methodist Church in 1910:

> It should not be forgotten that while many of these immigrants have deteriorated . . . they belong to a race which is the first among the strong ones of the earth – a race that hitherto has had no equal in the work of colonizing . . . [getting prairies cleared] and covered with yellow harvests; and with beautiful and rich possessions.
>
> Under the free sky of this Dominion . . . the children of these people will grow up into healthy and worthy manhood. Blood will tell. The race will assert itself and reproduce in the children of these people the old English character and the old English strength.[33]

The final point to be considered in this section is yet another ambiguity in the meaning of "race." In the days of Sir John A. Macdonald, to be Canadian was to be British, and the existence of Quebec was not a barrier to this unproblematic identification. As the decades wore on, however, Canada developed certain economic conflicts with Britain, mostly in respect to tariffs, and in the cultural realm there began to be an assertion of a Canadian nationalism. In a typical attempt to assert a national identity but still uphold the ideals of the Empire, the popular novelist Sara Jeanette Duncan presented a small-town Ontario hero who is a staunch imperialist but also a Canadian nationalist. Duncan's glorification of Canadian open spaces, healthy work, and democratic lack of class difference does not prevent her hero from waxing mystical about England: "I see England down the future the heart of the Empire, the conscience of the world, the Mecca of the race."[34] Other Canadian writers, however, began to see Canadians as a distinct "race"; as the Vancouver racist agitator Charles E. Hope put it, "we must remember we are trying to evolve a Canadian race as well as Canadian nation."[35] Hope and others, however, simultaneously believed in the Anglo-Saxons as a race: when they spoke of a Canadian "race" they probably meant a culture, and saw this culture as based on Anglo-Saxon "racial" characteristics.[36]

The nationalist view was vividly presented in a poem, published in the Methodist magazine *Missionary Outlook* in 1905, celebrating the defeat of Native peoples and the rise of a powerful, masculine Canadian nation/race:

> And still the tide flows westward,
> Toward the land of the setting sun;
> And the call goes forth into all the world,

Until now, where the smoke of the wigwam curled,
  A new life has begun.

For see! 'Tis the birth of a nation!
And the men who will mingle now
The blood of the nation of every land,
Are founding a race, 'neath whose sovereign hand
  The knee of the world shall bow.[37]

But an article a few months later in the same publication spoke matter-of-factly about the "English-speaking race," and this latter usage remained popular until World War One.[38]

Emily Murphy, the conservative feminist who as a magistrate of women's courts enforced social purity ideals, firmly believed the views about Anglo-Saxon superiority already described, but she added a peculiarly Canadian hypothesis:

> I think the proximity of the magnetic pole has something to do with the superiority of the Northmen. The best peoples in the world have come out of the north, and the longer they are away from boreal regions in such proportion do they degenerate.[39]

Making Strangers into Neighbours: Race, Ethnicity, and Sexuality in the Work of Home Missions

In the period under study, purity work was intertwined with church work on immigration, which ranged from lobbying the government to ensure "purer" immigrants, to face-to face work teaching immigrants or giving them help. This close connection, or indeed slippage, from sexual/ethical categories to immigration and race policy was facilitated both by the strong discursive links between racial and sexual purity analysed in the previous section and by the way in which the work of moral reformers was organized. The particular practical work most relevant for the study of this connection between sex and race/immigration is what was known as home missions.

Missionary work was one of the chief activities of Christian churches in Canada. It was particularly important for churches other than Catholic or Anglican, since both of these had a clear ethnic and national base and were in some ways not keen to disrupt their ethnic homogeneity by indiscriminate recruiting. Methodists, Presbyterians, and Baptists, by contrast, had organized not national churches but conversion-based groups that needed revivals and constant outreach to maintain and increase their base. These Canadian churches, like their counterparts in the U.S. and Britain, developed extensive foreign mission efforts from the mid-nineteenth century on, Canadians concentrating primarily on China, Japan, and India.[40] Unlike British churches, however, Canadian Protestants had the additional task of reaching out to those who had been made into foreigners in their native land, that is, the Native peoples; and, after Laurier's open-door policy came into effect in 1897, much effort was devoted to converting "foreigners" (non-British and non-American immigrants) to Canadian brands of Protestantism.

Foreign missions had been the first concern of both women and men in the Protestant churches, and from the beginning "foreign" included Native peoples. Although work with Native people was sometimes re-classified under the newer category of home missions, the original conceptualization of the missionaries as the real natives of Canada was retained. With the rise of the social gospel movement, a somewhat more progressive attitude developed, church people sometimes speaking against corruption among Indian Affairs officials or against extreme acts of racism. But even social gospel texts, which present the church as a maternal force mediating between the weak Indians and the sometimes harsh paternal government, portrayed Native peoples as savages who routinely killed their old people, tortured their slaves, and treated women as mere drudges.[41] (Evidence of matrilineality and egalitarian gender roles was, however, also treated as an index of *lack* of civilization.) Although the sexual practices of Native peoples were rarely mentioned, there were veiled references to their disregard for monogamous legal marriages, and more generally to their susceptibility to the passion of the moment. Trying to give these attitudes an anthropological veneer, the missionary educator Rev. Gunn stated that many Native "languages, while rich in combinations and names of material things, are poor or absolutely without such abstract words as faith, hope, and love."[42]

The work of church missionaries with Native peoples was thus firmly based on the belief that only European Christianity could provide the basis of character development. While some church people tried to prevent Native people from being wiped out or ruthlessly exploited, none even contemplated the possibility of self-determination. Even the self-appointed friends of the Indian carried out a contradictory policy best expressed by the deputy superintendent of the Department of Indian Affairs in 1924:

> The policy of the Dominion has always been to protect the Indians, to guard their identity as a race and at the same time to apply methods which will destroy that identity and lead eventually to their disappearance as a separate division of the population.[43]

Whether Native peoples were categorized under foreign or home missions, they were part of a vast group of people who came to be known, in the early twentieth century, as "strangers." The term applied paradigmatically to non-English speaking immigrants, but also, by analogy, to Native peoples and even to those whose poverty or vice made them appear as racially distinct. In 1899, a Presbyterian newspaper proclaimed that "a healthy morality"and "a national spirit" depended on making strangers into non-strangers: "It is not to be dreamed of that the Church is to neglect these strangers. Neglect means national peril and religious decline."[44]

Strangers had to be turned into "neighbours," a process sometimes captured by using the word "neighbour" as a verb, as was done by the historian of the Methodist Women's Missionary Society in her description of the contrast between foreign and home missions:

> It may be we find it easier, through our missionaries, . . . to *neighbour* with those thousands of miles away than we do to visit the foreign woman at the other end of the city. 'Love the *stranger*' is the command.[45]

This dichotomy was clearly set out in the work of J.S. Woodsworth, the foremost Canadian spokesperson on the morals of strangers: in 1909 he published his popular book on immigrants, *Strangers Within Our Gates*, and two years later he published a similar volume on urban problems titled *My Neighbor*.

As "foreign" immigrants began to claim more attention than Chinese and Japanese "heathen," the churches rearranged their budgets accordingly. For instance, the Methodist Women's Missionary Society (MWMS) tripled the number of its missionaries working in Canada between 1906 and 1916; the number of foreign missionaries also went up but far less dramatically.[46] Equally significant is the increasing amount of space devoted to home missions in church publications. And while the Methodist Missionary Society's annual reports put foreign ahead of home missions until 1909, in the year of Woodsworth's *Strangers Within Our Gates* home missions began to be listed first. That same year, the aims of home missions were described as follows: first, "sanitation"; second, "education"; and, a poor third, "evangelistic and social work."[47]

The term "sanitation" referred primarily to physical hygiene, but since in the minds of social reformers soap and water were spiritual as well as physical cleansers, sex hygiene and moral uplift were also intended. The degree of impurity affecting immigrants, however, was a hotly debated point. Some reformers thought immigrants were basically healthy and only needed some training in the English language, self-control, and self-government in order to become good Canadians, while others saw "foreign" immigrants as inherently degenerate in body and spirit. The latter, more racist view was often put forward by church leaders who did not directly work with immigrants but were responsible for lobbying the government and speaking to the public. Rev. S.D. Chown's view of non-Anglo-Saxon immigrants as a potential poison in the Canadian national bloodstream have already been cited; his views were echoed by an editorial in the Methodist *Missionary Outlook* on the topic of strangers:

> They come to us with a manhood that has been dwarfed; . . . with low ideals of family and social life; with a sullen dislike of law and government and those by whom the law is enforced . . . an ominously large number may be classed with the idle and vicious, the incapable, the physically and morally degenerate, the pauper and the criminal.[48]

The imminent danger to Canadian virility posed by strangers was also highlighted by the Presbyterian Church's Rev. G.C. Pidgeon, whose metaphors, however, were more gastronomic than sexual: "Any foreign substance in the body corporate [is] as fatal to its life as an indig.[estible] mass in a liv.[ing] organism. . . . Moral problems involved."[49]

Some of the front-line workers, nonetheless, had a more benevolent attitude. The home missions textbook issued by the interdenominational Canadian Council for Missionary Education Movement called for "hospitality" to be shown toward the new immigrants from southern and eastern Europe and stated that "we can avoid snap judgements on whole races, based on the few moral failures that are reported in our papers."[50] Without directly criticizing the white-slavery campaign or other moral/sexual panics in which the churches had taken an active role, Gunn tries to shift the onus of moral responsibility by claiming that quite often "pure" immigrants are corrupted upon their arrival in Canadian cities: "The immigrant has to meet the 'Devil's Missionaries' of the liquor traffic, the brothel and the corrupting politician." In this way, "races long known for purity of family life have seen their young women and young men fall down and become a notorious stain upon the national life."[51]

A similar note was struck by moral reformers when they timidly protested against parts of the Chinese exclusion policy on the basis that to allow only male workers to come to Canada was to encourage immorality. Although basically opposed to Chinese immigration, one wing of the missionary movement took the position that family life was better than all-male immigration: the threat of Chinese opium smokers and white slavers was the background myth in the apparently benevolent suggestion that "we do hereby earnestly advocate the free admission of the wives and children of the Chinese in Canada in the interest of justice and morality."[52]

The novel suggestion that it was Canada that degenerated immigrants and not the other way around was made by the main Italian Methodist missionary, M.C. Catalano, who worked in Toronto. Caught between two worlds, Catalano certainly believed that Italians had to be "properly Canadianized" before they could contribute to "this 'Great Canada', which is undoubtedly the Land of Promise," but he also pointed out that Italian peasants arriving in Toronto met "evil forces" that "are the cause of the degeneration instead of the social and moral standard of life of the newcomers."[53]

Despite some efforts to turn the discourse of degeneracy around, the hegemonic idea of Canada was that it was already a very pure nation, and that the challenge of non-Anglo-Saxon immigration had to be met mainly by Canadianizing and Christianizing the strangers – two processes that in practice merged into a single one. As Rev. Pidgeon put it, "our church is not only a Christianizing but a Canadianizing element."[54] Patriotic religiosity characterized not only the racist right wing but also the benevolent current of the missionary movement. For instance, the Rev. W.T. Gunn, whose criticisms of extreme racism have been cited above, began his home missions text with an epic evocation of "God's Foundation for Nation Building in Canada." Images of rumbling glaciers, geological shifts, and the formation of mineral deposits are suffused by a sense of a national destiny that is firmly Protestant and Anglo-Saxon. Completely erasing Native peoples from his history, he declares: "In the beginning God created Canada." Providence then sought to fill it properly:

> Races and centuries passed till men [i.e., Europeans], seeking westward a Continent they knew, found in their way a continent they knew not. . . . So through the nineteenth century slowly the pioneers came, hewed down the forests, laid the foundations of homes and law and order and righteousness, secured for themselves and their successors religious liberty and responsible government, mapped out the land and bound its scattered Provinces into one Dominion from Coast to Coast.[55]

This mythical account of the origins of a nation not only portrays the Americas as empty of people before 1492, but manages to naturalize British ideas about law, the state, and religion, as though the Magna Carta emerged from the glaciers. It is hence clear that even the progressive wing of the social gospel was intensely nationalistic, and the content of their nationalism was Anglo-Saxon Protestant hegemony.

This is also seen in the writings of J.S. Woodsworth. Woodsworth, who had spent his childhood in his father's missions to Indians in Canada's Northwest, was, according to his biographer, very concerned with "personal purity";[56] but his distinctive contribution to Canadian Methodism and social reform was his work with non-Anglo-Saxon immigrants in Winnipeg's All People's Mission from 1899 onward.[57] In the course of his work, he came to the conclusion that although some immigration from southern and eastern Europe was tolerable, particularly given the assimilative efforts of All People's and other missions, Canada's immigration policy ought to allow only such quantity and quality of immigrants as could be easily assimilated. The formation of distinct pockets of, say, Doukhobors or Russian Jews ought to be strongly discouraged, while Asians and blacks, the lowest races in Woodsworth's elaborate classification system, were strangers to such a degree that they should not be allowed into Canada. Asians and blacks, as "essentially non-assimilable elements are clearly detrimental to our highest national development, and hence should be vigorously excluded."[58]

The exclusion of non-whites is implicitly related to the exclusion of the non-moral. Woodsworth noted that Canadian immigration law already excluded criminals, beggars, and prostitutes, but he claimed that enforcement was not tough enough; he suggests employing Canadian immigration agents at European ports and having these agents investigate prospective immigrants to root out "paupers" and "prostitutes." He also suggests that in any case the law's provisions should be broadened, to exclude "persons of poor physique, persons mentally deficient, the hopelessly incapable, the morally depraved."[59]

People of colour were assumed to be potentially if not actually depraved: this is the implicit premise behind Woodsworth's claim that blacks and Asians are non-assimilable. If blacks and Asians are at the bottom of the racial hierarchy, eastern and southern European immigrants are assumed to be also "dark" in the moral sense. With these new immigrants, "whole families of degenerates were included among arrivals, and weaklings of all objectionable types are represented." Extreme poverty was also a cause, or perhaps a consequence, of moral depravation: denouncing British pauper child immigrants, Woodsworth states without argument that "any large immigration of this class must lead to the degeneration of our Canadian people," and furthermore that British pauper children have "inherited tendencies to evil."[60]

The inclusion of British paupers among degenerates emphasizes that Woodsworth's taxonomy of immigrants is not primarily based on physical anthropological criteria but rather on a combination of cultural perceptions. Although the people who end up at the top are largely fair and people of colour are at the bottom, the darkness of the skin is not the only or even main criterion, since it could not distinguish – as Woodsworth is so careful to do – between Turks and Greeks, or between Poles and Austrians.

Church women, who contributed vitally to the missionary movement through fund-raising and in organizational, publicity, and outreach efforts, were as patriotic as men, but their Christian patriotism was supplemented by a belief that non-Christian women were subjected to many indignities, sexual and otherwise, that would come to an end when enlightened Protestantism held away.

Nellie McClung, who was very active in the temperance movement, wrote a fund-raising pamphlet for the MWMS attacking the sceptics who thought mission work was useless because "our Christian civilization" was not worth exporting.

> Take the treatment of women! Even the most rabid suffragist who ever scorned our man-made laws, will agree that women are treated with greater respect in Christian and Anglo-Saxon countries than in any other. . . . Child marriages, the burning of widows, the throwing out of girl babies . . . are all, I believe, reasons for our efforts to extend Christianity and its humanities.[61]

Feminism, Christian chauvinism, and ethnocentrism were for McClung and her fellow feminists a unified whole: the superiority of the Anglo culture is not an incidental belief that could be excised, leaving a pure feminism behind. Rather, the very origins, as well as the form, of McClung's feminism are shaped by ethnocentric ideas about sexuality and civilization shared by non-feminist moral reformers.[62] The problematic character of "women's work for women," the slogan of the MWMS, can be seen in finer detail through an analysis of the work of an interesting organization devoting itself to turning strangers into neighbours: the Department of the Stranger of the Presbyterian Church.

The Department of the Stranger: Philanthropic Deportation

The Presbyterian Church shared the concern shown by Methodists and other representatives of respectable Canadian opinion for contacting and assimilating immigrants. Much of their work was with Scottish immigrants: it sent a minister to work in Glasgow to prepare immigrants and notify appropriate Canadian congregations of the impending arrival of new Scots Presbyterians, and after the Great War they became heavily involved in both obtaining and controlling Scottish single women coming as immigrant domestics. Nonetheless, they also funded a handful of projects for Ukrainian and other non-Anglophone immigrants in the Prairies, most notably schools and nearby boarding homes for rural children in Wakaw and Teulon, and a hospital in Vegreville.[63]

By 1911, the Presbyterian Home Mission Board was paying for Rev. Hunter Boyd in Glasgow and for three immigration chaplains in Quebec, Montreal, and Winnipeg. These tried to direct incoming immigrants to appropriate local churches, but they also helped with the practical details of arrival. That year, Mrs. Ethel West, who was on the executive of the Women's Missionary Society, tried to convince the male-dominated Home Mission Board that special work by women among women immigrants was necessary, adding that girls and women moving within Canada could benefit from an organization such as the proposed Department of the Stranger. The clergymen on the Board agreed that immigration was a key area of work; but they made it clear that they would expect a Department of the Stranger to concern itself "not only with the women and children, but with the men and boys," and they furthermore insisted that the new department be put under the supervision of the Home Mission Board, with the Women's Missionary Society acting in an "auxiliary" role.[64]

Despite the men's formal victory, Mrs. West got herself appointed as head of the Department of the Stranger, and although accountable to the Board of Home Missions she appears to have had considerable latitude in which to use her boundless energy and superior organizational skills. In 1912, the Home Mission Board prepared forms on which congregations could both report new arrivals or departures or be apprised of immigrants or other strangers in their area. By 1913, Mrs. West had nine Toronto agencies report Presbyterian (and possibly all Scottish) female strangers to her, and many congregations across the country had set up "Strangers' secretaries" to do similar work: the department as a whole handled over 15,000 names in 1913.[65]

Mrs. West, who appears to have been the wife of a Toronto businessman and who had much experience in home mission work, bombarded the Strangers' secretaries of local congregations with requests for reports and circulars giving advice on how to track down strangers. Throughout, her concern for the well-being of immigrants was overshadowed by her greater concern for the moral order of Canadian cities. Before her system of surveillance was established, "girls went to work where Chinamen were employed, where liquor was used," and to prevent these evils she gives suggestions:

> The strangers should be visited immediately and kept in close touch for about three months. . . . You will find that you need to study the environment of the stranger as much as the stranger. . . . We had a group of 62 Scotch girls come to Toronto in one batch, and we have followed their environment most closely.[66]

The "modern" flavour of Mrs. West's advice is not untypical of church workers in this period of transition between philanthropy and modern social work; along with similar organizations, the department pioneered techniques of social work later used by state officials.

In Toronto, where Mrs. West could keep a closer watch on the not always zealous labours of volunteer local Strangers' secretaries, the work of the department reached 8,000 people in 1919, including 1,000 returning soldiers and 254 domestics; in 1921, it reached over 5,000 people, 195 of these being immigrant domestics. The separate mention of domestics was not an accident: the Toronto co-ordinator of Strangers' work, Emma McDougall, shared Mrs. West's concern for the dangers posed to Canada by these single women living outside the family. She complained that "a great many of these girls are subnormal to a greater or less degree," adding that "in several cases the girls were engaged at a place where a Chinaman was also kept."[67] Mrs. West and her colleagues were perfectly aware of the fact that the Canadian government's tight post-war immigration policy forced many British single women to pretend they wanted to be domestics in order to be admitted to Canada, but they had little sympathy for these women's attempts to get factory or clerical work, insisting that they stay in domestic jobs and that they maintain their chaste character.

The department also assumed policing functions, seeking the deportation of immigrant domestics who had strayed from the straight and narrow path. The easy slippage from helping immigrants to deporting them is traced in Emma McDougall's 1923 report:

> Even if a girl leaves the city or takes a position without consulting them, these organizations [Strangers' local secretaries] retain an interest in her, and a good deal of my special work has been investigating cases of this kind. Very often this investigating is the means of putting a girl on her feet. In rare cases she has to be deported.[68]

Neither the Department of Immigration nor the shipping companies were keen to seek out and deport undesirable immigrants, according to the zealous philanthropists. The voluntary organizations hence assumed some of the coercive functions of the state under the banner of preserving national health and morality: McDougall stated in her 1922 report that "I cannot take time to tell of those who may be deported as undesirables because of ill-health or lack of moral training."

The philanthropic policing undertaken by West and McDougall was not as unsupported by the state as they claimed; the 1910 Immigration Act had added a clause allowing the deportation not only of pimps and prostitutes but also of all "women and girls coming to Canada for immoral purposes." And as Barbara Roberts has shown, many deportations for immorality were masked by immigration officials under the rubrics of "medical grounds" or "liable to become a public charge." Roberts concludes:

> On the one hand, there is much evidence that the Department routinely deported women for offences that were little more than sexual transgressions for which they had been caught (for instance by pregnancy or venereal disease). On the other hand, the Department from time to time issued instructions to its various agents cautioning them to be sure that women reported for deportation for offences connected with sexual immorality were not merely victims of other persons' desires to get them out of the way.[69]

The state may have on occasion been reluctant to deport a woman accused of immorality, but on many proven occasions no such reluctance was shown. Among the 2,169 "problem cases" singled out by the state among women brought in under the Empire Settlement Aftercare Agreement, 574 were deported for having illegitimate children, and fifty-four for the vague charge of "immorality."[70]

The state's work in moral regulation was facilitated by the allegedly philanthropic work of the Presbyterian immigration chaplain in Montreal, Rev. John Chisholm, "an exploring missionary in the interior of British Columbia" transferred from work among Native peoples and lumbermen to work in an urban setting. Hired in 1912, by 1913 he had already formulated his own sociology of immigrants, proclaiming that Canada might be improved by the addition of "the impulse of the Celt, the endurance of the German, the patience of the Slav, the daring of the Northman, and the romance of Italy." This parade of clichés, however, led him to worry about other character traits that were adding "seasoning" to Canada: "as we view the uncouth ways of many, their lusty morals, their alien ideas, their ignorance and superstition, we have reason to fear that to us is coming a tremendous contribution of the worse."[71] Both Chisholm and his Quebec colleague, Rev. Patterson, mentioned the dangers of "the white slave traffic" as being part of their work. This type of work has generally been described as philanthropic settlement and Canadianization, but it had a darker side that can be called "philanthropic deportation."

During the war there was little need for chaplains to meet the small numbers of immigrants, but after the war the work was renewed. In the meantime, Chisholm, wanting to know how many of the "129,480 immigrant girls" coming to Canada in the pre-war years "made contribution" to the social evil, had got in touch with "prominent social service workers in the USA, among them the late Anthony Comstock."[72]

In an interesting transition from philanthropy to the state, he says he was then "strengthened in his research work" by the "Department of Justice creating me a member of the Federal Secret Service." Since there was no such body, it is difficult to know what Chisholm meant; perhaps he was simply granted the powers of immigration officials. Be that as it may, his official status apparently gave him entry into venereal-disease hospitals, where he heard "from the lips of those poor girls, detailed descriptions" of the causes of their fall. His new status, however, did not merely strengthen his research: he also undertook direct "law enforcement." He mentions rescue work as something that is important but is being done by other church workers; his own specialization, law enforcement in clergyman's disguise, is described as a twofold task: "(1) For the stranger's protection. (2) For the stranger's correction."

As an example of protecting strangers, Chisholm tells a melodramatic tale of extreme exploitation of a domestic servant by an evil mistress, in which he plays the role of white knight rescuing the hapless woman. As an example of correction, he tells the story of a woman whose passage had been prepaid from Scotland by a "gentleman" requesting her services as a domestic. The woman (like many other single women immigrants) tried to avoid domestic service and took up with a returned soldier. Chisholm, alerted by the gentleman in question, claims to have traced the ex-soldier's past "and found that he was an ex-convict with a wife in the USA. I made these facts known to her, but she was inclined to be impertinent, saying she knew her own business." The irate Chisholm then threatened the woman with indentured domestic labour to pay the passage money back to the gentleman, saying:

> If you say no I shall phone for a policeman to come in the taxi and take you to the Immigration Headquarters and you shall be deported and never again allowed to enter Canada. I do this to keep you from acting fraudulently with the man who paid your

passage and also to keep you from acting immorally by marrying a man who has a wife already.[73]

Under such threats, the woman was forced to give up her relationship and take up domestic work. Since Chisholm claims to have "exercised law-enforcement on 54 different occasions" in one year, there were clearly quite a few women whose lives were drastically affected by the power of Chisholm's moral regulation procedures.

Two other organizations of the early twenties appear in the records of the Presbyterian Department of the Stranger.[74] Both show how easily the category of "stranger" allowed church workers to shift their targets from immigrants in general to single women and back again; and both show the coercive power of organizations set up ostensibly to protect those who were "strange" by reason of either their family/gender or ethnic status.

The first was the Travellers' Aid Committee, which in 1923 gathered under a single banner the work of WCTU, YWCA, and Methodist and Presbyterian women who had already been doing "stranger" work at train stations and other places frequented by immigrants and travellers. The Canadian National Travellers' Aid Committee was in close touch with its U.S. counterpart. In its first report it claimed to have saved hundreds of girls from white slavery; but the few actual cases reported in the documents gathered by Mrs. West (who represented the Presbyterian Church on the National Committee) indicate that more common than white slavery was the problem of runaway girls, who were sometimes semi-forcibly taken back to their parents' homes by Travellers' Aid workers.[75] A 1925 circular from the U.S. Travellers' Aid Society advised workers to watch out for young women travelling "without hat or baggage" or who show "unusual or irregular conduct of any kind"; the intricate instructions and sample questionnaire that followed were designed more to control than to help women travellers, and the class bias of the work is obvious from the first mention of hatless girls.[76]

The last organization in which Mrs. West was involved (prior to church union in 1925) was the Canadian Council for the Immigration of Women for Household Service, quickly and euphemistically renamed Canadian Council for the Immigration of Women (CCIW). This was set up in the post-war period, when many British women wanted to come to Canada at a time when the government – in part due to the high rate of venereal disease among its troops stationed in Britain – had come to believe that British women were more likely to be diseased prostitutes than healthy "mothers of the race."

This view was not merely the government's; Montreal's well-known social worker Helen Reid advocated "stricter measures" to keep out working-class British women who

> . . . in addition to their lack of training for domestic service, bring with them only too often, serious mental and moral disabilities. These women either glut the labour market here, reducing the wages of working men, or end up alas! too frequently in our jails, hospitals, and asylums.[77]

As Marilyn Barber shows, at this time the Immigration Department was responding to women's organizations by setting up a Women's Division. That women immigrants without families were perceived as moral deviants is best shown by the fact that compulsory medical examinations were first introduced for unaccompanied women, being extended to all immigrants later.

The CCIW's approach was described in 1920 by the Dominion WCTU president:

> This organization makes provision for not alone the safeguarding of the continental emigrant, but of the safeguarding of Canada as well – a point never emphasized in former years as it should be. . . . Another aim of this laudable organization is to ensure more careful scrutiny overseas that there may be fewer distressing cases of deportation.[78]

Its own minutes confirm this emphasis on protecting Canada from single women immigrants: "This Council was formed primarily to ensure Canada against the undesirable type of woman; secondly to provide proper housing for the women when they do come."[79] The CCIW was set up in 1919 as an official advisory body to the government; the context of female enfranchisement suggests that it represented the government's idea of how women (middle-class women, needless to say) might contribute to public policy. Its members included Lady Falconer, Mrs. Vincent Massey, Charlotte Whitton, and about a dozen other important women – as well as Rev. Shearer, of Winnipeg vice scandal fame, and Tom Moore from the Trades and Labour Congress. Rev. Chisholm also attended some of the Council's meetings.

Its main aims were to facilitate the wholesale importation of British women uprooted by the war or fired from their wartime jobs, and to set up a system to ensure that once in Canada the prospective domestic servants did not escape their fate and seek other kinds of work or enter into relationships with men. Eight hostels were set up across the country to provide the single female immigrants with both accommodation and supervision; matrons were also added to boats and trains for the same dual purpose. The Minister of Immigration, Mr. Calder, in his speech at the founding conference of the Council, first outlined the problem: "Homes are being broken up, our apartment houses flooded, and the energies of Canadian womanhood spent for lack of help."[80] This bleak picture of servantless middle-class women, which undoubtedly moved his audience, was mobilized to promote a great crusade for domestic servants: however, the selection of the "right type of girl" was crucial to keep out "undesirables" and "riff-raff." Calder stressed that although the government was prepared to fund this crusade, volunteer work by women would be "more effective." His reasons are not spelled out but undoubtedly he shared the ladies' belief that the work of volunteer women would appear as philanthropic rather than coercive; and of course the government would save money, because although the hostels received a per diem rate for their clients' room and board, they were managed by Local Councils of Women or YWCAs.

If British women whose passages had been partly paid by the Canadian government tried to escape the net of philanthropy, Toronto's new female morality police officer, Miss Carmichael, engaged in what was euphemistically titled "follow-up work." Miss Carmichael and Immigration Department officials were responsible for a very high rate of deportation cases among British female domestics. Barbara Roberts's research shows that

Taking only the legal deportations, which understates the case by what may be a considerable margin, the rate of deportation for British female domestics brought over under the Aftercare Agreement between January 1, 1926 and 31 March 1931, under supposedly stringent procedures of selection, supervision and assistance, was 4.6%. This is considerably more than the average of 1% cited by the Department in its published annual reports.[81]

Mrs. West, busy with her Department of the Stranger work and clearly outranked by Lady Falconer and Lady Pope, did not speak very much at CCIW meetings. One exception was a discussion in October of 1920 regarding the possible immigration of Jewish children whose families were starving in the Ukraine famine; Mrs. West helpfully stated that "the large majority of Jews are of Bolsheviki tendencies. The Jews will not assimilate. . . [they are] a menace to our country."[82]

Charlotte Whitton, then at the beginning of her long career in child welfare work, became increasingly prominent in the CCIW; her techniques for monopolizing the attention of government officials caused much resentment among other women. Her particular interest in the moral regulation of single mothers became correspondingly prominent in the Council's work. The joint work of the Council and federal officials resulted in the introduction of new bureaucratic methods (such as pink cards for single women) to identify immigrants posing a potential moral danger.[83] But whether because of the tensions caused by Whitton's autocratic method, or because the government came to depend less and less on philanthropic agencies for their immigration and deportation work, the CCIW disappeared by 1927.[84]

The career in home missions of Mrs. Ethel West, which is unusually well documented, allows some conclusions to be drawn about the transformation of moral reform work into the post-war period. First, there is clearly more collaboration by the state, and notably immigration officials, in the work that was previously done by volunteers for primarily evangelistic reasons. Far from the state supplanting philanthropy, however, what we see is a curious transformation – at its most extreme in Rev. Chisholm – of moral reform itself, and a conscious and deliberate use of volunteer organizations by the state for undertaking work that would otherwise be both too coercive and too expensive.

Second, we see how racial, class, and sexual fears were not only connected but were in some cases merged into a single moral panic – the unfit immigrant – which could be interpreted as primarily a gender/class problem (as in the case of British domestics unfit by reason of their low morals) or primarily a racial problem (as in the case of the "neurotic" Jews).

Third, we see that there was no clear distinction between the work of providing help for those in need – single women needing a place to stay, immigrants requiring basic survival information – and the work of controlling, regulating, and even deporting those deemed undesirable because of their sexual irregularities or because of their "race." The fact that the Department of the Stranger exercised coercive power should not lead us to the one-sided conclusion that nobody obtained generous help from it or was able to use it to track down lost friends or relatives. As in the case of so many of the moral reform projects undertaken in this time period, coercion and protection were but two sides of the same coin.

6

The City as Moral Problem

The Surface Crust of Civilization

Moral reformers played an important role in the development of both urban sociology and urban social work in Canada. The Methodist Wesley College in Winnipeg was the first higher education institution in Canada to offer sociology courses (in 1906), and the Methodist college in Toronto, Victoria, pioneered this discipline in Ontario, while the Baptist institutions of Acadia and McMaster began to offer sociology in 1907. Even when the first "secular" department was created (at McGill, in 1922), it was headed by the former Baptist minister Carl Dawson. To the then-combined fields of sociology and social work, moral reformers brought a unique perspective based on the ideals of purity, whiteness, and cleanliness. The extent to which medical and scientific "experts" took up these ideas and images as their own is proof that the moral reformers, while learning a great deal from lay sources, nevertheless left an important imprint in the social sciences. This success was facilitated by the fact that turn-of-the-century social scientists and urban planners were, for their own reasons, engaged in a re-visioning of society in general, and the city in particular, as organic wholes, rejecting the laissez-faire perception of society as a collection of individuals seeking their personal fortunes. The religious sense of community responsibility – the community surveillance of the immoral – was therefore congruent with developments in social science at the level both of theory (Herbert Spencer, Emile Durkheim) and of applied urban sociology and urban planning, two fields dating from the turn of the century and whose origins are intertwined with the moral reform movement.[1]

Hence, J.S. Woodsworth was appealing both to the social gospel and to developments in sociology when he stated, in his important 1911 work on urban problems, that it is only in recent years that we are beginning to learn that as the city is not a mere aggregation of independent individuals, but rather a certain type of social organism, so the physical city must be considered as a whole and the various parts must be subordinated to the whole.[2]

Concepts deployed by Woodsworth in his missions-education text-book ("Crime, immorality, disease and misery vary almost directly as the size of the plot, the breadth of the street and the number of parks"[3]) were virtually indistinguishable from those used in secular sources. One common link was the perception of the city as the obvious unit of sociological analysis (as opposed to the individual, or humanity as a whole). There was also a growing consensus that this unit was (a) an organism, and (b) in poor health.[4]

The lists of urban problems found in the literature may obscure the fact that more important than specific problems such as inadequate sewers or fire hazards was the underlying macro-problem: the city itself. Urban environments had been considered morally problematic at least since J.J. Rousseau and the English Romantics; in the late nineteenth century, however, the problem of the city was transformed by being intertwined with the fears about racial, moral, and social degeneration analysed in earlier chapters.[5]

Some reformers attempted to promote back-to-the-country schemes, at least for pauper children (who could be useful on farms, but who were surplus population in an urban setting). Dr. Barnardo's massive transport of British poor children to Canadian farms is perhaps the best-known example; as Joy Parr has shown, these schemes shared a mythology of the countryside as healthy, which was not discredited by repeated charges of child exploitation and child abuse.[6] The equa-tion of health with country life was echoed by a commission that in 1911 investigated Toronto charities and concluded that urban orphan-ages should send children to rural foster homes. Declaring that central heating and hot water baths were unnecessary luxuries in children's homes, the commission stated:

Strong, rugged, independent manhood is the need of this young country, and these qualities can be better developed in the bracing air of the farm and village home, than in the hot house atmosphere of the average orphanage.[7]

Despite the great mythological appeal of the rural solution, most reformers did not seriously advocate reverse migration to rural areas. Rather, they pragmatically focused their attention on making the city a healthier and more moral environment, often arguing that the hopeless conditions of English slums and New York tenements might be avoided in Canada if strong preventive measures were taken. This hopeful attitude was promoted by Woodsworth, who used the biblical dichotomy of Babel vs. the New Jerusalem to mobilize young Protestants to build cities of virtue throughout Canada. A similar dichotomy was used by his fellow Methodist educator, Rev. W.T. Gunn:

> Every city has been a Babylon, and every city has been a New Jerusalem; and it has always been a question whether the Babylon would extirpate the New Jerusalem, or the New Jerusalem would extirpate the Babylon.[8]

Moral reformers were indeed engaged in extirpating the Babylon lurking in the slums of every city; but they were also engaged in the more positive task Rev. G.C. Pidgeon called "Building the Holy City." Praising the hardy biblical Jews who returned to Palestine to rebuild Jerusalem, leaving behind lazy compatriots dazed by the glitter of Babylon, he stated that, "like the Jews," the modern reformers had three tasks before them. The first was to "clear away the rubbish," which in the Canadian context meant abolishing "liquor traffic, Sabbath-breaking, dishonesty, impurity." The second was to prepare the materials for the rebuilding of the walls of Jerusalem, by which Pidgeon meant not brick manufacturing but the shaping of human materials in Sunday schools and YMCAs. The third stage was the actual building process, including the erection of safeguards for "the moral welfare of the place."[9]

While some reformers spoke only through moral injunctions and biblical analogies, many others recognized that industrialization and urbanization were problems largely because they produced poverty for the many and wealth only for the few. Herbert Ames's pioneering study of Montreal industrial workers showed that 25 per cent of the families in his sample lacked steady work, being forced to scrape by on charity and loans during the winters while hoping for summer dock work. In Toronto, the industrial boom of the 1870s-1890s did not reduce the major inequality between rich and poor.[10] And in Winnipeg, social gospel leader J.S. Woodsworth produced a "Report on the Living Standard" proving that the prairie town's boom conditions were not benefiting its working class.[11]

Indeed, while the urban population of Canada went from 1.1 million in 1881 to 4.3 million in 1921 (which raised it from one-quarter to one-half of the country's population), this growth was not indicative of golden conditions for workers in the cities. Michael Piva's study of Toronto, for instance, concludes that during the period of greatest growth, 1906-19, the wages for male workers declined, while the housing crisis aggravated due to the influx of immigrants. The housing crisis in Montreal was even worse and contributed to infant mortality rates among the worst in North America.[12]

Urban growth, therefore, was linked not only to the rise of middle-class suburbs and department stores but also to the development in Canada of urban poverty. This type of poverty was conceptualized through the lens provided by European, and in particular English, studies of industrialization and poverty, which centred on the social construct of the slum. As Paul Rutherford has pointed out, much attention was devoted to this problem beginning in the mid-1890s;[13] from then until well into the twenties the slum was defined not only as an economic or public-health problem but as an essentially *moral* category. The slum, and by implication its population, was portrayed as the dark, seething mass of vice existing not beside but *underneath* the respectable neighbourhoods, posing a danger that was simultaneously sanitary and moral:

> Underneath the seemingly moral surface of our national life, there is a terrible undercurrent of unclean vice with all its concomitant evils of ruined lives, desolated hearth-stones, prostituted bodies, decimated constitutions, and early dishonored graves.[14]

The superintendent of the Methodist slum mission in Toronto produced a similar image in his 1908 report, quoting Thomas Huxley to the effect that slums could "create something worse than savagery – a great Serbonian bog, which in the long run will swallow up the surface crust of civilization."[15]

The bourgeoisie's fears that their civilization was but a thin veneer constantly threatened by a volcanic eruption from the proletarian id certainly lend themselves to a Freudian analysis. More relevant to present purposes, however, is the way in which the language of mythology and religion was seamlessly integrated with the cold language of social science in the definition and investigation of the slum. Toronto's Medical Officer of Health, Dr. Charles Hastings, a key figure in Canadian urban reform, attempted to move away from the moral discourse of nineteenth-century social investigation, but the moral definition of the slum continued to lurk, so to speak, under Hastings's scientific surface. A key early U.S. study had defined a slum as "an area of dirty back streets, especially when inhabited by a squalid and criminal population."[16] Reacting to this, Hastings's important 1911 study of Toronto slums provided a more "scientific" definition:

Originally the term was applied to low, boggy back streets, inhabited by a poor, criminal population. The term as used here, however, applies for the most part to poor, unsanitary housing, overcrowded, insufficiently lighted, badly ventilated, with unsanitary and in many cases, filthy yards.[17]

Hastings was partially successful in portraying the houses and yards, not the people, as deviant: the photographs in the report feature many more dirty outhouses than criminal human beings. And yet, this shift in focus from the poor people to their habitat reflects not a shedding of moralism in favour of science but simply the ascription of moral deviance to physical objects. "Rear" houses (built in backyards or back lanes) and unsanitary outhouses, Hastings says, "have become . . . a danger to public morals, and in fact, an offence against public decency." This deviant environment then naturally produces deviant people: "criminals and moral lepers are born in the atmosphere of physical and moral rottenness pervading the slums of large cities."[18]

Hastings's use of such phrases as "moral rottenness" allowed the explicitly religious reformers to join in the attack on unsanitary outhouses as Christian soldiers. The main Protestant practical plan for slum reform, the downtown city mission, was envisioned as an "army of occupation to move upon the forces of sin, especially upon the enemy's strongholds, where evil is massed in the crowded centres of city life."[19] Lurid passages from Hastings's slum report were reprinted in the annual report of the Methodist Department of Evangelism and Social Service, together with the conclusion that "overcrowded dwellings" were "hotbeds for germination and dissemination of disease, vice, and crime."[20]

The constant repetition of the phrase "disease, vice, and crime" created a very strong "horizontal linkage" (to use David Garland's phrase) between these three distinct social constructs. Occasionally reformers argued about whether physical poverty and disease caused moral decay – as in Herbert Ames's claim that drinking was generally a symptom or effect, not a cause, of poverty – or whether moral decay was the primary cause.[21] Most of the time, however, they ignored causality and simply linked together physical, moral, and juridical forms of degeneration under the overall rubric of "slum conditions."

What was objectionable about slums was not the mere presence of disease-crime-vice, but, perhaps more importantly, the perception that these problems were – like the rear houses so decried by Charles Hastings – in some ways hidden from view. The repeated use of analogies and allegories comparing slums to "darkest Africa" and other colonized places reinforced the assumption that the inhabitants of the slums, like those of Africa and the Americas, only began truly to exist when "discovered" and represented by the white male representatives of ruling classes. Gareth Stedman Jones has commented on the great middle-class desire to know the poor and expose both their habitat and their habits to the light of investigation: in the Canadian context we see the same anxiety about not knowing, not seeing, about losing control over the city.[22] J.J. Kelso put this most clearly: "the slums are exceedingly dangerous to the health and morals of a city because they are to the great majority of the people unknown and unexplored retreats." Refusing to grant subjectivity to the people living in the so-called slums, he takes it for granted that investigation will be undertaken by experts shining the searchlight of knowledge on the vices that secretly accumulate in the slum underbelly of the city – just as stones half-buried in the ground will accumulate under them a "nest of slimy and creepy things." "But let the sunlight in and they soon disappear. Is this not equally true of the slums?"[23]

The sunlight of knowledge was regarded by Kelso as itself a form of social control, making urban vices scatter like the bugs under an overturned rock. The theme of knowledge as control was echoed by Rev. S.W. Dean of the Fred Victor Mission, who said that the slum was "the *lurking place* of disease and impaired health, the *hiding place* of crime, the haunt of immorality," and then proceeded to quote the Bible: "Men love darkness rather than light because their deeds are evil."[24]

The evil deeds taking place in the secret darkness of the slum were legion: prostitution, alcoholism, thriftlessness, child neglect, gambling, stealing, lack of hygiene, irreligion, contagious diseases, swearing, bad eating habits, "the love of finery," and Sabbath-breaking all came under the gaze of the investigators. In the second half of this chapter we will examine the practical efforts of two organizations, the Methodist Church and the Salvation Army, to reform the slum dwellers and change all their vices into the opposite virtues. First, however, we will examine the slum vice par excellence, thought to exist nowhere else and to owe its existence to two typical features of this environment, namely overcrowding (the material cause) and moral degeneration (the moral cause – and effect). This was the vice (or crime, or sin) of incest, often highlighted as "the most unspeakable" of all slum conditions.

The Sexual Secret of the Slum

In England, the respectable reading public had become agitated about the moral and sexual dimensions of housing overcrowding in the wake of the sensationalist pamphlet by Rev. Andrew Mearns, *The Bitter Cry of Outcast London* (1883) and of the Royal Commission on the housing of the poor (1885), which was partly a response to the concern generated by Mearns's pamphlet. As urban reform historian Anthony Wohl explains, the health problems suffered by the urban poor were not news, but Mearns's dark allegations about the nameless crime were indeed news.

> Nothing brought more publicity and sense of urgency to the housing question than Mearns's statement that 'incest is common'. It shocked the nation, and when the Royal Commission on the Housing of the Working Classes met, it spent considerable time examining witnesses on the subject.[25]

After Mearns's accusations about the innermost secret lurking under what he unoriginally called "the thinnest crust of civilization" were publicized, both in the pamphlet itself and in reports of the Royal Commission hearings, the issue of incest remained publicly visible in Britain for several decades.

In the U.S., Linda Gordon's study of family violence argues that incest was recognized and discussed as a problem from the 1880s until the 1920s. After World War One, incest became invisible as professional social workers utilized a new therapeutic model in which the whole family was seen as deviant, or, alternatively, in which girls were often accused of being overly sexual. Since Canadian social work practices largely followed the U.S., her findings probably hold true for Canadian cities, and are corroborated by the not numerous but persistent references to incest in the moral reform literature. In the absence of historical studies of incest and family violence in Canada, it can be tentatively argued that from 1885 to the 1920s the issue was openly discussed, although the discussion did not reach panic proportions as it did in England. Also applicable to the Canadian context is Gordon's comment that incest was generally seen not as an abuse of either gender or parental power but as a uniquely working-class crime, to which philanthropists responded without acknowledging that upper- or middle-class fathers ever abused their daughters.[26]

That incest was hardly a secret can be seen from the explicit reference in a poem used by J.S. Woodsworth as the epigraph to the first chapter of the young people's textbook *My Neighbor*. In it, urban evils such as starving seamstresses are mentioned along with "the crowded couch of incest in the warrens of the poor."[27] But much more common than such direct references were hints and euphemisms that clothed themselves in modesty but fired the imaginations of the audience. Mearns's pamphlet employed a technique similar to that of W.T. Stead's "The Maiden Tribute." In bold letters, the pamphlet told readers that they were entitled to imagine the worst possible sexual crimes (including, of course, incest) with the author's full assurance that they were not engaging in pornographic fantasy but in serious social investigation:

> So far from making the worst of our facts for the purpose of appealing to emotion, we have been compelled to tone down everything, and wholly to omit what most needs to be known, or the ears and eyes of our readers would have been insufferably outraged.[28]

Also in England, the Archbishop of Westminster, in a pamphlet significantly entitled *The Child of the English Savage*, enumerated cases of parental cruelty in some detail but then referred darkly to "twelve cases of a kind of cruelty which cannot even be named."[29]

The English working-class crime that could not be named had, in Canada, a particular ethnic organization. The WCTU used the English view of working-class people as savages but applied it to immigrants:

> In communities of foreigners we find it almost the universal rule that the house consists of only one or at most two rooms, and where this last-named luxury abounds the one room is used as a kitchen and the other as a bedroom for the whole family and perhaps a boarder or two. What must be the inevitable outcome of such conditions as these?[30]

Thus incest was evoked in the audience's imagination without the writer having to utter the word: and its alleged unnameability gave it an aura of great importance, of being, in Mearns's words, "that which most needs to be known."

This last text, however, also raises the related but distinct issue of boarders or lodgers – generally single men – and their possible sexual abuse of children. This sexual possibility, not so much the inconvenience to both family and lodger of having to share already cramped quarters, is what was meant by "the lodger evil," a phrase used by Charles Hastings and others. Hastings, as reluctant to mention sexual matters as the most prim maiden, does not directly bring accusations against the Toronto poor but rather quotes from a Glasgow doctor who again uses the technique of the rhetorical question:

> I ask you to imagine yourselves, with all your appetites and passions, . . . suddenly shrivelled and shrunk into such conditions of space – I might ask you, I do ask you to consider and honestly confess – what would be the result to you?[31]

Toronto Mayor W.H. Howland had discussed the lodger evil quite a few years earlier and linked it to prostitution, mentioning that there was one lodging house in which "hundreds of children have been ruined."[32]

Whether the sexual abuse of children was undertaken by fathers, other male relatives, or unrelated boarders, the analyses presented by moral reformers tended to ignore the gender dimension and the issue of parental power. Instead, incest was portrayed as the natural product of both physical overcrowding and the moral degeneration typical of the poor. In this way, the perpetrators were simultaneously blamed and excused, since their abuse was portrayed with the same language used to describe the inevitable emergence of fevers from contaminated water. Incest – and also child sexual abuse by lodgers – naturally emerged from the deviant environment of the slums, and in particular from the one-room dwelling. Unlike working-class London, in which Charles Booth determined that only dwellings in which there were three people or more per room were truly overcrowded, neither Toronto nor Montreal had many one-room dwellings for the whole family: one room per person (giving each family four or five rooms) was a more common situation.[33] But the more spacious dwellings of the Canadian working class were seen through the eyes of Mearns and Charles Booth.

Just as Kelso had argued that sunlight would scatter the vices from their urban hiding places, public health inspectors seemed sometimes more concerned with invading people's privacy in pursuit of knowledge than improving their health. Even houses that looked to be in fairly good condition could be imagined to have many people inhabiting them, or other evils not visible without the searchlight of investigation. As the caption under a photograph of an ordinary Toronto house, Hastings writes: "External appearances are sometimes deceiving, as is manifest in this picture."[34] The picture, of course, cannot make anything except appearances manifest, but Hastings is implicitly relying on the discourse of the "thin crust of civilization" to legitimize his workers' massive house-by-house searches.[35] Winnipeg's public health inspector, Dr. Douglas, also appealed to the "appearances are deceiving" expert discourse to justify his employees' night-time raids on poor citizens asleep in their makeshift beds:

> The innocent looking couch by day is opened out at night and becomes a bed for two boarders. The disappearance of beds and bedding in the day time is one reason why day inspections for overcrowding are not sufficient unless supplemented by night inspections.[36]

As Dr. Douglas makes clear, even though the Canadian working classes had more rooms and hence more potential privacy than their English counterparts, they were not exempt from the other moral evil thought to lead to incest: the persistent use of large beds for several boarders or family members, instead of the bourgeois single bed. One upstanding citizen of Toronto claimed that people living on Elm Street (the heart of the slums) must surely be sleeping several to a bed, since he argued, "its sidewalks and doorways were crowded with people, male and female. It suggested to me that there was overcrowding which meant two beds in a room and two or more in a bed."[37] This logical leap, from seeing people gathering in doorways to imagining promiscuous sleeping practices, is typical of the urban-reform literature.

Although Hastings does not seem to have recorded the numbers of beds in houses, other reformers explicitly frowned not only on parents and children sleeping together but even on small children sharing a bed. The WCTU's Department of Health and Heredity, for instance, included in its plan of study of "the home" the topic of "the use of single beds"; and some sex hygiene educators even recommended that husbands and wives sleep separately, to prevent magnetic force being drawn from one to the other and to minimize sexual arousal.[38]

Condemnations of bed- or room-sharing by several people were thus not necessarily avowals of the rights of children, particularly girls, to be free from abuse. Rather, the conditions associated with poverty were used either to blame working-class parents or to medicalize whole working-class communities (or both). Saving children from slum conditions, and especially from incest – regarded more as sexual immorality than as abuse – was a task undertaken to some extent for the well-being of children, but more importantly for the sake of the nation. As an Anglican clergyman said at the 1912 Canadian Public Health Association meeting, "if Canada is to rear an imperial race, it will not be by children raised in slums."[39] On his part, Winnipeg's Dr. Douglas decried overcrowding as hampering the attempt to properly "bring up Winnipeg's most valuable asset – her children."[40]

A different perspective, very much a minority opinion, used the general knowledge of incest to point out both the gender bias of the legal system and its over-concern for property rights rather than personal safety. This view was confined largely to the WCTU, which fought for higher age of consent for girls throughout this period and also sought prosecutions for incest with stories such as the following:

A girl of 15 has lately been rescued from her own father, who threatened to kill her and her mother if thwarted in his wickedness. This man (or devil) got six months in jail as punishment of his crime, and at the same time a young man was sent to the penitentiary for three or four years for 'stealing some iron.' Such are our laws![41]

But for the majority of reformers, incest – the sexual secret of the slum – was the unmentionable vice lurking deep beneath the crust of civilization, lurking even below vices such as prostitution and alcoholism. The slum, organized around the archetypal sin of incest, functioned symbolically as the demonic opposite of the spacious homes of the bourgeoisie, organized around a central core of companionate, domestic marriage as sole sexual expression. And while the incest of the slums was thought to give rise to social and physical monsters, the marriage of the bourgeoisie was seen as giving birth to happy, clean, and obedient children with a responsible breadwinner father and a virtuous mother. With incest defined as a class vice originating in class degeneration and urban overcrowding, Canadian social reformers used people's honest anger about the sexual abuse of children by men of all classes as fuel for the fire of *class* regeneration and social purity, largely ignoring issues of gender and age power.

Colonizing the Slum

The efforts of moral reformers to colonize the slums can be traced back to the beginnings of city mission work in New York in the 1840s, when Protestant missionaries pioneered public health education while doing evangelistic work. As Carroll Smith-Rosenberg points out, this type of philanthropy was a continuation of the purely evangelical work of the tract societies, which had divided up the city into districts and sent "Biblewomen" or male missionaries to pray with families and entice them to read religious tracts. Exactly the same techniques were used by both social researchers and public health nurses sixty years later. Indeed, the New York City Association for Improving the Condition of the Poor, which in the U.S. led the campaign to rationalize philanthropy and restrain the charitable impulses of churchgoers confronted with beggars, was an offshoot of the Tract Society, which in 1843 split its philanthropic from its evangelical branches.[42]

In turn-of-the-century English Canada, city mission work consisted of two distinct though by no means separate approaches to the question of how best to civilize/colonize the slums. The church-based reformers argued that mere social development was not enough and that spiritual regeneration was a necessary precondition of prosperity. By contrast, reformers who, although usually practising Protestants, preferred to emphasize the social and political aspect of urban reform, developed approaches that shared many of the evangelical reformers' preoccupations but emphasized material results and scientific, not individual, work processes. Some promoted model housing, such as Octavia Hill in London or Herbert Ames in Montreal; some tried to co-ordinate and systematize charity and have municipal government take it over to a greater or lesser extent, like Goldwin Smith in Toronto; but perhaps the most innovative approach of all was the settlement house.[43]

Settlement houses broke away from the basic framework of philanthropy by refusing to give material aid and by breaking down the geographical boundaries between rich and poor: middle-class volunteers actually went to live in slums, and were more likely to be found running evening social circles for working girls than giving out loaves of bread. This settlement of the social frontier was, however, not meant to have the colonizers live just like the natives: the middle-class volunteers built nicely appointed houses, with many rooms and single beds for all, which were regarded as prototypes of the future social order. As Vicinus puts it, "the cultured middle-class volunteers would purify the stained slums of England by their very presence."[44] Many of these settlements were wholly or mostly occupied by single women who, as Vicinus points out, often described their work as analogous to their brothers' imperial adventures in colonization.

Despite the paternalism (or maternalism) inherent in the idea of the settlement house as a benevolent influence, the more progressive wing of the settlement movement, particularly in the U.S., went so far as to question the idea that reformers were morally superior to the people they were uplifting. Some of them, most notably Jane Addams, believed genuinely in democracy and pioneered forms of work that would later be known as community development. Mary Simkhovitch, a leading New York settlement worker, expressed the aim of the movement as one of raising the consciousness of a neighbourhood:

A settlement aims to get things done for a given neighborhood. It proposes to be the guardian of that neighborhood's interest, and through identification of the interests of the settlement group with the local interests, it forms a steadying and permanent element in a community which is more or less wavering and in flux. To work out the methods by which a neighborhood may become a consciously effective group is . . . the difficult task of the settlement everywhere.[45]

Jane Addams, whose own Chicago Hull House was from 1890 until World War One the shining light of settlement work, saw her work in the light of the organicist sociology she had learned from Comte and Herbert Spencer. For her, settlements were organic forces countering the fragmentation, individualism, and coldness of industrial capitalism. Stopping short of advocating socialism, Addams nevertheless believed that capitalism had many pernicious social effects; its creation

Toronto's Public Health Department continued the work done earlier by moral reformers in teaching proper mothering. Photo taken in 1912 in a downtown Toronto hall. (Courtesy City of Toronto Archives)

of class antagonisms and individualist competition had to be constantly counteracted, she thought, by forces promoting an organic form of democracy. Economics might fragment the social body, but cultural and social work could unify it. Reformers, stated Addams,

> are bound to see the needs of their neighbourhood as a whole, to furnish data for legislation, and to use their influence to secure it. . . . They are bound to regard the entire life of their city as organic, to make an effort to unify it, and to protest against its over-differentiation.[46]

Settlement houses along these lines, avoiding both religious preaching and charity and emphasizing service to the community, were established in major Canadian cities. Ottawa and Fort William each had one, Montreal had three, and Toronto had two non-religious settlements.[47] In the absence of secondary sources on the secular settlements, it is difficult to know to what extent they emulated Hull House or acted as simple charities; but it can be said with certainty that the religious settlements (also known as city missions) quietly integrated many of the features of their secular rivals. Hence, despite clergymen's protestations that "ordinary settlement work has not religious aim" and "neglects the culture of the soul,"[48] there was not a clear dividing line between the secular settlements and the church-sponsored city missions. Some of the latter were primarily evangelistic, but others, notably J.S. Woodsworth's All People's Mission in Winnipeg, were low-key about conversion. All People's undertook Chicago-style social research, for example, by mapping out patterns of ethnicity in the city, and organized community services such as English classes and childcare. The two examples of slum moral reform studied here in some detail, the Methodist Fred Victor Mission and the Salvation Army's slum rescue work, cannot be dismissed as old-fashioned evangelical-cum-charity projects: they were Canadian pioneers in "modern" techniques of social work even while speaking in the language of conversion.

The Fred Victor Mission

Methodist work in the slums of Toronto centred on the Fred Victor Mission. Originally started by a Mrs. Sheffield to instruct street "waifs and strays," in 1866 it was formally put under church authority, which meant that clergymen now directed volunteer women. In 1894, a grand downtown building (at Queen and Jarvis) was donated by farming equipment manufacturer Hart Massey in memory of his son, Fred Victor, who had died young. By 1906, the building held many community and social work activities: there were mothers' meetings, elocution and cooking classes for girls, clubs for boys and young men, and Bible classes for various age and gender groups. In addition, the

The Victor Home laundry business brought in a substantial sum, almost $700 in 1911; the Ontario government gave almost $400, the city $300, and the rest – close to $800 – was supplied by Fred Victor funds. The Home was, therefore, a substantial operation, and after the initial burst of evangelical zeal to convert prostitutes, increasing emphasis was put on the profitability of the laundry business and other mundane matters: the Toronto City Council's Charities Commission pronounced it, in 1911, to be a "splendid institution."[61] It is unfortunate that no case records exist since these would allow a testing of the hypothesis that the Home quickly transformed itself from an evangelical mission to prostitutes into a fairly modern social-work institution with a mix of public and private funding and an emphasis on sound administration. The secondary sources available on the work of Methodist deaconesses, however, suggest that this was the general trend.[62]

The highly gendered interactions between deaconesses on the one hand and fallen women and dirty households on the other, geared to the production of a class-specific form of respectable femininity, were supplemented by an effort to change ethnic cultural patterns, most notably through the Italian mission. By 1906, this mission could only boast of thirty-six converts, which obviously meant that out of the 170 children enrolled in the Sunday school, most never left Catholicism (their mothers may have sent them partly as free babysitting and partly to improve their English). Several male missionaries, all of Italian origin, quickly succeeded each other in the thankless job of attempting to convert Italian Canadians to Anglo-Canadian Protestantism: "there are peculiar and serious difficulties in reaching the Italian children," one of them said, because of the "untiring efforts on the part of priests and nuns." Even this institution, however, cannot be reduced to "social control," since it ran very popular evening English classes for adults, which undoubtedly helped many Italians in Toronto survive their immigration experience.[63]

Religiously based city missions, then, were clearly aimed first at converting and then at generally improving and regenerating the slum population. Some people were undoubtedly converted both in religious and in social terms. The popularity of the service programs – childcare, shelters, English classes – would suggest, however, that Toronto's poor people managed to get something of what they needed and wanted from these institutions and were not the passive objects of control strategies. The same tension between conversion and service can be found in the work of the organization that pioneered slum work: the Salvation Army.

Mission employed two nurse-deaconesses to do home visits (Charles Hastings's public health nurses had not begun their work yet), and another deaconess as a travellers' aid worker at Union Station, to "guard the young women coming for the first time to the city from the many nefarious traps that are set for them."[49]

The Mission also controlled the Italian Methodist missionary who worked out of the Agnes Street church; it was involved in "fresh air" work, that is, taking young children and nursing mothers on summer picnics and outings to the island; and it was responsible for the Victor Home for young women, housed in a separate building.

The staunchly middle-class clergymen and deaconesses – who were often ministers' daughters – did not mince words about the slum dwellers who were their clients: "What awful specimens of humanity. They are, speaking generally, the offscourings of society – tramps, criminals, outcasts, wrecks – living pictures of the awfulness of sin."[50] Although feeling responsible for the "wrecks," the reformers were more comfortable with the respectable working classes. From the scanty sources available it would appear that "wrecks" were often visited in their homes by the deaconesses, while the people who attended regular classes and clubs at the Mission were probably already respectable. In a special issue of the *Christian Guardian* devoted to city mission work, the editorial outlined the three types of work as follows: "(1) work with the self-respecting poor; (2) work with the degenerates; (3) rescuing the fallen and profligate."[51] The stories of reform published in the Mission's annual reports tend to indicate that work in the first category was the most successful and that instances of regeneration of degenerates and profligates were not numerous.

In 1908, the Mission was able to expand, thanks to a bequest in Hart Massey's will; among other things, the young women's home bought laundry equipment to rationalize its fairly significant laundry business, which had previously been based on the (unpaid) hand washing of the inmates. Around this time, they also opened a Salvation Army-style shelter for homeless men, in which male transients might get a meal or a night's lodging. Always wanting to avoid "pauperizing" the poor through charity, the Mission forced the men to do a certain amount of manual work for their bed or board (probably chopping firewood, like the Salvation Army); and the men were certainly not overfed, since the not-quite-free meal usually consisted of bread and coffee. In addition, an ad for the shelter humiliated potential clients by warning that "A bath may be required of any applicant for a bed."[52]

In 1911, a "Deaconess settlement" was opened, providing a home for the four to six deaconesses who worked at the Mission. While the Mission building itself was full of activities each afternoon and evening, the deaconesses were mapping out the vices of the nearby slums. One Miss Batchelor told a story typical of the genre of deaconesses' reports. Miss Batchelor first notices a drunken couple in a dwelling with a floor that "looked as if it had not been scrubbed for months."

> On a dirty greasy table was the remainder of their meal – crusts of bread and two tiny half-cooked fish. The husband was drunk, and storming because his two sons had been sent to prison.

The deaconess ignores the husband and turns to the wife:

> We pleaded with the mother to give up that which was ruining her life, not for her own sake only, but so that the boys might have a pleasant and helpful home on their return. With tears in her eyes she promised to send her little girl to our Junior League, and come herself to the Gospel service of the Mission.[53]

In interpreting this, it ought not to be assumed that Miss Batchelor invented the story. Nor should it be assumed that the interaction is adequately described by the phrase "social control." It could well be that the mother in the story actually wanted to stop drinking and took the opportunity provided by the deaconess to reform herself and send her daughter to Sunday school, so that she would not follow in her brothers' footsteps. Drinking and crime were problems for the poor themselves, not only for bourgeois observers, although the solutions offered by deaconesses and other reformers did not, admittedly, reflect the poor people's own values and interests.

One common feature of deaconesses' reports is their contempt for working-class and immigrant mothers whom they take to be inadequate nurturers. The sewing and cooking classes held at Fred Victor, taught by middle-class young women studying at the Lillian Massey School of Household Science, were aimed not only at the girls who attended them but at the whole family, with girls being used as a kind of fifth column for respectability and proper English cooking. For instance, a story is told about a girl who learned how to bake muffins; her mother resented the innovation, but the girl's father was quite pleased. The story ends with the mother acknowledging defeat and learning to cook from her own small daughter; the mother's pride and dignity counts for nothing in this narrative.[54] Elsewhere, the deaconesses openly avow their aim: "Time and again we have had direct proof of a new [household] regime instituted wholly through the efforts of these little girls, resulting in more cleanly habits, cleaner tables...."[55]

Here as elsewhere, cleanliness was but the visible manifestation of purity: "sewing can be taught so as to give excellent training to the

hand in deftness, the eye in accuracy, the intellect in creative best of all the moulding of character, and a love for the beautiful."[56] Purity, neat sewing, and proper cooking, howe not meant to turn the slum girls into Rosedale matrons. Th Massey student-teachers taught both mothers and daughter: not roast beef and Yorkshire pudding but "cereals," "peas an and "tough meats in order to make them tender" – an ackn ment that class distinctions were not to be erased but rather r in the rush toward better hygiene and spiritual health.[57]

The same class and gender biases were apparent among th ligious promoters of household science. The National C Women, for instance, declared that "the country is suffering' poor women lack domestic science.

> Of course, they all *think* that they know, but the conseq their cooking is that the husband goes out to the saloon ε are most wretched homes. We know this, in a measure, own servants and our cooks.[58]

The social construction of gender apparent in these lessons hold science was continued, in a more coercive vein, in the trave work performed by Fred Victor deaconesses from 1904. Repo this work emphasize working closely with police and other auth apprehend girls. For example, a nameless young woman was g Union Station by a deaconess because she "had a very bad rep the "bad" girl was turned over to "an official," while a young travelling with her, about whom no suspicions existed, was nev taken to the Victor Home, whether voluntarily or by force is n The deaconess simply concludes "we had every reason to believe the younger sister] was saved from a life of dishonor."[59]

This Victor Home was primarily designed, around 1900, as a rescue home for fallen women, but it seems that not ma women took shelter there except when about to give birth. 119 new young women were admitted, about half under twe apart from these, seventy-seven "respectable" adults and se children were also sheltered. In 1909, there were 251 adm and the report states that there were "respectable girls" as "moral unfortunates." The Home forced single mothers to six months and their babies for one year; the latter restrictio that most of the women preferred to stay for one year, a some went into domestic service. No rationale is given for about babies, but it was probably designed to prevent wl known as moral neglect of children, the type of child abuse o single mothers were automatically suspected.[60]

"The Blood and Fire in Canada": The Salvation Army

William Booth was a Methodist New Connexion revival preacher who, in 1865, formed his own mission in London's East End. He gradually transformed it into the headquarters of an international organization that rejected the bourgeois character of late Victorian Methodism, returning to the earlier concern for the poor and down-trodden but with distinctly modern techniques. The Salvation Army rejected theology in favour of what they called "red-hot" revival meetings; it rejected educated male ministers in favour of "soldiers" and "officers" of both sexes; it rejected grand churches and pew rents for plain halls where everyone was welcome to wander in and out, as in pubs; and it replaced solemn hymns and organ music with street brass bands and open-air singing. It also took a major role in pioneering social work among the non-respectable poor, who were often rejected by established charities but who came to form the Army's special constituency. The Army's success has been ascribed to its judicious mixture of "soup" and "salvation," and in this sense the Canadian Army was not substantially different from the parent body.[64]

The Canadian operation was begun impromptu by British immigrants who had been exposed to the Army prior to emigration. In the spring of 1882, London, Ontario, and Toronto both witnessed attempts to begin Army work; these were so successful that by September of 1883 a procession of members in Toronto numbered 700. Wanting to control the Canadian operation, General Booth sent Thomas Coombs to take over the leadership. By December of 1885, the Canadian *War Cry* had a circulation of 32,955, and at its tenth anniversary in 1892 the Army claimed about 10,000 members from coast to coast and stated that 60,000 people attended its meetings.[65]

The theatrical methods of the Army, dismissed by Methodist middle-class intellectuals as vulgar, were clearly designed to create as much of a sensation as possible, in the hope that some percentage of those who watched the spectacles would be persuaded to participate by "kneeling on the penitent-form" and declaring that they were saved. Evangeline Booth, daughter of the General and leader of the Canadian Army from 1896 to 1904, undertook remarkable public shows that played with gender and class conventions in ways which, if the context had not been so firmly religious, would have marked her as a fallen woman:

> In her unorthodox uniform and red wig, she would majestically lead a parade to the Toronto Temple, riding a pure-white horse . . . she suggested that she should give a lecture in the character of 'Miss

Booth in Rags' at Massey Hall, but to mix anything pertaining to religion with anything dramatic or out of the ordinary was an entirely new idea in conservative Toronto.[66]

Evangeline's mother, Catherine Booth, had already pointed out that saving souls did not have to imply rejecting popular culture. On the contrary, one could mobilize it for religious purposes:

> We think that the same enterprise which actuates business men with respect to their buildings should be incorporated into religion. What care and sagacity are exercised as to the situation and suitability of business premises . . . opening the theatres, dancing halls . . . and gin palaces every day, and making them attractive every night by flaring gas, music and other attractions.[67]

If Salvation Army halls looked more like dance halls than like churches, one aspect of working-class culture was quite unacceptable, that is, an interest in fashion, especially on the part of young women. In the early days, Salvationist men wore navy blue jerseys with red lettering, while women wore severe outfits from their own wardrobe with the simple addition of "S" badges on the collar. But after a few years uniforms were introduced, to heighten the military aspect of the organization. The men wore military-style jackets with braid, while the women wore highnecked, severe frocks, with bonnets that made young girls look old; in addition, all jewelry was strictly banned. The severe female uniform thus contrasted sharply with the pretty if cheap clothes favoured by urban working-class young women, and was the symbolic opposite of the "finery" by which fallen women were allegedly known.

A poignant story of failed rescue makes it apparent that "the love of dress" (unlike the love of music or of outdoor entertainment) was one feature of working-class life that women at least had to give up if they wanted to be saved. (The story, incidentally, also illustrates the Army's early efforts to interact with the prison system.)

> About 8:30 a.m. the doors of the jail were to be thrown open, and two girls who had served their time were to come out. . . . The heavy doors creaked and swung open, but instead of the coarse brown suit, we met them attired in the latest fashion, made of the most costly plush brocades, satins, fringes, ribbons, laces and feathers in profusion. Would they come with us [to the Rescue Home]? Not these two. A cab was waiting for them, they entered it and started for their old home, their old haunts.

As we walked sadly homeward, our minds queried. Why this love of dress? how did they learn to love it? and is it to gain the means to purchase this clothing that they adopt dishonest plans?[68]

The plain dress of Army women was not only a rejection of working-class showy fashions, however; it was also an attack on the consumerism of the upper classes, and thus cannot be seen as an anti-proletarian conspiracy. Florence Kinton, an early recruit to the Army from a middle-class Methodist family, wrote in her 1888 diary that disgust for fashionable feathered hats and fur coats drove her to the Army, in which women of all classes looked the same: "So I sat [in church] and listened to the sermon and looked at the people all wrapped in rich furs and murdered birds; and self-satisfaction, and scented handkerchiefs and silks and cushions . . . ."[69] Elsewhere Kinton, who became a leader in rescue work in Toronto, again highlighted the role of clothes in spiritual transformation:

I took my scissors and with ruthless fingers ripped off the superfluity of ornaments – bright bows, and lace and trimming. Thenceforth I must dress in all simplicity. I went to my wardrobe and lifted from the hooks things of which I had an unnecessary supply. I strapped them in a bundle, ready for the Rescue Home.[70]

The equation of finery with sin (especially female sin) was certainly not unique to Salvationists. A typical list of factors contributing to the downfall of working girls, drawn up by mainstream churches, included the "inordinate love of fine clothing and desire for the easy life"; and the Toronto WCTU stated that the Salvation Army was by no means unique in decrying finery, since the WCTU itself urged young women to form clubs eschewing "undesirable dress, deportment and conversation."[71] Unlike other organizations, however, the Salvation Army provided an alternative: a uniform that erased class differences and managed to appeal both to puritan sensibilities about women's dress *and* to popular interest in military regalia. Given Victorian social criticism of both the rags of the poor and the fashions of the rich, the Army's solution to the vexed question of clothes was a brilliant one.

If women had to give up jewelry and fashion, working-class men absolutely had to give up their gender-appropriate vice: drink. Despite the brass bands and gas lights, Army halls were different from dance halls in the absence of alcoholic drinks. But, as in the case of fashion, the Army did not, unlike the rest of the temperance movement, simply ask for bars to be closed: they provided alternatives. The most interesting example of this is the transformation of the famous Montreal dock workers' pub, Joe Beef's Canteen. This pub, whose important role in working-class male culture has been analysed by Peter De Lottinville, was renowned in the nineteenth century for its rowdy culture and bizarre pets, and its owner dubbed it the "Great House of the Vulgar People." After the owner's death it went into a decline, and in 1893 it was bought by the Army and turned into a working-men's club by the symbolic name of "Salvation Lighthouse."[72] There, food and non-alcoholic drink were provided, undoubtedly under the sort of large-character posters, with such messages as "God Saves," that graced every Army Hall and home. The Salvation Army considered its purchase and renovation of this proletarian landmark as quite a coup;[73] the transformation, analogous to the replacement of showy finery by uniforms, typifies the Army's approach to the problem of the slum. Unlike outside reformers seeking the demolition of unsanitary housing and the closing down of pubs, the Army considered itself to be living in the neighbourhood, not merely investigating it. They realized that moral reform would be powerless to affect the urban poor unless it managed to utilize, rather than suppress, working-class culture.

Until the late 1880s, the English Salvation Army had been basically an evangelical sect, with some *ad hoc* social services. The publication in 1890 of General Booth's *In Darkest England and the Way Out* marked the beginning of the Army's long commitment to social work. As the frontispiece to *In Darkest England* makes perfectly clear, this work was envisioned as the literal rescue by Salvationists in lifeboats of people shipwrecked in a dark ocean whose waves were marked "pauperism," "vice," "prostitution," "drunkenness," and so on. This powerful and complex image was not new, being a social version of the evangelical conversion allegories Booth would have learned during his Methodist years. The novelty was that Booth used such an elaborate allegory, reminiscent of medieval paintings, at a time when most religious discourse was growing increasingly abstract and even scientific. Exiled from liberal theology, highbrow literature, and social theory, allegories were nevertheless alive and well in the popular press (as W.T. Stead's "Maiden Tribute" demonstrates), and the language used by the Army was a successful combination of old-fashioned religious imagery organized through classical rhetorical tropes with the "modern" techniques of yellow journalism. The Army's preference for maritime metaphors, even prior to 1890, can be seen from texts such as the following:

Sinking souls upon fickle rafts are braving the tempests and storms of the social ocean, throwing out signals of distress which, for the most part, are unheeded and unseen, and the proud ship of worldly morality and perfunctory charity rides proudly by leaving the waifs of life to perish beneath the dark waters by which they are surrounded.[74]

But in the complex picture that appeared as frontispiece to *In Darkest England*, this metaphor of social work as rescuing people from shipwrecks is elaborated into a multi-layered allegory, in which Canada appears as the far-off land of rural health in which wrecked mariners can undertake a new life.

If shipwrecks provided a central image guiding the Army's work with the slum dwellers, another important image was that constructed by analogy with Stanley's *In Darkest Africa*, which had been published to much acclaim just prior to Booth's work. A long quotation from Stanley is found at the beginning of the first chapter, telling of the explorer's arduous journey through bogs and forests, using a machete to hack his way through what he called "the inner womb of the tropical forest." This masculinist birth metaphor is elaborated by Booth, who, preparing the way for his own account of English slums, warns the reader that in African forests full of "dark, dank air, filled with the steam of the heated morass, human beings dwarfed into pygmies and brutalized into cannibals lurk and live and die."[75] The rotting, threatening, mysterious – and hence female – decay of the Congo jungle provides the lens through which to explore the exotic slums. The challenge to social workers, Booth writes, is to clear the forest/slum so that light can penetrate and roads can be built that will not be "immediately choked up by the ooze of the morass and the luxuriant parasitical growth of the forest." Carried away by metaphor, Booth even claims that "Darkest England, like Darkest Africa, reeks with malaria."[77]

With knowledge acquired through courageous exploration, the Army colonizers set out to rescue the inhabitants of the bogs/slums. In their work, they generally divided their constituency into three distinct categories (similar but not identical to the three categories identified by the Methodist city missionaries): (1) the honest poor; (2) the vicious and fallen; (3) the criminal.[78] Unlike the Methodists, Salvationists built social agencies designed primarily for the latter two categories, believing that existing philanthropies catered only to what General Booth called "the aristocracy of the miserable."[79]

The vicious and fallen were in turn subdivided according to gender and vice. Fallen women were encouraged to go to rescue homes, which the Army successfully established – before the traditional churches – in Victoria, Toronto, London, Stratford, Saint John,

Winnipeg, Halifax, St. John's, Ottawa, and Hamilton. The reports do not put much stress on the reasons for women entering these homes; whether they were "illegitimate mothers," prostitutes wanting to leave the trade, homeless women, or aging and sick women was not very important to the Army, which ignored modern trends in social research such as the mania for classifying all cases according to cause. They were less interested in research and more interested in results. In an early year, 1892, these are reported as follows: 290 cases received across Canada, 135 sent to domestic service after a suitable period of penitence, five married, and "only 61 cases" unsatisfactory.[80]

A set of "Rules and Regulations" for rescue homes published in 1896 gives a sense of how these homes were run. Rising at six a.m., the women were kept working, either at housework or in productive labour, until the evening, which was usually taken up by religious meetings. Women were not allowed to go to their bedrooms during the day; were forced to "lay aside flowers, feathers, bangs and bustles while in the Home"; were not allowed to refer to their former life in any way; and were "expected" to stay for six months. But mere compliance with these onerous rules was not sufficient: the home officers demanded heartfelt commitment, stating that "every duty, however arduous it may be, should be performed in a spirit of cheerful willingness."[81]

For drinkers of both sexes there were also appropriate homes; and for those who were in the street because of drink or unspecified vices, there were night shelters. These – mostly for men, though there was a women's shelter in Toronto that housed 3,158 women in one year – generally compelled the men either to do manual work or to pay a small amount for a mattress in a communal dormitory and a frugal supper (bread and coffee, usually).[82]

Throughout, work with "the vicious" was marked by a cheerful and even comradely attitude suggesting that poverty and even vice (except perhaps prostitution) were usually due to misfortune or accident, not laziness or genetic degeneration. Stories such as "Fence Jack: Redeemed Burglar" and "A Pickpocket in Heaven"[83] spent much more time entertainingly recounting the misdeeds and adventures of these melodramatic characters than detailing their conversions, and would have appealed to the same people who enjoyed broadsides and pamphlets about famous outlaws. Many of the early converts were themselves very poor, some being reformed prostitutes and alcoholics, and hence were able to speak in the language of the slums (although the few sources available suggest that, especially among women, those who were in charge of rescue work were from a higher socio-economic class). An article titled "To the Rescue" happily proclaimed that "multitudes of drunkards and harlots have been washed in the Blood of Jesus" in a tone that might have struck a chord with John Wesley but would have horrified the Eatons, Masseys, and other respectable Methodists, who would also have been unamused by the adventures of a pickpocket in heaven.[84]

Perhaps the most unique contribution of the Army was in their work with offenders. Throughout Canada, the Army pioneered volunteer parole and probation services, believing that if they could convince judges and other court officials to leave offenders in their hands, true reformation would take place. Early in the twentieth century it began to get formal government grants for its probation work, but even before this, the Army had established its workers in or near police courts and jails. These workers brought such innovations as a "Red Maria," which was available to transport released prisoners to "prison-gate" homes.

In Army accounts of its own work no distinction is drawn between voluntary halfway houses and coercive institutions to which the police or the courts actually sentenced people. Since the same homes served both these roles, and the Army in any case believed that everyone was guilty until proven saved, it is impossible to determine to what extent this court and prison work was useful to prisoners and to what extent it merely added a new level of moral surveillance and regulation. That rescue homes could lead to longer and even indefinite sentences being imposed, especially on women convicted of morals offences, is suggested by such comments as this, from the Vancouver social survey of 1913:

> Central Mission and the Salvation Army have rescue homes for unfortunate girls. In this field the great need is an arrangement by which the courts will not impose fines on first offenders, neither imprison them, but shall *commit them to a rescue home for an indefinite period*. If on their dismissal they again offend and if longer terms at the rescue home seem ineffective, imprisonment would seem to be inevitable.[85]

In the absence of studies of the role of the Salvation Army in the criminal justice system, little can be said about why the state became interested in encouraging private agencies, even of a sectarian religious character, to take over some aspects of criminal justice work. David Garland's argument (developed in the English context) might provide an initial hypothesis for further study; he argues that when such programs as probation and parole were being developed,

> much care was taken to ensure that the agencies dealing with the welfare of offenders – reformatories, police court missions, discharged prisoners' aid societies and so on – retained their private

status and reputation, even when they were a de facto element in the normal routines of penal practice. Thus although private rescue work might be facilitated, it was made quite clear that the moral welfare of the offender was in no sense the duty, responsibility or proper concern of the liberal state.[86]

This is corroborated by the Canadian Army's own explanations of the division of labour between the state and philanthropy. Commenting that purely coercive measures such as imprisonment never amount to regeneration, they write that "although the law is very necessary to check these terrible vices, yet to a certain extent it is a failure, for our fair Dominion is more than ever over run by sin."[87] Hence, there is an important place for what Garland calls "private agencies of moralisation": "we," continues the Salvationist writer, "mean to arrest hell-bound sinners and make them think of the terrors of hell." These pseudo-arrests carried out not by the armed power of the state but by the theatrical techniques of the private Army potentially cover many more people, since the Army wants to save the multitudes sunk in vice, not just those few who happen to break a man-made law. But at the same time that the writer tries to give the Army's private work a veneer of officiality by using words such as "arrest" (meaning conversion), the writer acknowledges that the state often uses force instead of gentler methods: a picture shows a Salvationist tearing a criminal-looking man away from the clutches of a policeman, and sympathy is expressed for the "men and women," such as the poor vagrant, "who are pounced down upon by servants of the law."

This article (and its accompanying pictures) shows the complex relationship between philanthropy and the state, in the specific case of law enforcement. The Salvation Army collaborated with the state, and indeed obtained both funding and official powers from it; but it also made it clear that it was different from and more benevolent than the state. At the same time, Army benevolence had an insidious regulatory effect in stressing subjective feeling (witness the compulsory cheerfulness of rescue-home women) and not merely behavioural conformity. This somewhat contradictory position of the "private agencies of moralisation" vis-à-vis the Canadian state will be taken up in the next chapter.

7

Philanthropy, the State, and Moral Regulation

The transition from volunteer philanthropy to professional and scientific social work was neither smooth nor uncontroversial. The passions raised in the debate on how to approach the problems of poverty and vice, a debate whose participants did not know that state-organized social work would prevail while the churches receded into the background of Canadian society, are clearly visible in the mini-debate sparked by the controversial figure of Alice Chown.

Alice Chown was born in 1866 to a Kingston Methodist family including many doctors, lawyers, and high-ranking clergymen, including her uncle, S.D. Chown. She spent years caring for a sick mother but happily shed her spinster daughter role when her mother died in 1906. She then travelled to England, Chicago, and New York, volunteering for suffrage organizations and becoming acquainted with new social and sexual theories. This led to a disenchantment with both her family's religion and the philanthropic endeavours to which the females of the family were expected to devote themselves. She attempted unsuccessfully to introduce Freudian ideas into Toronto's middle-class suffrage circles and greatly admired Edward Carpenter's radical ideas on love and sex. An ardent feminist and pacifist, she helped to organize support for the Eaton's strikers in 1912. In quest of dress reform she threw away corsets, tight dresses, and uncomfortable shoes in favour of loose Grecian tunics and bare feet. And, more relevant to present purposes, she waged a one-woman campaign to revolutionize philanthropy.[1]

As early as 1899, Chown had argued in both Methodist and feminist circles in favour of the adoption of scientific philanthropy. She was the secretary of the Charity Organization Society in Kingston and gave a speech praising COS methods at the annual meeting of the National Council of Women. This speech, also printed as an article in the Methodist *Christian Guardian*, highlighted Canada's need for "data for dealing with [social] conditions, that we may substitute the

The Kingston feminist Alice Chown had few allies in her quest for a purely secular and scientific approach to the problems of poverty and vice. (Courtesy Queen's University Archives)

diagnosis of the trained physician for the empirical knowledge of the well-meaning but ignorant amateur."[2]

These views were strengthened in the course of her travels and in her conversations with modern American reformers such as Florence Kelley. In 1911, seeking to emulate Kelley and the women of the Chicago school, Chown set out to investigate the training of Methodist deaconesses. Her report, published in *The Christian Guardian* probably only because of her family name, was scathing. The sociology taught at the Deaconess Training School was "unscientific," "emotional pap" that not only served to further pauperize the poor by providing charity rather than scientifically studying poverty, but also helped to imprison deaconesses in the gender structure of the church. Chown acidly speculated that perhaps the real purpose of the women's training was

> to furnish nice little satellites for Methodist ministers, women who will clasp their hands in admiration at the greater knowledge of the pastor.... It seemed to me that the course of study was aptly framed to fill Ruskin's ideal education of women, the ability to appreciate other people's learning, not to be competent oneself.[3]

Chown's acerbic remarks provoked a counterattack by Rev. Bartle Bull of the Fred Victor Mission. Outraged that such an article would appear in the official Methodist weekly, Rev. Bull stated that deaconesses do not need "abstract sociological theories."[4] Undeterred, Chown published a second article advocating the scientific study of economics, political science, history, and hygiene (the omission of sociology likely indicates not ignorance but rather a low opinion of her uncle's sociology lectures at Victoria College). Such a course of study, she believed, would produce modern social workers, who might perhaps be assisted by deaconesses trained in "personal service."[5]

With typical tactlessness, Chown reproduced the subordination of deaconesses, expected in her scheme to defer to secularly trained social workers. Furthermore, Chown failed to acknowledge that modern social work might be just as intrusive as charity: she optimistically wrote that "the girl receiving insufficient pay would be encouraged, friends and recreation provided, but she would also be studied."[6]

This latter statement provoked a reply from a *Christian Guardian* reader, a Mrs. Morrison in rural Saskatchewan, who defended the methods of charity work and added: "And anyway, does the girl receiving insufficient pay wish to be studied? Would Alice A. Chown wish to be studied herself? Would you? Would I?"[7]

In a third article, Chown acknowledged that she had been too harsh on the deaconesses themselves, but defended her stand against charity and for modern social work in a passage whose theorization of gender and philanthropy deserves being quoted at length:

> I am too much of a lover of my own sex not to understand how our very weakness of self-sacrifice and self-negation has come from long years of regarding other people before ourselves. I am not criticizing the women who, yielding to this feminine characteristic of self-denial, devote their lives to service, but the Methodist Church, which accepts the service of these fine-spirited women, gives them such a poor preparation for their work and then so inadequately remunerates them.[8]

This critique of gender relations was followed by an attack on the way traditional philanthropy, by supplementing inadequate wages with charity and such services as low-cost boarding homes for women workers, propped up exploitative capitalist relations:

> It is no new view – that charity pays part of the cost of manufacture . . . our charity, although intended for the victims of the present industrial system, sometimes indirectly benefits the employers. . . . In conclusion, let me say, what the poor want is not charity, but justice.

As the controversy escalated, more prominent Methodists joined the fray: J.S. Woodsworth put forward his views on the church's role in social service. Trying to find a middle ground, he acknowledged that Miss Chown had been overly critical, but added that she had "rendered a valuable service to the Church by daring to frankly criticize things as they are." In the U.S., he pointed out, secularly based settlements were supplanting church-run city missions: such an outcome could be avoided in Canada if the churches modernized their methods sufficiently.[9]

This heated debate brought to the surface disagreements, which usually remained unspoken or at least unpublished, among various camps: conservative charity workers, socialist advocates of justice instead of charity, feminists who sought to end women's subordinate role in social service, and promoters of scientific sociology and social work. Chown's campaign for modernity, science, and gender equality was not very successful, among other reasons because she consistently antagonized other women with her airs of intellectual superiority and American connections.[10] But the ideas presented by her, particularly in regard to the need for scientific training of social workers and for structural rather than individual approaches to social change, were by no means unique, and were taken up – generally cleansed of radical and feminist elements – by other reformers.

One of the main currents in the philanthropy reform movement was what was known as "charity organization." This movement to co-ordinate and rationalize charity, whose aims were to cut down on actual aid and maximize the thrift and self-reliance of the poor through education and moral reform, was pioneered in Toronto by the Women's Christian Association (WCA). The WCA believed that the publicly run House of Industry did not investigate its "clients" sufficiently. They fought pauperization by refusing to give money to the poor, giving donations in kind and only after investigation of potential "impostors."[11] In the 1880s, middle-class women continued to visit and investigate the poor, but now the slogan of charity organization was taken up by such male notables as the retired Oxford professor Goldwin Smith, known locally as "the sage of the Grange."[12] At this time, before the waves of non-British immigration, the fears about the lower orders focused not on the racially other but on British slum types such as "the beggar and the tramp" and "the girl outcast."[13] These characters were believed to be descending upon Canada on the same boats that brought literary and journalistic accounts of English urban "barbarians."

Efforts to set up clearinghouses for all charity cases and prevent the poor from getting help from several sources were not very successful, due to sectarian suspicions and lack of bureaucratic organization. Further, the idea that one should give advice instead of money was theoretically coherent but in practice resulted in losing one's clientele to more generous competitors. Since in most parts of Canada there was no threat of the workhouse because there were no Poor Laws, private charities found it difficult to uphold the British distinction between the worthy and the unworthy poor in their actual work. (In Britain, private philanthropy concentrated on "honest" poor while those regarded as thriftless were generally sent to the parish.)[14] The popular Kingston writer and charity activist Agnes Machar explained that the dilemma faced by Canadian philanthropists was the need to "relieve distress without either encouraging pauperism by indiscriminate almsgiving, or bringing anything that might saddle the country with a poor law."[15] In Montreal, the philanthropic manufacturer Herbert Ames also expressed a distaste for state relief in the Poor Law tradition but agreed that "some Central Charity Board, upon which representatives of every race and creed might sit, should be here established."[16] How co-ordination and rationalization of relief might be achieved without developing a fully public system that would inevitably pauperize rather than uplift the poor was the constant worry of philanthropists.

It is unclear whether the seven cities that had charity organization societies in 1900 actually managed to co-ordinate charity and establish the casework method.[17] But if the charity society groupings in various cities did not share common administrative practices – a development hampered by the inherent dilemmas of maintaining the private character of philanthropy while centralizing and modernizing it – they were unified in their theory. Winnipeg's Associated Charities typically portrayed itself (as shown in a diagram in Woodsworth's *My Neighbor*) as a giant lens gathering the rays of churches, hospitals, correctional agencies, and other sources of social sunlight into a single beam illuminating "The Home of a Needy Family." This body put forward the belief that "the large majority of applications for relief are caused by thriftlessness, mismanagement, unemployment due to incompetence, intemperance, immorality, desertion of the family and domestic quarrels." It ominously added: "In such cases the mere giving of relief tends rather to induce pauperism than to reduce poverty."[18]

The city of Toronto had moved to co-ordinate charities and have the municipality assume some control over relief as early as 1893, although for the first two years of this plan the city's relief officer had his salary paid by Goldwin Smith personally, a peculiar reversal of the practice of municipal funding of private charities.[19] The attempt at co-ordination was not a success, however, for the Charities Commission appointed by City Council in 1911 reported that there was much "indiscriminate charity" and recommended that "a central registration and investigation bureau be established."[20] The lack of such a central body was remarkable given the substantial sums of money given to privately run charities by the city ($71,000 in 1908 alone).[21] Only after 1912 did the city organize a modern social service (welfare) department, although as we shall see church-based charity workers continued to exercise a great deal of leadership into the 1930s.

The extremely uneven development both of centralized public relief and of bureaucratic methods to standardize the investigation of what came to be known as "cases" puts in question mythical accounts of a smooth rise of the welfare state. Insofar as a welfare state did rise, it was in fits and starts, and the private charities were leaders as well as followers in the campaign to modernize and rationalize both relief and social research – as seen, for instance, in Goldwin Smith's contribution of a municipal welfare officer's salary, in the face of a city council unwilling to take power away from philanthropy. Philanthropic funds were also responsible for paying all of the costs of the School of Social Work at the University of Toronto for the first few years of its operation, a fact indicating that philanthropy and science, private and public, were neither antagonistic nor mutually exclusive categories.[22]

Private moral and social reformers, therefore, often pioneered modern relief methods and made important contributions to social research. The National Council of Women undertook innovative research, such as the 1880s survey of "feeble-minded" women, which foreshadowed later surveys by state and medical authorities. In this and similar activities (whose effect on ordinary people was not necessarily beneficial, as in the case of the hapless women recommended for institutionalization and/or sterilization), the NCW encouraged middle-class Protestant women to learn how to do policy-oriented research. President Lady Aberdeen gave simple lessons in research methods:

> In the Executive of a Local Council some subject is mentioned which seems to call for action. . . . The lady will probably be asked to gather statistics on the subject, and read a paper before the next meeting of the General Council. She does so . . . probably a subcommittee will be appointed to deal with the matter and bring the request and opinion of the Council before the proper authorities.[23]

But perhaps the best example of the contribution of moral reformers to social science is the social survey or case study in urban sociology, conceived and funded by the Methodist and Presbyterian departments of moral reform at a time when university-based social research was almost unknown.[24] From 1911 to 1913, these two churches, aided by various philanthropic bodies, conducted partial social surveys measuring variables such as sanitation, housing, working conditions, and, last but not least, "social purity: white slave traffic, houses of ill fame, and other forms."[25] Despite the desire to measure purity (put into practice in wild guesses about the numbers of women stolen by white slavers and in attempts to observe and count how many times bar patrons swore), the surveys done by churches in Sydney, Vancouver, London, Fort William, and other places were far more sociological than the non-religious Toronto Social Survey of 1915, which focused almost exclusively on female sexual deviance.[26] The university students and clergymen conducting these surveys copied the most advanced American methods: for example, they drew detailed maps showing the distribution of ethnic and family types on a particular city block ("38 families, 165 boarders, 201 Poles, 130 Russians").[27]

The churches undertook this social research work partly because of the fear (voiced by Woodsworth during the Alice Chown debate in the *Christian Guardian*) that if the churches did not lead in this new field of work, they would be superseded by secular agencies, as was already happening in the U.S. Also, as morality came increasingly to be understood as environmentally determined, social knowledge of environments, particularly in urban areas regarded as hotbeds of vice, came to be seen as a necessary component of the work of moral reform.

The knowledge gathered was not meant to be shared with the poor themselves to serve in their own emancipation; rather, it was a weapon in the crusade against disease-crime-vice, giving the reformers a tactical advantage in the moralization campaign. Rev. George Pidgeon typically compared the vicious to rats, on the basis that both were disturbed by the flashlight of philanthropic knowledge: "The late Bishop Fowler said, 'when you flash a ray of light into a rat-hole you spoil it for rat purposes.' Naturally the rats are disturbed." The rat analogy was translated into philosophical speech as follows: "the higher life kn[ow]s the lower better than the lower kn[ow]s itself; while the lower cannot underst[and] the higher."[28]

The privately initiated schemes for quantifying social and moral problems were thus primarily means of organizing a harmonious social formation: but the university- or government-based research and social work techniques that came later were not necessarily more objective or less rooted in a desire to moralize the poor and sustain a particular system of class, race, and gender domination.

The interactions between moral reform and the emerging modern system of public welfare are clearly seen in the case of Toronto's Neighbourhood Workers' Association (NWA), described as the "most prestigious and influential agency in the city."[29] This was a hybrid public/private organization whose story demonstrates that there was no smooth transition from amateur philanthropists to state professionals, but rather a complex series of relationships that eventually resulted in the state assuming financial responsibility for the relief of poverty – without eliminating either the moral-reform ethos or the practical importance of private agencies, which continued to flourish even if their relation to the state changed.[30]

The man who steered the NWA through its first few decades, Methodist minister Rev. F.N. Stapleford, traced the NWA's origins to the charity organization methods of the Associated Charities of the late 1880s, which he – erasing the WCA women from the record – identifies as the invention of Goldwin Smith.[31] Stapleford omits to mention the persistent failures of charity organization projects in Toronto and elsewhere, painting a picture of smooth continuity between 1888 and 1912, when the Associated Charities met its (unexplained) demise. Be that as it may, soon afterwards secular settlements and church-run missions came together – partly due to their own need for co-ordination and partly because of the pressure put on them by the municipal Charities Commission of 1911 – and formed the Neighbourhood Workers' Association. The brand-new municipal Social Service Committee (run out of Charles Hastings's public health empire) paid the salaries of three secretaries appointed to run the NWA; but the NWA secretaries were responsible to a board representing the various private philanthropies, which led to frictions between private and public.[32]

Both Stapleford and Toronto Mayor Horatio Hocken constructed a public image of harmony between the two spheres, with Hocken assuring the philanthropies that municipal controls over grants ("a systematic kind of management") would very rarely lead to cuts.[33] Nevertheless, by 1917-18 the conflicts were publicly admitted, and the Bureau of Municipal Research suggested that "the work of the NWA fundamentally requires private control – at least in this stage in its evolution – and there should certainly be no difficulty in raising from private sources the small sum annually necessary.[34]

This privatization plan was carried out, and from 1918 on the NWA paid its own staff of four caseworkers. Their work was the investigation of the private-sphere equivalent of welfare fraud, that is, people getting charity from more than one source. For instance, in 1919 the NWA, concerned about the proliferation of "fresh air" schemes for inner-city children, established a Fresh Air Exchange to hunt down parents who sent their children to more than one such camp, and created a new camp, Bolton, to facilitate centralization. The casework was organized by dividing the city into nine districts and encouraging the geographical specialization of charities. Stapleford, a great believer in the virtues of casework, seems to have encouraged Toronto social workers to learn their methods from Mary Richmond's *Social Diagnosis*, an early and well-known American textbook of modern social work. (As well as running the NWA, Stapleford taught casework in the early days of the University of Toronto's Social Service Department, later Faculty of Social Work.)[35]

The NWA thus became a privately run watchdog over charities that, though also privately run, were to a significant extent publicly funded through both provincial and municipal grants. As the NWA expanded its operations, it devoted more fund-raising efforts to paying its own staff, in keeping with the new social-work philosophy of investigating, educating, and providing some services for the poor without actually giving them material aid.

Stapleford continued to head the organization into the 1930s. Under the pressure of depression-caused changes in the relief system, the city welfare department assumed (in 1934) both financial and investigatory control over the unemployed, but it left the NWA in charge of the "social cases where unemployment is not a factor, such as desertion, illness, etc.," as well as the "cases where unemployment is a factor but where family demoralization" existed.[36] Thus, whereas the professional workers hired by the city clearly preferred to deal with strictly economic problems, the 1934 division of labour was based on the principle "That the emphasis of the Neighbourhood Workers' Association shall be on family rehabilitation and a constructive effort to stay those processes of demoralization due to prolonged unemployment."[37]

The attempt to separate moral from economic intervention into the sphere of the family, with philanthropy in charge of moralization services and the state in charge of unemployment relief, was not a stable one. Brigitte Kitchen and Veronica Strong-Boag have shown in another context that new state benefits such as mothers' allowances were granted only after the state constructed them as payment for specific services, entitling the state to moral surveillance of the recipients. The Ontario commission that in 1920 investigated the feasibility of mothers' allowances put it most starkly:

> The mother is regarded as an applicant for employment as a guardian of future citizens of the state, and if she does not measure up to the State's standards for such guardians, other arrangements must be sought in the best interests of the children and to prevent increase in the number of dependents of this nature [single mothers].[38]

The state, then, was clearly willing and able to exercise a great deal of moral regulation, particularly where women and reproduction were involved.

Thus, even if there was a common-sense view that the work of moralization (for instance, in rescuing fallen women or changing domestic cooking and drinking habits) was best performed by private philanthropies, the state did not dispense with moral categories in its own welfare apparatus. Meanwhile, the private charities continued to specialize in reforming prisoners, drunks, and fallen women; but their "talking cures" were carried out partly through quasi-state coercive and economic powers exercised by a growing number of full-time employees.[39] The statements of both state officials and philanthropists suggested that philanthropy was wholly privately funded and oriented by benevolent aims, while the state had jurisdiction over those requiring correction and those, such as lunatics, who would not benefit from moralization schemes. But in practice philanthropy received much of its funding from the state and exercised many of its functions, while the state used moral distinctions not only as rhetorical but as practical categories. This does not mean, however, that the distinction between philanthropy and welfare, the state and civil society, was entirely illusory: it only means that it was far more complex and mobile than people imagined. Private philanthropies continued to exist outside of the state, even through the halcyon days of the welfare state, because there were good reasons on both sides to maintain the fences even while moving them back and forth.

Conclusion: The State, Civil Society, and Moral Regulation

This picture of the symbiotic – though sometimes conflicting – relationship between philanthropy and the state differs substantially from both liberal and Marxist accounts of the inexorable rise of a welfare state growing from its centre outwards and superseding both the values and the work methods of the charities. Liberal accounts dismiss the moral categories persistently used by both charities and the welfare state as quaint remnants of a bygone era, which only slow down but do not shape the growth of modern state methods. Marxist accounts (and in Canada this chiefly means accounts produced by the political economy school) explain the rise of welfare as due to the perpetual conflict between the accumulation and the legitimation functions of the state: that is, since the naked domination of the bourgeoisie for the sake of capital accumulation might produce social revolt, the state carries out the work of smoothing the sharp edges of capitalism by giving some minimal relief to those who do not earn wages.[40] The state is, in this view, the servant of the bourgeoisie, since even when state officials are sincerely convinced that they are helping ordinary people, the *real* effect of social welfare is to manage the inherent contradictions of capitalism, which, unmanaged, would result in class war.

Neither liberal nor Marxist accounts, however, consider the possibility that moral regulation might be an important social process, which is intertwined with but is not an effect of either the economic or the political. Moral regulation is very closely linked to state formation, as the British school of historical sociology has argued;[41] but as Foucault and his followers have pointed out, the state has no monopoly on moral regulation, and private organizations – notably, the medical and legal professions and the philanthropic groups – have exercised crucial leadership in the regulatory field. David Garland has taken the debate one step further by reminding us that general discussions of the state or even the capitalist state do not help in understanding the specific questions faced by *liberal democratic* states; such states, structurally committed to constructing ethics as a field of private opinion and behaviour, have historically found it convenient to leave moral rehabilitation to private agencies that face no such constraints.[42]

But Garland's framework, though largely correct, is not sufficient to capture the complexities inherent in the public funding of private agencies, or in the negotiations surrounding the Toronto Neighbourhood Workers' Association. He tends to assume that moral regulation is the province of philanthropy, while coercion and scientific knowledge belong to the state. Even if there is some truth to this generalization, one has to be careful to point out exactly how moral regulation came to be perceived as best performed by agencies in civil society, not the state, and one has to be sceptical of any claims that envision a clear separation between moral and economic regulation.

Both the state and the philanthropies have a vested interest in delineating their respective jurisdictions in a clear-cut manner; but in fact the state does not restrict itself to giving unemployment insurance or putting the insane in asylums, and the philanthropies do not merely preach morality. Economic, social, and moral functions are not strictly divided up, even if the public realm tends to avoid direct regulation of morality – at least in times when the liberal and democratic character of capitalist states predominates over the repressive and undemocratic aspects – and agencies in civil society emphasize their own role in shaping the subjectivity of individuals. The distinction between the state and civil society is a flexible one and is articulated differently at the level of rhetoric, at the level of administrative practice, and at the level of people's experience. Similarly, the distinction between different modes of regulation (moral vs. economic vs. political) is not found ready-made but is constantly produced, in varying ways, by agents located outside as well as inside the state. A study of social purity – a moral reform project undertaken largely by private organizations but supported to some extent by the state and the ruling class generally – thus helps to problematize both the state/civil society dichotomy and the interplay between different modes of regulation.

Moral regulation is an important aspect of ruling, helping to constitute class, gender, sexual, and race relations by interpreting both social action and individual identity as fundamentally ethical. It is of course true that the quest for a self-regulated sexuality in young people (or, more generally, for the kind of ethical subjectivity idealized by moral reform) had beneficial effects on Canadian capitalism; but capitalism is not always and everywhere rooted in Protestant social purity, being perfectly compatible with other systems of moral regulation. To see social purity as explained by the value of self-regulated sexuality to capitalism would be functionalist in the extreme – as well as being reductionist, since we have seen that race, gender, and sexuality are best understood not as secondary, adjectival features of class subjects but rather as relatively autonomous categories that can be constructed and experienced as more basic than class.

Moral reform is hence not a singular stage in the history of capital accumulation: if secular modernity had been as powerfully successful as both Marxist and liberal accounts would have it, advanced capitalist states would not at the end of the twentieth century be undertaking moral projects to strengthen the family, remove prostitutes from city streets, and build character in post-permissive schools. Neither is it an ideology explainable through its functional role in the capitalist system of class relations. Moral reform, like moral regulation generally, seeks to construct and organize both social relations and individual consciousness in such a way as to legitimize certain institutions and discourses – the patriarchal nuclear family, racist immigration policies – from the point of view of morality. Its relationship to production, or for that matter to the state, cannot be theorized *a priori*, for these relations shift with changes in social regulation generally. The fact that there have been such shifts – for instance, in the reformulation of "the problem" of immigrants as an economic rather than sexual/health threat – shows that moral regulation does not occupy a social space distinct from that occupied by "the economic" or "the social": it is a mode of regulating social and individual life generally, not pretagged moral issues. In the present day, the scope of moral reform has been narrowed, and only issues such as abortion (which was not, interestingly enough, a major concern of the social purity movement) are perceived as constitutive of the nation's moral character. An examination of social purity and philanthropic moral reform shows that practically every social issue was understood as moral in a not very distant historical period, which implies that all these issues can potentially be reconceptualized as moral.

The present study shows not only that there have been predecessors to today's anti-pornography crusaders and other moral reformers – that would be a trivial conclusion – but, more importantly, that social regulation has undergone some major shifts, both in terms of the relationship between the state and private agencies of regulation and in terms of the framing of social problems. We no longer regard any and all social problems as moral; and we have come to expect the state to initiate both research and action on practically all such "problems." These are profound discontinuities between the age of purity and the present day, which can be contrasted with continuities in popular fears of a national decay rooted in sexual decadence. Some of the tools used here to analyse the workings of social purity – for instance, the tracing of slippages between racial and sexual categories, or the problematic nature of the relation between civil society and the state in philanthropic work – may be useful in other contexts. The scope and the mode of operation of moral regulation, however, do not remain constant, and require separate analysis in each instance.

Notes

Abbreviations

CTA	City of Toronto Archives, Toronto
NAC	National Archives of Canada, Ottawa
PAO	Public Archives of Ontario, Toronto
SA	Salvation Army Heritage Centre, Toronto
UCA	United Church Archives, Victoria College, Toronto

Note on Archival Sources

At the time the research was conducted, two of the record collections used were in the process of being classified (records of the Woman's Christian Temperance Union, in the Public Archives of Ontario, and those of the Canadian Council of Churches, National Archives of Canada). Therefore, the box and file numbers listed in the following notes were temporary numbers and may or may not correspond to the permanent numbers assigned later by archivists.

Preface

1. Hayden White, *Tropics of Discourse: Essays in Cultural Criticism* (Baltimore, 1978); Joan Scott, "On Language, Gender and Working-Class History," *International Labor and Working-Class History Journal*, no. 31 (Spring, 1987), pp. 1-13. Gareth Stedman Jones has also articulated a view of history privileging discursive relations as creating social relations; but in his own work he does not always practise what he preaches. See his *Languages of Class: Studies in English Working-Class History 1832-1892* (Cambridge, 1983).
2. "In many of its incarnations, 'language' theory is simply the flip side of crude materialism. Language is still separated from the social, but the causality is reversed." Christine Stansell, "Response to Joan Scott," *International Labor and Working-Class History Journal*, no. 31 (Spring, 1987) p. 27.
3. Joan Wallach Scott, *Gender and the Politics of History* (New York, 1988); Mary Poovey, *Uneven Developments: the Ideological Work of Gender in Mid-Victorian England* (Chicago, 1988); Denise Riley, *'Am I that name?': Feminism and the Category of 'Women' in History* (Minneapolis, 1988).

4. For one aspect of the social construction of female vice through the classification of non-verbal signs (namely clothes), see Mariana Valverde, "The Love of Finery: Fashion and the Fallen Woman in Nineteenth-Century Social Discourse," *Victorian Studies*, 32, 2 (Winter, 1989) pp. 168-88.

Chapter 1

1. H. Clare Pentland, *Labour and Capital in Canada 1650-1860* (Toronto, 1981); Allan Moscovitch and Jim Albert, eds., *The "Benevolent" State: The Growth of Welfare in Canada* (Toronto, 1987); Leo Panitch, "The role and nature of the Canadian State," and Reg Whitaker, "Images of the state in Canada," in Leo Panitch, ed., *The Canadian State* (Toronto, 1977).
2. G. Kealey, *Toronto Workers Respond to Industrial Capitalism* (Toronto, 1980); G. Kealey and B. Palmer, *Dreaming of What Might Be: The Knights of Labor in Ontario 1880-1900* (Toronto, 1987); B. Palmer, ed., *The Character of Class Struggle* (Toronto, 1986); Michael Piva, *The Condition of the Working Class in Toronto* (Ottawa,1979).
3. Ramsay Cook, *The Regenerators: Social Criticism in Late Victorian English Canada* (Toronto, 1985).
4. Rev. C.W. Watch, "Social Purity Work in Canada," in A. Powell, ed., *National Purity Congress* (Baltimore, 1895), pp. 272-77.
5. These included Dr. Elizabeth Blackwell, Anthony Comstock, and Frances Willard (president of the U.S. Woman's Christian Temperance Union and one of the foremost reformers of her time).
6. Rev. Flint, in Powell, ed., *National Purity Congress*, p. 140.
7. See for instance F.S. Spence, *The Facts of the Case: A Summary of the most Important Evidence and Argument presented in the Report of the Royal Commission on the Liquor Traffic* (Toronto, 1896). Spence claims that the first temperance convention in Canada was held in Halifax in 1834; but the movement only began in earnest in the late 1870s, and the Dominion WCTU was not founded until 1885.
8. The main source is Richard Allen, *The Social Passion: Religion and Social Reform in Canada 1914-1928* (Toronto, 1971). See also Dennis Guest, *The Emergence of Social Security in Canada* (Vancouver, 1985), pp. 31-34; Cook, *The Regenerators,* ch. 7.
9. See Gareth Stedman Jones, *Outcast London* (London, 1971), esp. pp. 244ff. See also Christine Stansell, *City of Women: Sex and Class in New York City 1789-1860* (New York, 1986), ch. 4; and C. Smith-Rosenberg, *Religion and the Rise of the American City: The New York City Mission Movement 1812-1870* (Ithaca, N.Y., 1971).
10. Quoted in Eli Zaretsky, "Rethinking the Welfare State," in J. Dickinson and B. Russell, eds., *Family, Economy and State* (Toronto, 1987), p. 100.
11. Jacques Donzelot summarizes this shift as follows: "In general, philanthropy differed from charity in the choice of its objects, based on this concern for pragmatism: advice instead of gifts, because it cost nothing; assistance to children rather than to old people, and to women rather than to men." *The Policing of Families* (New York, 1979), p. 66. Donzelot's analysis, based on the work of

Foucault, has had a strong influence on many current analyses of nineteenth-century philanthropy.

12. Quoted in Stedman Jones, *Outcast London*, p. 244. See also Mariana Valverde, "French Romantic Socialism and the Critique of Political Economy" (Ph.D. thesis, York University, 1982), esp. ch. II, "The Debate on Misery and the Critique of Political Economy."

13. See Donzelot, *The Policing of Families*, for a lengthy analysis of the constitution of the social.

14. David Garland, *Punishment and Welfare: A History of Penal Strategies* (London, 1985), p. 153.

15. A well-known Canadian example of the treatment of economic questions as social questions is W.L. Mackenzie King, *Industry and Humanity* (1919). See also J.S. Woodsworth, *My Neighbor: A Study of City Conditions, A Plea for Social Service* (1911; reprinted 1972).

16. Donzelot, *The Policing of Families*, argues that poverty, the family, and population are the main three "problems" that made up the social in the early nineteenth century.

17. See Anna Davin, "Imperialism and Motherhood," *History Workshop*, no. 5 (1978), pp. 9-57.

18. Bryan S. Green, *Knowing the Poor: A Case-Study in Textual Reality Construction* (London, 1983).

19. James Kay, *The Moral and Physical Condition of the Working Classes* (1832), quoted in Frank Mort, *Dangerous Sexualities: Medico-Moral Politics in England since 1830* (London, 1987), p. 22.

20. See Anthony Wohl's introduction to the reprint of Mearns's pamphlet *The Bitter Cry of Outcast London* (New York, 1970). This topic will be developed in the first section of Chapter 6.

21. B.G. Jefferis and J.L. Nichols, *Light in Dark Corners: Searchlight on Health* (Naperville, Ill., various editions from 1880s on). The 1922 edition was given the more modern title of *Safe Counsel or Practical Eugenics*.

22. Dennis Guest, in *The Emergence of Social Security in Canada* (Vancouver, 1985 [2nd ed.]), has a liberal framework that presupposes that whenever state benefits were organized on a philanthropic basis, this was either a mistake or a leftover of the past. The essays in A. Moscovitch and J. Alpert's edited collection *The "Benevolent" State*, however, demonstrate that many of the great new programs of the welfare state, such as mothers' allowances, were introduced for what one could only call philanthropic reasons such as concern for the eugenic future of the Canadian "race."

23. For instance, see James H. Gray, *Red Lights on the Prairies* (Saskatoon, 1971, 1986).

24. Frances Willard, in A. Powell, ed., *National Purity Congress* (Baltimore, 1896) p. 127; president's address (to the Dominion WCTU), in *White Ribbon Bulletin*, 13 December 1913, p. 180.

25. "Fewer Criminals with Pure Milk," *Daily News*, 19 October 1911, p. 13.

26. Advertisement for Canada Bread's four Toronto bakeries, in *Daily News*, 30 September 1911, p. 18. It should be noted that good bread was then assumed to be white; the association of health with brown bread is a very recent one.

27. On the campaigns to clean up the city's water supply and ensure safe milk, see Paul A. Bator, "Saving Lives on the Wholesale Plan: Public Health Reform in the City of Toronto, 1900-1930" (Ph.D. thesis, University of Toronto, 1979). The protagonist of Bator's thesis, Dr. Charles Hastings, believed in the moralizing effects of pure milk and water.

28. E.M. Knox, *The Girl of the New Day* (Toronto, 1919), p. 5.

29. Paul Rutherford, "Tomorrow's Metropolis: The Urban Reform Movement in Canada, 1880-1920," Canadian Historical Association, *Historical Papers*, 1971, p. 215.

30. W.L. Mackenzie King, *Industry and Humanity* (Toronto, 1919), pp. 330-31. See also Chapter IX, "Principles Underlying Health," which is concerned not with the health of individual bodies but with the health of the labour force as a whole, or, as King himself put it following Comte, the health of the "social organism."

31. CTA, RG-11, Box 167, Monthly Report of the Medical Officer of Health for October, 1914, p. 235.

32. W. L. Clark, *Our Sons* (1914; 5th ed.), pp. 24-25. As we shall see below, Clark's counterpart, A.W. Beall, who lectured to schoolchildren on behalf of the Ontario WCTU, not only agreed with Clark but even calculated the value of each young Canadian person at $50,000.

33. For an elaboration of this argument, see M. Valverde and L. Weir, "The Struggles of the Immoral: More Preliminary Remarks on Moral Regulation," *Resources for Feminist Research*, 17, 3 (September, 1988), pp. 31-34.

34. This point is made, from a somewhat different perspective, in an important article by Nikolas Rose, "Beyond the Public/Private Division: Law, Power and the Family," *Journal of Law and Society*, 14, 1 (Spring, 1987), pp. 61-75. In Philip Corrigan and Derek Sayer, *The Great Arch: English State Formation as Cultural Revolution* (Oxford, 1985), the role of the state in moral regulation is highlighted, and their theorization has been influential here; but the agencies of regulation internal to civil society are obscured.

35. Bruce Curtis, "Preconditions of the Canadian State: Educational Reform and Construction of a Public in Upper Canada, 1837-1846," in A. Moscovitch and J. Alpert, eds., *The "Benevolent" State* (Toronto, 1987), pp. 47-67. Curtis's insistence that educational reform was not merely social control or suppression of the working classes parallels the claim made above that social purity was more geared to moulding the subjectivity of citizens than simply controlling their behaviour. If the public education system was assigned the task of creating rationality and political subjectivity, the social purity movement sought to create an ethical/moral subjectivity.

36. Quoted in Michael Owen, "Keeping Canada God's Country: Presbyterian Perspectives on Selected Social Issues" (Ph.D. thesis, University of Toronto, 1984), p. 46.

37. David Garland, *Punishment and Welfare: A History of Penal Strategies* (London, 1985). Garland links the "modern" penal strategies centred on treatment to social work and eugenics in an analysis that is extremely relevant to social purity even though he neglects to analyse the modernization of sexual and gender regulation. He also stresses that the liberal state, though obviously in charge of the prison system, had to leave the moral reformation of prisoners in the hands of private

agencies such as the John Howard and Elizabeth Fry Societies and the Salvation Army.

38. On the medicalization of poverty in nineteenth-century philanthropy, see Christine Stansell, *City of Women: Sex and Class in New York 1789-1860* (New York, 1986); this idea is explored in Mariana Valverde, review-essay on Stansell's book, *Labour/Le Travail*, 22 (Fall, 1988), pp. 247-57. On the medicalization of crime, see Garland, *Punishment and Welfare*, and Michel Foucault, *Discipline and Punish* (New York, 1979). For the medicalization of sexuality, see Lorna Weir, "Sexual Rule, Sexual Politics: Studies in the Medicalization of Sexual Danger 1820-1920" (Ph.D. thesis, York University, 1986); Frank Mort, *Dangerous Sexualities: Medico-Moral Politics in England Since 1830* (London, 1987).

39. A.W. Beall, *The Living Temple: A Manual on Eugenics for Parents and Teachers* (Whitby, Ont., 1933). Although this book was not published until the 1930s it purports to collect the lectures that Beall had given to Ontario schoolchildren during the first three decades of the century.

40. Michel Foucault, *A History of Sexuality*, vol. I (New York, 1979); George Moss, *Nationalism and Sexuality* (New York, 1985); Jeffrey Weeks, *Sex, Politics and Society: The Regulation of Sexuality since 1800* (London, 1981); Gary Kinsman, *The Regulation of Desire: Sexuality in Canada* (Montreal, 1987).

41. King, *Industry and Humanity*, p. 485. King shares the concern of social purity activists (with whom he had earlier collaborated on some issues, such as suppression of the opium traffic) for regulating not only the work but also the spirit and the leisure time of young Canadians: people "require Education to teach them the right use of leisure."

42. Mrs. Spofford, in National Archives of Canada (NAC), National Council of Women of Canada (hereafter NCW), *Yearbook*, 1907, p. 85.

43. John Charlton, MP, April 10, 1899, quoted in T. Chapman, "Sex Crimes in Western Canada 1890-1920" (Ph.D. thesis, University of Alberta, 1984), p. 44.

44. Michael Owen's study of the Presbyterian wing of the movement, "Keeping Canada God's Country," bears this out. Paul Bator, "Saving Lives on the Wholesale Plan," found that all public health activists identified by him were of Anglo-Saxon origin, and the vast majority were either Methodist or Presbyterian; see also Linda Kealey, ed., *A Not Unreasonable Claim: Women and Reform in Canada 1880s-1920s* (Toronto, 1979). For the new middle class, see Robert Wiebe, *The Search for Order 1877-1920* (New York, 1967).

45. The American feminist, urban reformer, and social theorist Jane Addams did seek to homogenize American urban society through cultural means; but even she, who was more radical in class, gender, and racial terms than the leading social purity activists in Canada, did not envision abolishing the economic basis of bourgeois class formation. This will be explored in Chapter 6.

46. The goals of the social purity in terms of gender organization are captured in the statement made by the Methodist Board of Temperance and Social Reform in the context of the white slavery panic; the clergymen vowed not to cease in their struggle against white slavery until "[we can] restore the victim to her home and to a life of honor, purity, and helpfulness." UCA, Methodist DESS, Annual Report, 1911, p. 33.

47. Carolyn Strange, "The Toronto Social Survey Commission of 1915 and the Search

for Sexual Order in the City," in Roger Hall *et al.*, eds., *Patterns of the Past: Interpreting Ontario's History* (Toronto, 1988).

48. Ann Douglas, *The Feminization of American Culture* (New York, 1977). See also Carroll Smith-Rosenberg, *Religion and the Rise of the American City* (Ithaca, N.Y., 1971); Paul Johnson, *Shopkeepers' Millennium: Society and Revivals in Rochester, N.Y., 1815-1837* (New York, 1978); Nancy Hewitt, *Women's Activism and Social Change: Rochester, N.Y., 1822-1872* (Ithaca, N.Y., 1984); Mary P. Ryan, *Cradle of the Middle Class* (London, 1981).

49. Leonore Davidoff and Catherine Hall, *Family Fortunes: Men and Women of the English Middle Class, 1780-1850* (London, 1987), pp. 110-13.

50. Sylvanus Stall, *What a Young Husband Ought to Know* (Philadelphia, 1907 [1899]), p. 53. Note that the laborious components of domestic work, especially in the kitchen, are still thought to be exclusively female.

51. *Ibid.*, pp. 68-71.

52. Johnson, *Shopkeepers' Millennium,* shows that men who were born again in the revivals of the 1830s and 1840s fared quite a bit better in business than their unconverted counterparts, partly because of the formal and informal credit and business links forged among members of the same congregation.

53. See Sander Gilman, *Difference and Pathology: Stereotypes of Race, Sexuality, and Madness* (Ithaca, N.Y., 1985).

54. I have adopted the term "moral regulation" from Philip Corrigan and Derek Sayer, *The Great Arch: English State Formation as Cultural Revolution* (Oxford, 1985). However, they do not differentiate between moral and other modes of social regulation; by contrast, I restrict the term to mean the formation of *ethical* subjectivity.

Chapter 2

1. Mrs. Spofford, "Address," NAC, NCW, *Yearbook*, 1907, p. 86.

2. This hidden subject lies in what Teresa de Lauretis, following cinematic convention, calls the "space off," i.e., the space not directly shown on the screen but implied by the arrangement of objects on it. See T. de Lauretis, *Technologies of Gender: Essays on Film, Theory, Fiction* (Bloomington, Indiana, 1987), p. 26.

3. Rev. Virgin, in A. Powell, ed., *National Purity Congress* (Baltimore, 1896), pp. 39-40.

4. Sex educator A.W. Beall was fond of saying that "sowing character" was necessary in order to "reap destiny." Beall, *The Living Temple.*

5. "The Mighty Niagara of Souls," *War Cry*, 9 November 1895, p. 1.

6. Roland Barthes, *Mythologies* (London, 1973).

7. "The Mighty Niagara of Souls," p. 4.

8. For a long and sentimental account of a trip to the Falls, see Agnes Machar, *Down the river to the sea* (New York, 1894).

9. See the frontispiece of General Booth's *In Darkest England* (1890), which features a shipwreck in an ocean whose waves are labelled "sin," "pauperism," "gambling," and so on; Army officers are busy in life rafts pulling people out. The whole ocean scene is illuminated by a beacon representing the Army itself. This will be analysed in Chapter 6.

10. See advertisements on back page of *The War Cry*, numerous issues in 1890.

11. "Light in Darkest England," *The Deliverer* (June, 1891), p. 189.

12. Public Archives of Ontario (henceforth PAO), *The Woman's Journal* (July, 1898), p. 5.

13. The American WCTU's superintendent of social purity, Dr. Mary Wood-Allen, wrote in her popular book, *What a Young Girl Ought to Know* (Philadelphia and Toronto, 1897), p. 133, that evil thoughts poisoned the blood and it was thus necessary for one's health to think only "beautiful thoughts."

14. PAO, *The Woman's Journal* (October, 1900), both issues, p. 17.

15. Wood-Allen, *What A Young Girl Ought to Know*, p. 187.

16. Joseph Gusfield, *Symbolic Crusade: Status Politics and the American Temperance Movement* (Urbana, Ill., 1963).

17. This discussion is strongly influenced by Clifford Shearing, "Toward a Tropological Theory of Action," unpublished ms., Centre of Criminology, University of Toronto.

18. Gareth Stedman Jones, *Languages of Class* (Cambridge, 1983); Joan W. Scott, "On Language, Gender, and Working-Class History," *International Labor and Working Class History*, no. 31 (Spring, 1987) pp. 1-13. Scott presents a different approach in "Deconstructing Equality-Versus-Difference: or, the uses of Poststructuralist Theory for Feminism," *Feminist Studies*, 14, 1 (Spring, 1988), pp. 33-49.

19. Louis Althusser, "Ideological State Apparatuses," in *Lenin, Philosophy, and Other Essays* (London, 1972).

20. See the picture of the World's Missionary Conference that is reproduced as the frontispiece of John R. Mott, *The Decisive Hour of Christian Missions* (New York, 1911).

21. Chris Weedon, *Feminist Practice and Poststructuralist Theory* (Oxford, 1987); Mary Poovey, "Feminism and Deconstruction," *Feminist Studies*, 14, 1 (Spring, 1988), pp. 51-65. Poovey rightly remarks that in the absence of political commitments deconstruction could remain "an ahistorical master strategy" that subjects everything to its critical gaze except its own history and socio-economic coordinates (p. 61).

Chapter 3

1. John McLaren, "Chasing the Social Evil: Moral Fervour and the Evolution of Canada's Prostitution Laws, 1867-1917," *Canadian Journal of Law and Society*, 1, 1 (1986), pp. 125-60. This view is implicitly assumed by many other writers. See, for instance, Jay Cassel, *'The Secret Plague': Venereal Disease in Canada 1838-1939* (Toronto, 1987).

2. R. Whitaker, "Images of the Canadian State," p. 53. That the temperance movement, a large mass movement lasting over 100 years, is here dismissed as "an idiosyncratic obsession" indicates a refusal to theorize those aspects of society that do not easily fit into the categories of economic class.

3. The Canadian Conference on Charities and Corrections, an early social science/social work organization of secular reformers, appears to have differentiated itself from the Moral and Social Reform Council of Canada (MSRCC) primarily on the

grounds that the latter was initiated by the churches – although further research would have to be done to clarify the relation between the two groups. In the early twenties, the Social Service Council of Canada (successor to the MSRCC) also had a falling out with the more scientific National Committee for Combatting Venereal Diseases (NCCVD), after an initial period of collaboration.

4. Cook, *The Regenerators*. Cook makes a sharp distinction between secular and religious discourses and builds his book around the replacement of the latter by the former. His study, however, covers theological debates around Darwin and other intellectual changes, in which there was indeed a conflict, but it is almost silent on the social purity movement, which functioned at a less highbrow level and chose deliberately not to see any conflict between science (or at least social science) and religion.

5. Flyer entitled "The Church and Social Service: Programme [of] Social Study: Social Institutions, Economics, Public Hygiene," UCA, Fred Victor Mission file, n.d., but c. 1920.

6. See, for instance, Rev. S.D. Chown's typed notes for a series of lectures in sociology at Victoria College, n.d., UCA, Chown Papers, Box 13, files 377-383.

7. Mrs. Archibald (Nova Scotia), "The Importance of the National Council in Fostering and Developing the Patriotism of Canadian Women," in NAC, NCW, *Yearbook*, 1896, pp. 76 and 73.

8. Mary Joplin Clarke, of Central Neighbourhood House, Toronto, speaking for the Standing Committee on Neighbourhood Work of the Canadian Conference of Charities and Corrections in 1917. Document reprinted in Paul Rutherford, ed., *Saving the Canadian City: the First Phase, 1880-1920* (Toronto, 1974), p. 189.

9. *Christian Guardian*, quoted in M. Barber, "Nationalism, Nativism and the Social Gospel," in R. Allen, ed., *The Social Gospel in Canada* (Ottawa, 1975), p. 221.

10. See, for instance, the articles by R.L. Schnell and James Struthers in Moscovitch and Alpert, eds., *The "Benevolent" State*. On Charlotte Whitton, see Patricia T. Rooke and R.L. Schnell, *No Bleeding Heart: Charlotte Whitton, a Feminist on the Right* (Vancouver, 1988).

11. The United Church Archives has a collection of these; the most interesting (and complete) one was that of London, Ont., which was carried out by the local Men's Federation. The surveys typically studied vice and poverty with the same methodology, for instance, by counting how many people were swearing in a pool hall in a given evening, and then going on to calculate the budgets of poor urban families.

12. Frank Mort, *Dangerous Sexualities: Medico-moral Politics in England since 1830* (London, 1987).

13. Quoted in A. Wohl, *Endangered Lives: Public Health in Victorian Britain* (Cambridge, Mass.,), p. 7. Wohl states that this belief in the production of moral vice by dirt and poverty was a firmly held belief long before the germ theory of disease.

14. NAC, Mrs. Drummond, NCW, *Yearbook*, 1896, p. 486.

15. J.O. McCarthy, in *Social Service Congress* (Ottawa, 1914), p. 121.

16. J.J. Kelso, "Can slums be abolished or must we continue to pay the penalty?" (Toronto, n.d.); reprinted in P. Rutherford, *Saving the Canadian City*, p. 167.

17. Rev. S.W. Dean, "The Church and the Slum," *Social Service Congress* (Ottawa, 1914), p. 128.

18. NAC, Canadian Council of Churches Collection (henceforth CCC), Box 32, unnumbered file; Dr. Bates in minutes of meeting of the Social Hygiene Commission of the Social Service Council of Canada, 19 May 1921.

19. Biographical information from *The Canadian Who's Who*, 1936-37 edition, pp. 855-56; Jean Bannerman, *Leading Ladies* (Belleville, 1977), pp. 157-58; Rose Sheinin and Alan Bakes, *Women and Medicine in Toronto Since 1883* (Toronto, Faculty of Medicine, Univ. of Toronto, 1987), pp. 75-76. She also appears very often in the records of the Social Service Council of Canada (NAC, CCC, Boxes 29 and 32).

20. Dr. Margaret Patterson, *Social Service Congress* (Ottawa, 1914), p. 227.

21. Patterson did not invent the "moral hospital"; she was relying on international developments in criminology and medical sciences. See, for example, Havelock Ellis, *The Criminal* (London, 1910), and Phyllis Grosskurth, *Havelock Ellis: A Biography* (New York, 1980), for the source of many of Patterson's ideas on hospitals for morals offenders. Ellis had earlier been much influenced by Lombroso's view that criminals were anthropological oddities, throwbacks to earlier stages of evolution, but in the 1910 edition of his 1890 work he speaks of crime as based not so much on physiology, or for that matter on low intelligence, but rather on inherent moral flaws.

22. Paul Bator details the pressure brought to bear on federal authorities to institute medical screening of immigrants, pressure that resulted in the appointment of an inspection service headed by Bryce. Bator, "Saving Lives," pp. 33-34, 67-69.

23. See P. Bryce, "Saving Canadians from the Degeneracy Due to Industrialism in Cities of Older Civilizations," *Public Health Journal*, III, 12 (December, 1912), 686-92. For biographical information on Bryce, see also *The Canadian Who's Who*, 1910 ed., p. 29; Henry James Morgan, *The Canadian Men and Women of the Time* (Toronto, 1912), pp. 163-64; Heather MacDougall, "'Enlightening the Public': The Views and Values of the Association of Executive Health Officers of Ontario 1886-1903," in Charles G. Roland, ed., *Health, Disease and Medicine: Essays in Canadian History* (Toronto, 1984), pp. 436-64.

24. For biographical information, see Sheinin and Bakes, *Women and Medicine*, p. 29; Women's College Hospital Annual Reports 1914-1918, Series A7, Container 7, Women's College Hospital Archives; and her graduate file, RG A73-26, Box 107, File 10, Univ. of Toronto Archives.

25. For biographical information, see Sheinin and Bakes, *Women and Medicine*, p. 37; Women's College Hospital Annual Reports 1912-1914; Community Clinical Association "Minute Book" 1913-1927, Women's College Hospital Archives; and graduate file RG AS73-26, Box 136 File 34, Univ. of Toronto Archives.

26. For biographical information, see Sheinin and Bakes, *Women and Medicine*, pp. 106-07; Ontario Medical College for Women, "Annual Announcement," 1888-1906, Series A7 Container 7, Women's College Hospital Archives; Community Clinical Association "Minute Book" 1923-1927, Women's College Hospital Archives, and graduate file RG AS73-26, Box 126, File 65, Univ. of Toronto Archives.

27. Lorne Pierce, *Albert Durrant Watson* (Toronto, 1924). See also *Who's Who in Canada*, 1918 and 1926 editions; Morgan, *Canadian Men and Women of the Time*, p. 1147; W. Stewart Wallace, ed., *The Macmillan Dictionary of Canadian Biography* (Toronto, 1978), pp. 873-74.

28. On R.M. Bucke, see Cook, *The Regenerators*, ch. 6.

29. Jay Cassel, *The Secret Plague*, p. 115, states that it was formed in 1906 in Toronto, and was active for a decade; my own research tends to confirm this.

30. UCA, Methodist DESS, Minutes of Executive, Jan. 23, 1912.

31. In October of 1912, B.S. Steadwell, president of World's (i.e., U.S.) Purity Federation, announced that a coalition was lobbying for a provincial purity bureau. This coalition was said to include three leading Methodists and Rev. Shearer from the Presbyterians; but church records do not mention this plan, which appears to have been stillborn. See Public Archives of Ontario, WCTU collection, [Mrs. Asa Gordon] "The Suppression of Vice," *White Ribbon Bulletin*, November, 1912, pp. 4-5.

32. Ryerson was the foremost lobbyist for state-sponsored education in nineteenth-century Ontario. On the development of public education and the collaboration of the state and church leaders, see Bruce Curtis, *Building the Educational State: Canada West, 1836-1871* (London, Ontario, 1988).

33. UCA, Pidgeon Papers, Box 52, File 2970, "The Church and Moral Reform" (1907).

34. See UCA, Minutes and Annual Reports of Methodist DESS, 1906 and ff. Abortion was briefly mentioned in 1907 but was not a priority; drinking, gambling, smoking, prostitution, and obscene plays and literature were the main enemies against which the DESS fought.

35. UCA, Annual Report of Methodist DESS, 1915-16, p. 29.

36. In 1891, 17.5 per cent of Canadians were Methodists, 15.6 per cent Presbyterians, 13.4 per cent Church of England, 6.7 per cent Baptist, and most of the remaining third were Catholic. (Figures from Wendy Mitchinson, "Aspects of Reform," p. 56n.)

37. Quoted in Cook, *The Regenerators*, p. 195. Cook states that an American social gospeller heard Chown give a lecture in 1895 that was "word for word Toynbee" (*ibid.*, p. 202). Toynbee's work was also taken up enthusiastically by W.L. Mackenzie King, who studied political economy at the University of Toronto in the mid-1890s.

38. Charlotte Whitton, child welfare worker extraordinaire in the 1930s and 1940s and later mayor of Ottawa, began her working life as Shearer's assistant, in 1918. She did not share Shearer's evangelism – being a middle-of-the-road Anglican – but she did share his sexual conservatism and profound racism. See Rooke and Schnell, *No Bleeding Heart*, pp. 20-44.

39. Thomas Fisher Library, Univ. of Toronto, Lord's Day Alliance Papers, Box 135, "The Lord's Day Act and Seventh Day People," n.d. This pamphlet was mailed to Prime Minister Wilfrid Laurier by Shearer (NAC, Laurier Papers, vol. 319, Reel c-812, letter, 19 May 1904 with enclosure). Shearer wrote frequently to Laurier on the topic of Sunday observance, and the two men met at least once, on 13 December 1905 (NAC, Laurier, Vol. 391, Reel c-828, Shearer to Laurier, 4 December 1905).

40. Thomas Fisher Library, Univ. of Toronto, LDA Papers, Box 135; Annual Report of the Executive of the LDA, 1911. In western Canada, the Alliance sought out small Chinese food vendors who worked on Sundays and had them prosecuted. This was not the isolated work of a few fanatics; the Alliance had, in 1911, about 50,000 members in over 800 branches (mostly in Ontario, and usually linked to Presbyterian churches).

41. J.G. Shearer, "Right Kind of Puritanism," *Dominion Presbyterian*, May 6, 1906, p. 9.

42. Minutes of evidence, Royal Commission [on vice] in Winnipeg, 1910-1911, p. 694.

43. *Globe*, 12 November 1910; see also "Vice in Winnipeg Open and Defiant," *The Mail and Empire*, 12 November 1910.

44. Gray, *Red Lights on the Prairies*, p. 55. The Winnipeg vice panic is discussed in more detail in Chapter 4.

45. See *Globe*, 12 November 1910; for Shearer's testimony before the Royal Commission, see minutes of evidence, pp. 513ff.

46. Gray, *Red Lights on the Prairies*, p. 147. The Mounties proceeded to raid Calgary brothels on a large scale a month later (city police were never particularly zealous in anti-vice campaigns, and moral reformers often sought to call in the federal or provincial police forces, in keeping with their view of the provincial and federal states as more pure than the municipalities).

47. UCA, Pidgeon Papers, Box 52, File 2073, undated notes headed "Moral and Social Reform."

48. On the WCTU, see Mitchinson, "Aspects of Reform," pp. 146ff.

49. PAO, WCTU, *The Woman's Journal* (later titled *White Ribbon Tidings*), December, 1886.

50. PAO, WCTU, *White Ribbon Bulletin*, June, 1912, p. 1.

51. In the United States, the purity department of the WCTU eventually evolved into the National Parent-Teacher Federation.

52. PAO, WCTU, *White Ribbon Tidings*, 15 February 1899, p. 4.

53. PAO, WCTU, "President's Address," Dominion WCTU Annual Report, 1890, p. 42.

54. Lists of departments and their superintendents appeared in every issue of *White Ribbon Tidings*. See also annual reports of each department in the *Yearbooks* of the dominion WCTU.

55. Willard had singled out "Hygiene" as the first of the WCTU objectives; for her, abolishing the demon rum was only the prelude to "the reign of a religion of the body." Frances Willard, *Woman and Temperance* (Hartford, Conn., 1884 [fourth ed.], p. 42.

56. PAO, WCTU, Mrs. John Currie, "Moral Education Department," *White Ribbon Bulletin*, December, 1910, pp. 5-6.

57. PAO, WCTU, S.R. Wright, *White Ribbon Bulletin*, July, 1912, p. 6. See Angus McLaren, *Our Own Master Race: Eugenics in Canada, 1885-1945* (Toronto, 1990).

58. See Mariana Valverde, "'When the mother of the race is free': race, sexuality and reproduction in first-wave feminism," in F. Iacovetta and M. Valverde, eds., *Expanding Boundaries: New Essays in Women's History* (Toronto, forthcoming).

59. In the 1890s, WCTU women ran shelters for released women prisoners and reformed prostitutes in Montreal and in Victoria, and some of this work continued into the new century. Very few of the twenty or thirty thousand WCTU members were involved in these endeavours, however.

60. References to Travellers' Aid work (which was often done jointly by the WCTU and the YWCA) are found in the Minutes of the Ontario WCTU Executive for 1920 (PAO, WCTU, Box 3P-507, File 7).

61. On the NCW, see Mitchinson, "Aspects of Reform," pp. 253ff., and Veronica

Strong-Boag, *The Parliament of Women: The National Council of Women of Canada 1893-1929* (Ottawa, 1976).

62. Lady Aberdeen's opening speech at the 1896 general meeting stated that "if the NCW had done nothing beyond warning the fathers and mothers in Canada concerning the possible dangers awaiting their children in circulation of vile literature . . . and in the discussion on the teaching of some simple facts of physiology to children, it would have amply justified its existence." NAC, NCW, appendix to 1896 *Annual Report*.

63. Carolyn Strange, "From Modern Babylon to a City Upon a Hill: The Toronto Social Survey of 1915 and the Search for Sexual Order in the City," in Roger Hall, William Westfall, and Laurel Sefton MacDowell, eds., *Patterns of the Past: Interpreting Ontario's History* (Toronto, 1988), pp. 255-77.

64. NAC, NCW, "Report of Standing Committee on Objectionable Printed Matter," in 1913 *Annual Report*, pp. 79-81.

65. NAC, NCW, Mrs. Stevenson, 1896 *Annual Report*, p. 345.

66. NAC, NCW, 1913 Annual Report, p. 81.

67. The processes of networking can be discerned in a report compiled by the NCW for the Paris International Exhibition of 1900, *Women of Canada: Their Life and Work* (reprinted by the National Council of Women of Canada, 1975). This is both a directory of women's organizations and a somewhat rosy overview of women's participation in the creation of the "modern" Canada promoted abroad by the Canadian government (the report was compiled at the request of the Minister of Agriculture). French Catholic organizations are represented but in a subordinate position; this directory, like the NCW, attempted to include non-Anglophone and non-Protestant women but without letting this inclusion challenge the image of Canada as basically British and Protestant.

68. On the YWCA, see Wendy Mitchinson, "The YWCA and Reform in the 19th Century," *Histoire sociale/Social History*, XII, 24 (1979), pp. 368-84; Diana Pedersen, "'Keeping Our Good Girls Good': the YWCA and the 'girl problem' 1870-1930," *Canadian Women's Studies*, 7, 4 (1985), pp. 20-24; Diana Pedersen, "'The Call to Service': The YWCA and the Canadian College Woman 1886-1920," paper read at the Canadian Historical Association annual meeting, June, 1988.

69. Quoted in Terry Crowley, "Madonnas Before Magdalenes: Adelaide Hoodless and the Canadian Gibson Girl," *Canadian Historical Review*, LXVII, 4 (1986), pp. 525-26.

70. Quoted by Mitchinson, "The YWCA and Reform in the Nineteenth Century," pp. 382-83.

71. Lynne Marks, "Hallelujah Lasses: Women in the Salvation Army 1882-1892," in Iacovetta and Valverde, eds., *Expanding Boundaries*.

72. PAO, WCTU, *White Ribbon Bulletin*, October, 1912, p. 7.

73. P. Whitwell Wilson, *Evangeline Booth: The General* (London, 1935), p. 21.

74. Army supporters typically gave between twenty-five cents and a dollar, with the notable exception of the distiller Gooderham, who contributed thousands. The small amounts contrast with the donations of $5 or $10 that were common in Methodist records. (See SA, lists of donations published in *The War Cry*, 1890s).

75. "The Force of Love," *War Cry*, 20 October 1888, p. 1. The picture illustrating this article shows people literally adrift in the ocean.

76. Michael Bliss, "Pure Books on Avoided Subjects: Pre-Freudian Sexual Ideas in Canada," Canadian Historical Association, *Historical Papers*, 1979, p. 105. Later on he admits that purity educators were not simply suppressing sexual knowledge and experience, and describes their work as "creative sexual repression" – which is a more accurate term but still presupposes Freud's framework.

77. See, for instance, Havelock Ellis, "The Meaning of Purity," in *Little Essays of Love and Virtue* (New York, 1922); Maurice Bigelow, *Sex Education* (New York, 1916).

78. Bigelow, *Sex Education*, p. 73. The Columbia University Teachers' College, where Bigelow taught, was seen as the best in the U.S. at this time. See Christabel Pankhurst, *The Great Scourge* (London, 1913; published in the U.S. under the title *Plain Facts about a Great Evil,* 1913).

79. This point has been made, albeit in a very partisan and one-sided manner, in the critique of sexology presented by Sheila Jeffreys, *The Spinster and Her Enemies* (London, 1985).

80. J.A. Thomson and P. Geddes, *Problems of Sex* (New York, 1912), p. 41. This booklet, issued as part of a series mainly devoted to popular eugenic education, shows the artificiality of Bigelow's distinction between purity education and sex education, since it would fit equally well under both headings.

81. B.G. Jefferis and J.L. Nichols, *Light on Dark Corners: Searchlight on Health* (Naperville, Ill., 1894; edition quoted here 1922 and re-titled *Safe Counsel, or Practical Eugenics*).

82. A.W. Beall, *The Living Temple: A Manual on Eugenics for Parents and Teachers* (Whitby, 1933), p. 11.

83. Stall, *What a Young Husband Ought to Know*, pp. 39-41.

84. E. Blackwell, "The Human Element in Sex," in Vol. I of *Essays in Medical Sociology* (London, 1902), pp. 18-19.

85. Alice Stockham, *Karezza: Ethics of Marriage* (Chicago, 1896; reprinted 1903), p. 23.

86. The feminist contributions to sex hygiene were developed by women writers who were close to the sex reform movement but whose roots in social purity, particularly its feminist wing, are very strong. See, for instance, Grete Meisel-Hess, *The Sexual Crisis: A Critique of Our Sex Life*, trans. E. and C. Paul (New York, 1917). While Marie Stopes and Margaret Sanger definitely broke with social purity and took sides with the sex reform movement that developed after World War One, other less known feminist writers on sexuality show that there was significant continuity across what has generally been regarded as a great divide. This is an example of the more general historiographical point that periodization is never gender neutral.

87. J. H. Kellogg, a doctor working in his brother's vegetarian sanatorium in Battle Creek, Mich. (a resort known to history mostly because of the cold cereal invented there, corn flakes), was an extremely influential early purity advocate. See his *Plain Facts for Old and Young* (Burlington, Iowa, 1882 [orig. ed. 1877]). Kellogg popularized the "Jukes" study, a questionable piece of eugenic research that supposedly demonstrated that acquired traits or even habits such as drunkenness are inherited. He took an extreme line on the question of the frequency of sexual intercourse, advising that it happen only for reproduction; believing that semen was concentrated blood, he saw all "wasted" semen as a serious danger to male health.

88. See PAO, Ontario WCTU Annual Reports, 1905-1911, and *White Ribbon Bulletin*, January, 1911, p. 4.

89. Beall, *The Living Temple*, pp. 22, 75.

90. W.L. Clark, *Our Sons* (1914; 5th ed.). Hall's introduction states that the growth of boys recapitulates the development of "the race" (undoubtedly meaning the Anglo-Saxon race as paradigm, and the human race in general by analogy). For instance, from ages 11-15, "the lad is living all over again, in his own impulses and instincts, the barbaric period of race history." The four periods of both phylogenesis and ontogenesis are savagery, barbarism, chivalry, and modernity.

91. Clark, *Our Sons*, p. 229. In his report of 1916 to his employers, he reiterated that his work was "in the interest not of the fallen, but of the ever-bubbling streams of youth throughout Canada and Newfoundland." UCA, Methodist DESS, 1916 Annual Report, p. 122.

92. W.T. Gunn, *His Dominion* (1917), p. 181.

93. UCA, Methodist DESS, 1916 Annual Report, p. 122. This is the only year in which the sex educators gave an extended report.

94. Joan Sangster, "The Making of a Socialist-Feminist: The Early Career of Beatrice Brigden, 1888-1941," unpublished paper, History Dept., Trent University. I would like to thank Joan Sangster for making her paper available to me.

95. UCA, Methodist DESS papers, box 3 (B. Brigden), File 48.

96. UCA, Brigden papers, File 45, Brigden to T.A. Moore, 28 January 1914.

97. See Richard Allen, *The Social Passion: Religion and Social Reform in Canada, 1914-1928* (Toronto, 1971), pp. 104ff.

98. UCA, Brigden papers, File 56, Brigden to T.A. Moore, 12 July 1920.

99. See Joan Sangster, *Dreams of Equality: Women on the Canadian Left, 1920-1950* (Toronto, 1989).

100. In the United States, some public school systems introduced sex education in the 1910s, but apparently with much reluctance. See Patricia Vertinsky, "Education for Sexual Morality" (Ed.D. thesis, University of British Columbia, 1975), esp. ch. 9.

101. PAO, WCTU, Report from Adelia Lucas, Dominion Superintendent of Purity for WCTU, in *White Ribbon Tidings*, 1 April 1900, p. 3.

102. NAC, NCW, Annual Report 1918, p. 87. Sex hygiene was to be undertaken in the context of military drill and physical training, a suggestion that again makes the link between personal purity and patriotism.

103. PAO, WCTU, *Report of the 21st Convention of the Canadian WCTU* (Windsor, N.S., 1920), p. 108.

Chapter 4

1. There is an important historic link between the physical and medical control of prostitutes and the development of municipal government. See Jill Harsin, *Policing Prostitution in Nineteenth-century Paris* (Princeton, N.J., 1985)

2. This can be seen in the novels of Zola in France and those of Mrs. Gaskell in Britain and Theodore Dreiser in the U.S.

3. Quoted in C. Armstrong and H.V. Nelles, *The Revenge of the Methodist Bicycle*

Company: Sunday Streetcars and Municipal Reform in Toronto 1888-1897 (Toronto, 1977), p. 114. In C.S. Clark's famous *Of Toronto the Good* (Montreal, 1898), the argument was explicitly made that increased access to the islands and to parks through Sunday streetcars encouraged illicit sex.

4. Paul Craven, "Law and Ideology: The Toronto Police Court 1850-1880," in D. Flaherty, ed., *Essays in the History of Canadian Law*, vol. II (Toronto, 1983), pp. 248-307.

5. See Constance Backhouse "Nineteenth-Century Canadian Prostitution Law: Reflection of a Discriminatory Society," *Histoire sociale/Social History*, 18 (1986), pp. 387-423.

6. See Harsin, *Policing Prostitution*, for the Paris system. See also Mark Connelly, *The Response to Prostitution in the Progressive Era* (Chapel Hill, 1980), which details the shifts in U.S. municipal policy in the first decade of the twentieth century; and Barbara Meil Hobson, *Uneasy Virtue: The Politics of Prostitution and the American Reform Tradition* (New York, 1987), which despite its title covers some European countries as well.

7. See Mort, *Dangerous Sexualities*; Judith Walkowitz, *Prostitution in Victorian Society* (Cambridge, 1980).

8. The Canadian and Australian governments, concerned that their "healthy country boys" were acquiring venereal diseases from women camp followers in Britain, pressured the British to institute compulsory public health measures affecting all women in potential contact with troops. The British, however, resisted this. See Jay Cassel, *The Secret Plague: Venereal Disease in Canada 1838-1939* (Toronto, 1987), pp. 125-41.

9. See Deborah Gorham, "The Maiden Tribute of Modern Babylon Re-examined: Child Prostitution and the Idea of Childhood in Late Victorian England," *Victorian Studies*, 21, 3 (Spring, 1978), pp. 353-80; Mort, *Dangerous Sexualities*.

10. Provincial Royal Commission [on vice in Winnipeg, chaired by Judge H.A. Robson] (Winnipeg, 1911); Minutes of the Evidence, 20-50. (This document is in the Legislative Library in Winnipeg.)

11. John McLaren, "Chasing the Social Evil: The Evolution of Canada's Prostitution Laws 1867-1917," *Canadian Journal of Law and Society*, I,1 (1986), p. 127. See also Backhouse, "Nineteenth-Century Canadian Prostitution Law."

12. See McLaren, "Chasing the Social Evil," p. 127; Backhouse, "Nineteenth-Century Prostitution Law," pp. 390-93. Nevertheless, the fact that the Acts were still in the books in the 1890s was used by the Montreal moral reformer D.A. Watt to stir up Canadians against creeping toleration: "These unmentionable acts are nominally upon the Canadian Statute book," he said, due to British "missionary efforts for the propagation of vice." D.A. Watt, "The Canadian Law for the Protection of Women and Girls," in Aaron Powell, ed., *The National Purity Congress* (Baltimore, 1895), p. 449.

13. Between 1900 and 1914 the morality squad charged 2,363 male brothel customers and 1,617 female "inmates," also charging 1,238 women as "keepers." The courts, however, probably treated male customers more leniently than women. Figures compiled from *Annual Report of Chief Constable* [of Toronto] (ARCC), 1900-1914.

14. ARCC, 1901, p. 15. That same year only one man was charged with incest, and none with rape.

15. See Lori Rotenberg, "The Wayward Worker: Toronto's Prostitute at the Turn of the Century," in Janice Acton *et al.*, eds., *Women at Work 1850-1930* (Toronto, 1974), pp. 33-70. For the toleration of brothels in Montreal, see Andrée Lévesque, "Le Bordel: Milieu de Travail Contrôlé," *Labour/Le Travail*, 20 (Fall, 1987), pp. 13-32.

16. Clark, *Of Toronto the Good,* pp. 14, 106.

17. "Rev. R.B. St. Clair Relates His Remarkable Experience – Says Children are Walking Directories of Vice," *Toronto Daily News*, 1 November 1911, p. 12.

18. See John McClaren, "'White Slavers': The Reform of Canada's Prostitution Laws and Patterns of Enforcement, 1900-1920," paper read at the American Society for Legal History, Toronto, October 24, 1986; McLaren, "Chasing the Social Evil."

19. From 1900 to 1914, 829 men were charged as keepers (with more than a quarter of these in 1913, the year that new procuring legislation was passed), while 1,238 females were charged as keepers. In 1898, one man and one woman were charged with procuring; in 1899, three women were charged and one man; then one man was charged in 1905, and one female in 1907. Even at the height of the white slavery panic, 1910-14, only fourteen men and seven women were charged. See ARCC, 1910-14.

20. *Report of the Social Survey Commission of Toronto* (Toronto, 1915), p.12.

21. "They may be found in numbers loitering about the fruit stores, drug stores . . . crowding into the dance halls, the theatres and other amusement resorts; also in the saloon restaurants and the chop suey palaces." These girls, the commissioners said, were not exactly prostitutes but were "on the direct road." *Report of the Minneapolis Vice Commission* (Minneapolis, 1911), pp. 75-76.

22. *Mail and Empire*, 20 December 1911, p. 1. This article states that the city of Winnipeg has 79,017 men to 57,971 women; "in Toronto, however, a fair percentage of the ladies will never obtain husbands unless they seek them elsewhere." The ratio of men to women in cities of the settled eastern and central portions of the country was typically the inverse of Winnipeg's sex ratio during its boom years. This was especially true of cities such as Toronto and Montreal, whose bourgeois households and light industrial sector provided employment for large numbers of young, single women in the late nineteenth and early twentieth centuries.

23. Chief of Police McRae, in *Royal Commission . . .* (Winnipeg, 1911); Minutes of Evidence, p. 53. McRae was somewhat sympathetic to prostitutes; when questioned about why he did not close down houses the neighbours thought were brothels, he said, "I know of no law which permits me to dynamite, cremate or eject immoral women" (p. 58). This is probably a reference to the Winnipeg moral reformers' threat of privately burning down brothels.

24. Alan Artibise, *Winnipeg: A Social History of Urban Growth 1874-1914* (Montreal, 1975), p. 251.

25. See testimony of Lila Anderson, Marjory Morrison, Amy Morris, Alice Penchant, Louise Dupont, and Edna Hamilton, *Royal Commission . . .* , pp. 78 -154.

26. Adjutant McElhaney, in *Royal Commission . . .* , Minutes of Evidence, p. 8.

27. *Royal Commission . . .* , p. 126.

28. Gray, *Red Lights on the Prairies*, pp. 109, 118.

29. *Macleod Gazette*, 16 March 1886, reprinted *ibid.*, pp. 193-94.

30. For discussions of Native women's roles in the fur trade, see Sylvia Van Kirk, *Many*

Tender Ties: Women in Fur Trade Society in Western Canada, 1670-1870 (Winnipeg, 1980); Jennifer Brown, *Strangers in Blood: Fur Trade Company Families in Indian Country* (Vancouver, 1980).

31. Emily Murphy, *The Black Candle* (Toronto, 1922). This exposé of the drug trade in Canada argued that opium facilitated seduction but at the same time eventually caused impotence. The sexual qualities of opium resulted in "the amazing phenomenon of an educated gentlewoman, reared in a refined atmosphere, consorting with the lowest classes of yellow and black men" (p. 17).

32. Tamara Adilman, "A Preliminary Sketch of Chinese Women and Work in British Columbia, 1858-1900," in B. Latham and R. Pazdro, eds., *Not Just Pin Money: Selected Essays on the History of Women's Work in British Columbia* (Victoria, 1984), p. 57. To put these figures in context, between 1876 and 1884, 17,000 Chinese came into Canada. Most of these were destined to be railway labourers; a few were male merchants, and these were the only ones allowed to bring their families.

33. Before 1919 the obstacles were primarily financial, but in that year a special regulation was passed banning both skilled and unskilled women from coming in on their own. This forced women into fictitious marriages and increased dependence on their alleged husbands. Adilman, "A Preliminary Sketch," p. 61.

34. See the chapter on "the orientals" in J.S. Woodsworth, *Strangers Within Our Gates* (orig. 1909; reprinted Toronto, 1972). Woodsworth's assimilationism strikes the late twentieth-century reader as extremely condescending, but one must remember that in his time white Canadians only perceived two choices, exclusion or assimilation, and had not developed the idea of multiculturalism.

35. Karen Van Dieren, "The Response of the WMS to the Immigration of Asian Women, 1888-1942," in Latham and Pazdro, eds., *Not Just Pin Money*, pp. 79-98.

36. *Ibid.*, p. 84.

37. Apart from the WMS Annual Reports, which had a circulation of between 5,000 and 10,000 (they were lavishly illustrated and served as educational books on both geography and religion), the WMS had a regular section in *The Missionary Outlook*, a mass-circulation magazine published by the Methodist Church. This regular section concentrated on work in China and Japan but often mentioned the Victoria Rescue Home.

38. Elopement among adults could not be prosecuted as such, but people who had immigrated to Canada and left a husband or wife in another country could be, and often were, charged with the serious crime of bigamy; in one case of elopement the police managed to charge the couple with the theft of a suitcase (*Toronto Daily News*, 27 and 30 November 1911). For the Chinese man at the CNE, see *Toronto Daily News*, 26 September 1911, p. 15. Bigamy cases were reported in the *Daily News*, 15 September, 6 October 1911, and in the *Mail and Empire*, 21, 27, 29 December 1911.

39. *Toronto Daily News*, 7 December 1911, p. 7. That this acquittal was by no means unusual is corroborated by Carolyn Strange's research into criminal assize indictments. See Strange, "The Perils and Pleasures of Urban Living: Single Wage-earning Women in Toronto, 1880-1930" (Ph.D. thesis, Rutgers University, in progress). Karen Dubinsky has uncovered similar evidence in her analysis of rape and other sexual crimes in rural Ontario. See Dubinsky, "Maidenly Girls or

Strumpets? Prosecutions for Seduction in Ontario, 1880-1929," *Canadian Histori-cal Association*, 1 June 1989.

40. UCA, Annual Report of Methodist DESS, 1909, p. 4.

41. *Ibid.*, 1911, p. 31.

42. The techniques used by Stuart Hall *et al.*, in *Policing the Crisis: Mugging, Crime and the State* (London, 1978), have been useful in this study, although unlike Hall and his colleagues I would not want to claim that class conflict is necessarily the basis of all moral panics. See also Stuart Hall, "The Toad in the Garden: Thatcher-ism Among the Theorists," in C. Nelson and L. Grossberg, *Marxism and the Interpretation of Culture* (Urbana, Ill., 1988), pp. 35-74, which does not emphasize class as much and has fruitful suggestions for how to use discourse analysis.

43. See M. Valverde and L. Weir, "The Struggles of the Immoral: More Preliminary Remarks on Moral Regulation," *Resources for Feminist Research*, 17, 3, (Fall, 1988), pp. 31-35.

44. British Library (BL), *Pall Mall Gazette*, 4 July 1885, p. 2.

45. Stead later explained: "Mrs. Butler was very anxious lest the virtue of the recently reclaimed convert should be exposed to the strain of too great a temptation. . . . Jarrett pleaded to be spared this burden. I was inexorable." BL, W.T. Stead, *The Armstrong Case: Mr. Stead's defence in full* (1885), p. 9.

46. *Ibid.*, p. 3.

47. Judith Walkowitz has shown that by blaming the mother for selling her daughter, Stead manages to turn forced prostitution into a tale with a *female* villain and a male hero (himself). See her analysis of Stead's exposé, "Melodrama, Sexual Scandals and Victorian Political Culture," paper given at the Seventh Berkshire Conference on the History of Women, Wellesley College, June 19, 1987.

48. "The Maiden Tribute," p. 2.

49. Catherine Booth, in *The Truth About the Armstrong Case and the Salvation Army* (1885), pp. 22-23. The theme of agents in disguise would be a fruitful one for further study. Jarrett's peculiar role in the scandal highlights the ambiguity inherent in the popular pastime of cross-class cross-dressing for the purposes of social investiga-tion; since she had been an immoral woman, her dressing up as one was bound to be a different operation than, say, Beatrice Webb pretending to be a working girl. When Jarrett went to Canada to help set up rescue work operations for the Canadian Salvation Army, she was denounced (à la Stead) by a Canadian officer who claimed she was not *really* reformed. Moral ambiguity thus pursued the unhappy Jarrett.

50. Dubinsky, "Maidenly Girls Or Strumpets?"

51. These resulted in the Criminal Amendment Act of 1913, which among other things instituted whipping as the punishment for procurers.

52. See, for instance, *Report of the Vice Commission of Minneapolis . . .* (Minneapolis, 1911), and The Vice Commission of Philadelphia, *A Report on Existing Conditions with Recommendations* (Philadelphia, 1913).

53. Rev. J.G. Shearer, "The Canadian Crusade," in E. Bell, ed., *The War of White Slave Trade* (orig. 1911; reprint, Toronto, 1980), p. 334.

54. Clark, *Our Sons*, p. 126.

55. "The clean sheet sent in from some communities may possibly be due to the singular innocence of sessions sending in reports . . . with reference to certain public evils some of our church leaders may be living in a fool's paradise rather than a heaven

of social and political purity." UCA, Pidgeon Papers, Box 52, file 2073, n.d. but circa 1913.

56. NAC, NCW, Annual Report 1912, p. 49.

57. *Ibid.*, p. 50.

58. *Ibid.*, p. 51. The WCTU's *White Ribbon Bulletin* reprinted an allegation of white slavery produced by the Methodist Department of Temperance and Moral Reform (PAO, *White Ribbon Bulletin*, March, 1911, p. 5), and then referred back to this alleged fact in highlighting white slavery as an issue at its 1911 annual convention (*White Ribbon Bulletin*, November, 1911).

59. NAC, NCW Annual Report, 1913, p. 124.

60. *Ibid.*, pp. 52-53.

61. See Deborah Gorham, "Flora MacDonald Denison: Canadian Feminist," in L. Kealey, ed., *A Not Unreasonable Claim: Women and Reform in Canada 1880s-1920s* (Toronto, 1979), pp. 47-70.

62. Much suffrage propaganda pointed out that unworthy immigrant and Native men could vote while middle-class women could not. See Carol Bacchi, *Liberation Deferred? The Ideas of the English Canadian Suffragists* (Toronto, 1983), ch. V.

63. NAC, Canadian Council of Churches Collection, Box 29; minutes of annual meetings of Moral and Social Reform Council of Canada (which changed its name to Social Service Council of Canada in 1913).

64. See McLaren, "White Slavers," for arrest statistics, which never amounted to more than a handful.

65. NAC, CCC, Box 29, Minutes of the AGM of the Social Service Council of Canada, December, 1914. This story is typically not attributed to any source, which gives the impression it was personally witnessed by the speaker although he never claims this.

66. Rev. R.B. St. Clair, in Ernest Bell, ed., *War on the White Slave Trade* (1911; reprint, Toronto, 1979), p. 359. The reading public would be aware that department store work was perceived as putting women in contact with questionable men and at the same time stimulating their desires for the luxuries sold there, a combination fatal to their virtue. See, for instance, Jane Addams, *A New Conscience and an Ancient Evil* (New York, 1912). For an analysis of the portrayal of female consumerist frivolity, see Rachel Bowlby, *Just Looking: Consumer Culture in Dreiser, Gissing and Zola* (New York, 1985).

67. For similar stories, see UCA, Reginald Kauffman, "The Girl That Goes Wrong," pamphlet issued by the Methodist DESS, n.d.; Clifford G. Roe, *The Girl Who Disappeared* (American Bureau of Moral Education, 1914). See also white-slavery stories published in *White Ribbon Bulletin*, 1911-13.

68. "Canadian Girls in White Slave Traffic," *Toronto Daily Star*, 11 December 1911, p. 9.

69. Karen Dubinsky, "'The Modern Chivalry': Women and the Knights of Labor in Ontario 1880-1891" (M.A. thesis, Carleton University, 1985), pp. 176-87. I would like to thank Karen Dubinsky for sharing her research with me.

70. The association of Italian and Chinese men with abduction and forced prostitution is repeatedly made in newspaper headlines, and seldom justified by the news story itself. A good example is a large-headline story about a woman in New York, married to a Chinese man, who was caught in a drug heist; when questioned by

police she claimed that "she is weary of the 'life of white slavery' she has been leading." The story, however, makes it clear that she married the man of her own free will, and nothing is said about her being forced into prostitution. ("Was Enslaved by a Chinaman To Whom She Taught Religion," *Toronto Daily News*, 28 September 1911, p. 11.) In another incident, an Italian Canadian charged with murder was suddenly asked by the prosecutor: "Have you ever taken any part in the white slave traffic?", a question that undoubtedly tarred his character regardless of his negative answer. (*Toronto Daily News*, 15 November 1911, pp. 1, 11, 15.)

71. NAC, CCC, Box 29, text of pamphlet reproduced in the minutes of the AGM of the Social Service Council of Canada, December, 1914.

72. See Richard Ericson *et al.*, *Visualizing Deviance: A Study of News Organizations* (Toronto, 1987).

73. UCA, Annual Report of Methodist DESS, 1911, p. 32.

74. See Mariana Valverde, "The Love of Finery: Fashion and the Fallen Woman in Victorian Social Discourse," *Victorian Studies*, 32, 2 (Winter, 1988).

75. UCA, Annual Report of the Methodist DESS, 1915, pp. 7-8.

76. David Garland, *Punishment and Welfare: A History of Penal Strategies* (London, 1985), p. 177.

77. Royal Commission [on vice in Winnipeg], Minutes of Evidence, p. 122.

78. A Magdalen Asylum was set up in Toronto in 1852; see Susan Houston, "The Impetus to Reform: Urban Crime, Poverty and Ignorance in Ontario 1850-1875" (Ph.D. thesis, University of Toronto, 1974), p. 232.

79. J.W. Langmuir, quoted in R. Splane, *Social Welfare in Ontario 1792-1893* (Toronto, 1965), p. 247.

80. W.H. Howland, testimony in *Royal Commission on Capital and Labour* (1889), volume 5 of Evidence, p. 168.

81. D.A. Watt, "The Canadian Law for the Protection of Women and Girls," in A. Powell, ed., *The National Purity Congress* (Baltimore, 1895), pp. 450-51. See also his *Moral Legislation: A Statement Prepared for the Information of the Senate* (Montreal, 1890), which deals primarily with the need for higher age-of-consent provisions.

82. Garland, *Punishment and Welfare*, p. 46.

83. SA, "Rescue Notes," *War Cry*, 22 September 1888, p. 3. In the English Salvation Army there was a little more critical thought about the Salvationists' relationship to the state, probably as an historic result of the struggle against the Contagious Diseases Acts. For instance, an article published in the wake of the Jack the Ripper murders envisioned female Salvationists as "sisters" siding firmly with the prostitutes and against a hypocritical and sensation-loving public ("Our Murdered Sisters," *The Deliverer*, 15 August 1889, p. 19).

84. SA, "Our Rescue Home," *War Cry*, 24 December 1887, p. 1.

85. SA, *War Cry*, 30 June 1888, p. 2. The paper carried a regular column entitled "Rescue Facts."

86. Ads for the "Victor Home Household Laundry" ("Satisfaction Guaranteed") appeared regularly in the Methodist press. See, for example, the article and photograph in UCA, Fred Victor records, 1909, pp. 28-29.

87. UCA, Fred Victor records, *Twenty-One Years of Mission Work in Toronto 1886-1907*.

88. *War Cry* carried regular reports and figures concerning their own rescue work. Reports of other refuges also tend to stigmatize all women inmates whether or not they were guilty of sexual transgressions; for instance, Toronto's Haven and Prison Gate Mission reported in 1911 that it had seventy-one maternity cases, of which not all were single mothers (eighteen were not), but concluded that "the work is mostly among women who have erred, and those who by reason of deficient intellect or a similar cause are a menace to society." Reported in *Toronto Daily Star*, 1 December 1911, p. 16.

89. Wendy Mitchinson, "The WCTU: For God, Home, and Native Land," in Kealey, ed., *A Not Unreasonable Claim*, pp. 151-68.

Chapter 5

1. UCA, Pidgeon Papers, Box 32, File 529, notes for a sermon on "National Righteous-ness," first preached in 1907.

2. Quoted in Rooke and Schnell, *No Bleeding Heart*, p. 25.

3. J.S. Mill, *On the Subjection of Women* (Cambridge, Mass., 1970 [1869]), p. 67. For the acceptance of this view of the Anglo-Saxon "race" among English-Canadian intellectuals, see S.E.D. Shortt, *The Search for an Ideal: Six Canadian intellectuals and their convictions in an age of transition 1890-1930* (Toronto, 1976).

4. See N. Chabani Manganyi, "Making strange: race, science, and ethnopsychiatric discourse," in Francis Barker *et al.*, eds., *Europe and its Others* (Essex, 1985), vol. I, pp. 152-70; Sander L. Gilman, "Black Bodies, White Bodies: Toward an Iconography of Female Sexuality in Late 19th century Art, Medicine and Litera-ture," in H.L. Gates, Jr., ed., *'Race', Writing, and Difference* (Ithaca, N.Y., 1986), 223-61.

5. See Valverde and Weir, "The Struggles of the Immoral," pp. 31-35.

6. James Mavor quoted in Shortt, *The Search for an Ideal*, p. 134.

7. The self-image of British people as inherently self-regulated is critically explored in Geoffrey Pearson, *Hooligan: A History of Respectable Fears* (London, 1983).

8. NAC, CCC, Box 29, Minutes of Annual General Meeting of Moral and Social Reform Council of Canada, September, 1912. English chauvinism and racism was of course not new; there was a great deal of anti-Irish racism in the 1840s and 1850s. Houston, "The Impetus to Reform." Post-Darwinian theories of racial evolution, however, changed the character of English, Canadian, and American racism toward the end of the century.

9. UCA, S.D. Chown Papers, Box 13, File 376, undated address, "Law and Morality."

10. UCA, Presbyt. WMS, Dept. of the Stranger Papers, Box 4, File 41, Minutes for 7 October 1920 of the Canadian Council on the Immigration of Women. Emphasis mine.

11. Barbara Roberts, "Purely Administrative Proceedings: The Management of Cana-dian Deportation, Montreal, 1900-1935" (Ph.D. thesis, University of Ottawa, 1980), p. 313.

12. See McLaren, *Our Own Master Race*.

13. UCA, Pidgeon Papers, Box 32, File 529, sermon on "National Righteousness," first preached in 1907.

14. See Eric Hobsbawm and Terence Ranger, eds., *The Invention of Tradition* (Cam-

bridge, 1983). Terence Ranger's essay in this volume on the way in which British colonial administrators managed to invent not only British but even "African" traditions is quite relevant to the white Canadian project to imagine "Indians" and try to sell these images back to Native people as their own.

15. Quoted by Peter Ward, *White Canada Forever: Popular Attitudes and Public Policy Toward Orientals in B.C.* (Montreal, 1978), pp. 90-91. For the political economy of race, see B. Singh Bolaria and Peter S. Li, *Racial Oppression in Canada* (Toronto, 1988; 2nd ed.).

16. Alicya Muszynski, "Race and gender: structural determinants in the formation of BC's salmon cannery labour forces," *Canadian Journal of Sociology*, 13, 1-2 (1988), p. 105; Ward, *White Canada Forever*, p. 15. See also Donald Avery, "Canadian Immigration Policy and the 'Foreign' Navvy, 1896-1914," in Michael Cross and Gregory Kealey, eds., *The Consolidation of Capitalism*, Readings in Canadian Social History, vol. 4 (Toronto, 1983), pp. 47-73. On the political economy of Native people's relations with whites, see Ron G. Bourgeault, "Race and Class under Mercantilism: Indigenous People in 19th century Canada," in Bolaria and Li, *Racial Oppression in Canada*, pp. 41-70.

17. Howard Palmer, *Patterns of Prejudice: A History of Nativism in Alberta* (Toronto, 1983).

18. See Allen Chase, *The Legacy of Malthus: The Social Costs of the New Scientific Racism* (Chicago, 1980); Mort, *Dangerous Sexualities*; George Moss, *Nationalism and Sexuality* (New York, 1985); Robert Nye, *Crime, Madness and Politics in Modern France* (Princeton, N.J., 1984); Jeffrey Weeks, *Sex, Politics and Society: The Regulation of Sexuality Since 1800* (London, 1981). There is a pioneering discussion of nationalism and sexuality in the Canadian context in Gary Kinsman, *The Regulation of Desire: Sexuality in Canada* (Montreal, 1987), but the period before 1925 is not covered in any detail.

19. On Clarke's study, see Neil Sutherland, *Children in English-Canadian Society: Framing the Twentieth-Century Consensus* (Toronto, 1976), ch. 5. See also Angus and Arlene McLaren, *The Bedroom and the State* (Toronto, 1986), ch. 5, for the influence of eugenics on Canada's birth control movement. MacMurchy's thoughts on eugenics were summarized in her *Sterilization? Birth Control? A Book for Family Welfare and Safety* (Toronto, 1934), in which she praises the Third Reich's sterilization policy.

20. Moss, *Nationalism and Sexuality*; Nye, *Crime, Madness and Politics in Modern France.*

21. Max Nordau, *Degeneration* (New York, 1895), p. vii. Nordau claimed among other things that Impressionist painting practices were due to a disease of the retina, which caused painters to see the world as a collection of coloured blotches.

22. King, *Industry and Humanity*, p. 323. Emphasis mine.

23. Woodsworth, *Strangers Within Our Gates.*

24. For an examination of the origins of this, see Edward Said, *Orientalism* (New York, 1979); see also R. Valerie Lucas, "Yellow Peril in the Promised Land," in Barker *et al.*, eds., *Europe and its Others*, vol. I, pp. 41-57. Peter Ward, in *White Canada Forever*, mentions that white British Columbians saw Japanese immigrants as a slight variation on the Chinese, at least until the Russo-Japanese War of 1905, which

caused them to think of Japan as a much more successful and aggressive nation than China.

25. Roosevelt quoted in Richard Hofstadter, *Social Darwinism in American Thought 1860-1915* (Philadelphia, 1945), p. 155; Royal Commission quoted in Ward, *White Canada Forever*, p. 60. Asian Canadians, even if born in Canada, were not allowed to vote as late as World War Two.

26. Pedersen, " 'The Call to Service,' " p. 21.

27. Avery, "Canadian Immigration Policy and the 'Foreign' Navvy," p. 52.

28. See Bolaria and Li, *Racial Oppression in Canada*, ch. 5.

29. On Alberta riots, see Palmer, *Patterns of Prejudice*, pp. 20, 34; on the Vancouver riot, see Ward, *White Canada Forever*, pp. 67-74.

30. Staff Inspector Kennedy, in *Annual Report of the Chief Constable*, 1910, p. 31.

31. Quoted by Palmer, *Patterns of Prejudice*, p. 36.

32. William Calderwood, "Pulpit, Press and Political Reactions to the Ku Klux Klan in Saskatchewan," in S.M. Trofimenkoff, ed., *The Twenties in Canada* (Ottawa, 1972), pp. 191-215.

33. UCA, 86th annual report of the Missionary Society of the Methodist Church, 1910, p. 36. These views were similar to those held by Sara Jeanette Duncan's protagonist Lorne Murchison. In his visit to London he recognizes the "degeneration" of the English working classes and of the English nation as a whole, seeing Canada as offering a place for the "race" to regenerate itself, growing wheat and making steel under blue skies. S.J. Duncan, *The Imperialist* (Toronto, 1971 [1904]), esp. pp. 122-23.

34. Duncan, *The Imperialist*, p. 124.

35. Quoted in Ward, *White Canada Forever*, p. 137.

36. See Carl Berger, *The Sense of Power: Studies in the Ideas of Canadian Imperialism 1867-1914* (Toronto, 1970).

37. UCA, *Missionary Outlook*, March, 1905, p. 58.

38. UCA, *Missionary Outlook*, January, 1906.

39. Emily Ferguson [Murphy], *Janey Canuck in the West* (Toronto, 1910), p. 38.

40. Ruth Compton Brouwer, *New Women for God: Canadian Presbyterian Women and India Missions, 1876-1914* (Toronto, 1990).

41. See, for instance, the missionary textbook by Rev. W.T. Gunn, *His Dominion*, pp. 143-46. Gunn states that the Riel rebellion would not have happened if missionaries had had more power.

42. *Ibid.*, p. 134.

43. Duncan Scott, in *Handbook of Canada* (Toronto, 1924), p. 19.

44. Quoted in Marilyn Barber, "Nationalism, Nativism and the Social Gospel: The Protestant Church Response to Foreign Immigrants 1897-1914," in R. Allen, *The Social Gospel in Canada* (Ottawa, 1975), p. 192.

45. Elizabeth S. Strachan, *The Story of the Years* (Vol. III, 1906-1916) (Toronto, Women's Missionary Society of the Methodist Church, 1917), pp. 308-09.

46. In 1906 the MWMS paid for thirty-two missionaries in Japan and China, and twenty-one in Canada; in 1916, there were fifty-six in Japan and China, and sixty-four in Canada. *Ibid.*, p. 309.

47. UCA, *86th Annual Report of the Missionary Society of the Methodist Church in Canada*, p. 33.

48. UCA, *Missionary Outlook*, January, 1906, editorial, p. 3.

49. UCA, Pidgeon Papers, Box 33, File 583, "Our Dominion – God's Dominion," sermon, July, 1916.

50. Gunn, *His Dominion*, p. 206.

51. *Ibid.*, pp. 218, 221. This theme of North American cities corrupting European immigrants, especially their young people, was also pursued in the U.S. by progressive reformers such as Jane Addams.

52. This was a unanimously passed resolution at the 26 May 1911 meeting of the General Society of the Presbyterian Women's Missionary Society (PWMS). UCA, PWMS, Box 2, Minutebook.

53. UCA, MWMS, Pamphlet, "Italian Methodist Missions," n.d.

54. UCA, Pidgeon Papers, Box 32, File 34, "The Church's Problem in Canada," speech given in Glasgow in 1912. Strangers, Pidgeon reiterated, cannot vote properly until they become "Canadian and Christian Canadians at heart."

55. Gunn, *His Dominion*, pp. 3, 4.

56. Kenneth McNaught, *A Prophet in Politics: A Biography of J.S. Woodsworth* (Toronto, 1959), p. 25.

57. See Barber, "Nationalism, Nativism and the Social Gospel," pp. 194ff.; and also her preface to the reprint of Woodsworth's *Strangers Within Our Gates* (Toronto, 1972; orid. ed. 1909).

58. Woodsworth, *Strangers Within Our Gates*, p. 279.

59. *Ibid.*, p. 275.

60. *Ibid.*, pp. 231, 61. Elsewhere he states: "We need more of our own blood to assist us to maintain in Canada our British traditions and to mould the incoming armies of foreigners into loyal British subjects" (p. 50).

61. UCA, MWMS pamphlet, Nellie McClung, *An Insistent Call*, n.d., p. 5.

62. British and American feminists shared these racist and ethnocentric definitions of feminism; see Mariana Valverde, "The Concept of 'Race' in First-wave Feminist Sexual Politics," paper presented at the Social Science History Association, Chicago, November 5, 1988.

63. UCA, PWMS, Department of the Stranger (henceforth PDS), Box 1, and also reports of the Board of Home Missions, in the annual *Acts and Proceedings of the General Assembly of the Presbyterian Church in Canada*, 1910-1925.

64. UCA, PDS, Box 5, File 43 (typescript history of PDS); and Report of the Board of Home Missions (in *Acts and Proceedings* . . . , 1913, p. 18).

65. It is unclear whether this includes the immigrants met by the immigration chaplains (who had risen to six by 1913); the chaplains reported directly to the Home Mission Board and not to Mrs. West. But be that as it may, the bureaucratic network of the Department of the Stranger was remarkable.

66. UCA, PDS, Box 4, File 40, circular dated 22 January 1920.

67. UCA, PDS, Box 1, Toronto Reports for 1919 and 1921. In 1922, the PDS lobbied Mackenzie King for a more restrictive immigration policy. Despite their personal interest in getting more domestic help, the women argued that immigrants ought to be subjected to strict tests for their mental and physical health (PDS, Box 4, File 38).

68. UCA, PDS, Box 2, File 19, Emma McDougall's 1923 Report for Toronto. Barbara Roberts's excellent thesis, "Purely Administrative Proceedings: The Management of Canadian Deportation, Montreal 1900-1935" (Ph.D. thesis, University of

Ottawa, 1980), studies the Immigration Department's deportations for immorality, but is not aware of the important role of philanthropic groups in this area.

69. Roberts, "Purely Administrative Proceedings," p. 207. Some of the cases studied by Roberts include a twenty-five-year-old British immigrant woman deported in 1903 for being "addicted to masturbation" and various "illegitimate mothers" deported overtly for being "feeble-minded" but in fact for their sexual transgression (pp. 90, 195, 216).

70. *Ibid.*, pp. 226-27.

71. UCA, Rev. John Chisholm's report, included in the Report of the Board of Home Missions, in *Acts and Proceedings . . .* , 1913, p. 62. The reports of Chisholm and other immigration chaplains indicate that they performed many of the functions later taken over by immigration officials, from giving information about accommodation or money exchange to singling out undesirables. For biographical information, see his obituary in the Presbyterian Montreal-Ottawa Conference Minutes for 1936.

72. UCA, PDS, Box 2, File 15; typescript report, undated but undoubtedly 1922.

73. *Ibid.*, p. 6. Prosecutions for bigamy were not uncommon; men and women sometimes left legal husbands or wives behind when immigrating to Canada, and the courts – although undoubtedly unaware of the vast majority of such cases – zealously prosecuted those who came to official attention. Bigamy cases were given prominent newspaper coverage (in the last four months of 1911 alone, see *Toronto Daily News*, 15 September, 6 October; *Mail and Empire*, 21, 27 December).

74. The Methodists also had a Department of the Stranger, but it was started later and does not seem to have been nearly as active.

75. UCA, PDS, Box 4, File 42. See "First Report of the National Traveller's Aid Committee" (1925) and other papers in this file.

76. For instance, under "Home and Family Life," the proposed questionnaire has fourteen questions relating to "The Father," six relating to "The Mother," and so on; there are also eight questions on "mental and physical condition," which – in keeping with the obsession about feeble-mindedness characteristic of the mid-twenties – include "Has she had a physical examination or mental test or observation by a skilled physician?" UCA, PDS, Box 2, File 42, circular dated New York, May 25, 1925.

77. Quoted in Marilyn Barber, "The Women Ontario Welcomed: Immigrant Domestics for Ontario Homes 1870-1930," *Ontario History*, 72, 3 (1980), p. 159.

78. PAO, WCTU, Box 2N-103, "President's Address," in *Report of the 21st Convention of the Canadian WCTU* (1920). The middle-class desire for female servants was understood to be the primary factor in immigration policy regarding women: "The work outlined by this Council is of a very fine nature, with, *of course*, particular reference to the woman emigrant coming to enter upon household service of any type" (emphasis mine).

79. UCA, PDS, Box 2, File 41, Minutes of CCIW meeting, 12 January 1920.

80. UCA, PDS, Box 4, File 41, Minutes of founding conference of CCIW, Ottawa, September 9-10, 1919.

81. Roberts, "Purely Administrative Proceedings," p. 232.

82. UCA, PDS, Box 4, File 41, Minutes of First Annual Meeting of CCIW, October 5-7, 1920. Mrs. West's comments were followed by the reading of a long letter from

Canada's leading psychiatrist, Dr. C.K. Clarke, who argued that Jews were a "neurotic race"; to this letter Rev. Chisholm added that Jews were also largely involved in organized prostitution.

83. See Charlotte Whitton, "Unmarried Parenthood and Social Order," *Social Welfare*, April and May, 1920. Whitton particularly blames English women for being immoral and producing illegitimate children. *Social Welfare*, Canada's leading social work and social problems magazine at this time, also published articles on the immigration of British women, e.g., "Immigration of British Women," December, 1919, p. 66, and Una Saunders, "British Women Immigrants," May, 1920, p. 204. Saunders's article disagrees with that by Whitton in the same issue, arguing that Canada had a patriotic duty to take in ex-service women.

84. Roberts, "Purely Administrative Proceedings," pp. 213-14.

Chapter 6

1. See Robert Wiebe, *The Search for Order 1877-1920* (New York, 1967); Allen F. Davis, *Spearheads of Reform: The Social Settlements and the Progressive Movement 1890-1914* (New York, 1967); Philip Abrams, *The Origins of British Sociology 1834-1914* (Chicago, 1968); Mary Jo Deegan, *Jane Addams and the Men of the Chicago School 1892-1918* (New Brunswick, N.J., 1988). For Canada, see Douglas Campbell, *Essays in the History of Canadian Sociology* (Port Credit, Ont., 1983); Marlene Shore, *The Science of Social Redemption: McGill, the Chicago School, and the Origins of Social Research in Canada* (Toronto, 1987); Lorna Hurl, "Building a Profession: The Origin and Development of the Department of Social Service in the University of Toronto, 1914-1928" (Working Papers of Social Welfare, University of Toronto, Faculty of Social Work, 1983).

2. Woodsworth, *My Neighbor*, p. 28.

3. *Ibid.*, p. 30. Woodsworth had been asked to write his urban sociology textbook for the series of Methodist mission textbooks edited by F.C. Stephenson. The young people's groups that were the main target of Stephenson's efforts had over 62,000 members, but the book was also used in men's and women's missionary societies. This shows that *My Neighbor* probably received closer reading by more people than any Canadian urban sociology book since, and highlights the key role of extra-school education systems.

4. See Michael B. Katz *et al.*, *The Social Organization of Early Industrial Capitalism* (Cambridge, Mass., 1982), ch. 6.

5. Raymond Williams, *The Country and the City* (London, 1973).

6. Joy Parr, *Labouring Children: British Immigrant Apprentices to Canada 1869-1924* (London, 1980).

7. City of Toronto Archives (henceforth CTA), RG-11, Box 2, *Report of the Charities Commission (1911-1912)*, p. 7.

8. Lyman Abbott, quoted by Gunn, *His Dominion*, p. 188. See also Woodsworth, *My Neighbor*, p. 24.

9. UCA, Pidgeon Papers, Box 32, File 518; sermon, "Building the Holy City," first preached in 1898. This is based on the book of Nehemiah, which details the rebuilding of Jerusalem and the repopulation of Israel by Jews alone; once the city is built and the Law declared, everyone of foreign descent is excluded from Israel

(Neh. 13:3). This racial purity theme is not highlighted in Pidgeon's sermon but, given his and his audience's knowledge of the Bible, is nevertheless present as a subtext.

10. For Montreal, see Herbert B. Ames, *The City Below the Hill* (Toronto, 1972; orig. 1897), p. 72. For Toronto, see Gordon Darroch, "Early industrialization and inequality in Toronto, 1861-1899," *Labour/Le Travail*, 11 (Spring, 1983), pp. 31-61. For much of the period, the wealthiest 20 per cent owned 65-70 per cent of all Toronto wealth, while the lowest 40 per cent had a mere 8 per cent of the wealth. See also Greg Kealey, *Toronto Workers Respond to Industrial Capitalism 1867-1892* (Toronto, 1980), ch. 2.

11. J.S. Woodsworth, "Report on Living Standards, City of Winnipeg, 1913," reprinted as Appendix D in Artibise, *Winnipeg: A Social History of Urban Growth*, pp. 308-19.

12. Paul Rutherford, "Tomorrow's Metropolis: the Urban Reform Movement in Canada 1880-1920," Canadian Historical Association, *Historical Papers*, 1971, p. 203. Michael Piva, *The Condition of the Working-Class in Toronto 1900-1921* (Ottawa, 1979), pp. 87, 34. Piva's tables unaccountably exclude women workers. For Montreal, see Terry Copp, *The Anatomy of Poverty: The Condition of the Working Class in Montreal 1897-1929* (Toronto, 1974).

13. Rutherford, "Tomorrow's Metropolis," p. 210.

14. SA, *War Cry*, 24 December 1887, p. 1.

15. UCA, Fred Victor Mission papers (henceforth FVM), Rev. S.W. Dean in the annual report of the FVM for 1908, p. 11.

16. *The Slums of Great Cities* (1894), quoted in Edith Abbott, *The Tenements of Chicago* (Chicago, 1936), p. 156. Abbott's study is, unlike Hastings's, much closer to contemporary "value-free" sociology.

17. CTA, RG-11, Box 2, *Report of the Medical Health Officer on slum conditions in Toronto* (Toronto, 1911), p. 3. In this study Hastings makes numerous references to British slum literature and states that "there are few conditions found in the slums of European cities or in the greater American cities that have not been revealed in Toronto, the difference being only one of degree" (p. 4). On Hastings, see Bator, "Saving Lives on the Wholesale Plan," pp. 43ff.

18. [Hastings], *Report*, 1911, pp. 4, 24. Compare George Grant's fear that Canada as a whole might be in the process of becoming "a city of pigs" through rural depopulation and too much (rather than too little) urban material prosperity. Quoted in Doug Owram, *The Government Generation: Canadian Intellectuals and the State, 1900-1945* (Toronto, 1986), p. 15.

19. UCA, Rev. B.E. Bull (superintendent of the Fred Victor slum mission), in *Christian Guardian*, 20 December 1899, p. 1.

20. UCA, Annual Report of Methodist DESS, 1911, p. 48.

21. Ames, *The City Below*, pp. 73-74. But Ames, not wanting to alienate the temperance movement, ends up concluding that no causal chain need be determined, because what is important is the evidence that "drink is inseparable from idleness and poverty." Ames's position on drink, incidentally, contrasts favourably with that of Charles Booth, whose discussions of pauperism put drink as the first *cause*; see Charles Booth, *Life and Labour of the People in London*, vol. VIII (London, 1896), appendix B.

22. Gareth Stedman Jones, *Outcast London* (Penguin, 1984; orig. 1971), part III.

23. J.J. Kelso, "Can slums be abolished or must we continue to pay the penalty?" reprinted in P. Rutherford, *Saving the Canadian City: the first phase 1880-1920* (Toronto, 1974), p. 167.

24. S.W. Dean, "The church and the slum," in *Social Service Council of Canada Congress* (Ottawa, 1914), p. 127.

25. Anthony S. Wohl, introduction to *The Bitter Cry of Outcast London* (New York, 1970; orig. 1883), p. 16. See also his "Sex and the Single Room: Incest among the Victorian working classes," in Anthony Wohl, ed., *The Victorian Family: Structure and Stress* (London, 1978), pp. 197-216, which explores this issue as a bourgeois moral panic but omits to mention that feminists raised the incest issue as one of gender power.

26. Linda Gordon, *Heroes of Their Own Lives: The Politics and History of Family Violence* (New York, 1988), ch. 7.

27. Woodsworth, *My Neighbor*, p. 9.

28. Andrew Mearns, *The Bitter Cry of Outcast London*, pp. 56-57.

29. Cardinal Archbishop of Westminster, *The Child of the English Savage* (National Society for the Prevention of Cruelty to Children, 1890), p. 6.

30. PAO, WCTU, Olivia Fairchild, "One Phase of Home Missionary Work," *White Ribbon Bulletin*, December, 1912, p. 5.

31. CTA, RG-11, Box 167, article "Room Overcrowding and the Lodger Evil," quoted by Charles Hastings in his Monthly Report as Medical Officer of Health for February, 1914.

32. Royal Commission on Capital and Labour of 1889, Evidence, vol. 5 (Ontario), p. 166. Although the number of cases of carnal knowledge and rape that came before York County's criminal courts was nowhere close to the "hundreds" estimated by Howland, there was a significant link between the presence of male boarders and the vulnerability of resident girls to sexual assault, according to Carolyn Strange's research. Children's Aid and social work case files, such as the ones studied by Linda Gordon in *Heroes of Their Own Lives*, would undoubtedly provide a broader glimpse into the phenomenon.

33. In 1897, Montreal's industrial working class seems to have lived in families averaging about four individuals and in households averaging just over four rooms: Ames, *The City Below*, p. 47. In Toronto, where immigrants put much pressure on housing in the first two decades of the twentieth century, Charles Hastings was hard-pressed to find many instances of families living in a single room (in his 1911 slum report he found 198 families, but these were mostly couples without children since the number of individuals came to 472). See also his monthly reports, 1911-1918 (CTA, RG-11, Box 167).

34. CTA, Charles Hastings, *Report . . .* , 1911, p. 15.

35. For instance, in April of 1914, public health nurses paid 3,812 home visits; in January, 1914, there were 2,339 housing inspections (CTA, RG-11, Box 167, Hastings's monthly reports).

36. Dr. Douglas, *Bulletin*, 1913, quoted in Artibise, *Winnipeg*, p. 242.

37. "The Slum Evil," letter to editor of the *Toronto Daily News*, 9 December 1911, p. 6.

38. PAO, WCTU, *White Ribbon Bulletin*, 15 May 1900, p. 5.

39. Quoted in Bator, "Saving Lives," p. 167.

40. Dr. Douglas, *Health Bulletin*, 1911, quoted in Artibise, *Winnipeg*, p. 244.

41. PAO, WCTU, Annual Report (1897), p. 57.

42. C. Smith-Rosenberg, *Religion and the Rise of the American City: The New York City Mission Movement 1812-1870* (Ithaca, N.Y., 1971). See also Christine Stansell, *City of Women: Sex and Class in New York City, 1789-1860* (New York, 1986).

43. For an account of English reform, see Martha Vicinus, *Independent Women: Work and Community for Single Women 1850-1920* (London, 1985), esp. ch. 6, "Settlement Houses." For the growth of modern charity in the U.S., see Michael B. Katz, *In the Shadow of the Poorhouse: A Social History of Public Welfare in America* (New York, 1986).

44. Vicinus, *Independent Women*, p. 219.

45. Quoted in Allen F. Davis, *Spearheads for Reform*, p. 75.

46. Jane Addams, *Twenty years at Hull House* (New York, 1910), pp. 126-27; for a larger theoretical argument, see Jane Addams, *Democracy and Social Ethics* (New York, 1905). See also the autobiography of the founder of another famous settlement and social research agency, the Chicago Commons: Graham Taylor, *Pioneering on Social Frontiers* (Chicago, 1930).

47. See report by a Toronto Central Neighbourhood House worker (1917) reprinted in Rutherford, *Saving the Canadian City*, pp. 171-93.

48. UCA, *Christian Guardian*, 20 December 1899, p. 6.

49. UCA, FVM, pamphlet, *These Twenty Years (1886-1906)*. See also *Twenty-One Years of Mission Work in Toronto 1886-1907*.

50. UCA, FVM, *These Twenty Years*, p. 27.

51. UCA, *Christian Guardian*, 20 December 1899, p. 6.

52. See ad in 1912 annual report. Methodist publications ran this and other ads, for instance encouraging readers to send their laundry to the Victor Home, to be cleansed by the fallen women purifying their souls through unpaid washing work.

53. UCA, FVM, *Lights and Shades of City Life* (1900 annual report), p. 30.

54. UCA, FVM, 1901 annual report, p. 19.

55. UCA, FVM, 1900 annual report, p. 21.

56. UCA, FVM, 1902 annual report, p. 23.

57. UCA, *Christian Guardian*, 20 December 1899; Eva S. Pike, "Domestic Instruction in the Homes of the Poor," p. 8.

58. NAC, NCW, *Yearbook*, 1895, pp. 96-97. The same point was repeated the following year, when poor men were said to be driven to pubs due to "badly cooked food and a scolding wife." (NCW Yearbook, 1896, p. 94.) However, a feminist voice from the floor questioned this and said women ought not to be blamed.

59. UCA, FVM, 1911 annual report, pp. 30-31.

60. See Gordon, *Heroes of Their Own Lives*.

61. UCA, FVM, annual reports 1907, 1908, 1909; CTA, RG-11, Box 2, *Report of the Charities Commission*, pp. 33-34.

62. Ruth Brouwer, "The Methodist Church and the Woman Question 1902-1914" (York University, 1976, paper deposited at United Church Archives); J.D. Thomas, "Servants of the Church: Canadian Methodist Deaconess Work, 1890-1926," *Canadian Historical Review*, LXV, 3 (September, 1984), pp. 371-95.

63. UCA, FVM, *Twenty Years of Mission Work* (1906), p. 32.

64. R.G. Moyles, *The Blood and Fire in Canada: A History of the Salvation Army in the Dominion 1882-1976* (Toronto, 1977), p. 5. For an account of the English Army's social work, see Jenty Fairbank, *Booth's Boots: The Beginnings of Salvation Army Social Work* (London, 1983).

65. Moyles, *Blood and Fire*, pp. 7-11; see also Herbert P. Wood, *They blazed the trail: An account of the adventures of seven early-day officers of the Salvation Army in the Canadian Territory from 1882 to 1910* (Salvation Army, n.d. but c. 1963).

66. Moyles, *Blood and Fire*, p. 17.

67. Catherine Booth, quoted in Catherine Bramwell-Booth, *Catherine Booth: The Story of her Loves* (London, 1970), p. 247.

68. SA, *War Cry*, 11 October 1890, p. 14, "Why Should we Dress Plain?" On the belief that love of dress caused prostitution, see Valverde, "The Love of Finery," pp. 168-88.

69. Florence Kinton, quoted in Wendy Mitchinson, "Aspects of Reform" (Ph.D. thesis, York University, 1976), p. 91.

70. SA, Florence Kinton, "Every Chain," in *The Deliverer*, January, 1892, p. 121. The irony of this story is that the inmates of rescue homes were strictly forbidden to wear bows, lace, and finery of any sort.

71. Evangelical and Social Service Report quoted in Alice Klein and Wayne Roberts, "Besieged Innocence: the 'Problem' and the Problems of Working Women, Toronto 1896-1914," in Acton, *Women at Work*, p. 217. WCTU statement in *Toronto Star*, 1 May 1912, p. 16. (Thanks to Carolyn Strange for this reference.)

72. Peter De Lottinville, "Joe Beef of Montreal: Working-Class Culture and the Tavern," *Labour/Le Travail*, 8-9 (Autumn-Spring, 1981-82), pp. 9-40. De Lottinville does not seem to understand the specific character of the Salvation Army, however, and lumps it in with "middle-class reformers."

73. Moyles, *Blood and Fire*, p. 261. "May 1892: The Army takes over Joe Beef's Canteen in Montreal and turns it into the Salvation Lighthouse, a hostel for working men."

74. SA, *War Cry*, 20 October 1888, p. 8, "The Force of Love."

75. Booth, *In Darkest England*, p. 15. This book sold 200,000 copies in its first year alone and went through numerous reprints. There are suggestions that much of the book was ghost-written; but Booth and the Army claimed full credit for it and used it in their work, so that whether it was written by the General or not is not important.

76. Africa was generally treated as feminine, undoubtedly because of its "savage" passions and lack of European reason. The colonization process could thus be compared to (and legitimized by) the seduction/rape of the archetypal female by the archetypal male. For instance, a Canadian missionary textbook states: "Today, as for thousands of years past, Africa is drawing men to herself by the mystery of her ancient history, by the fascination of her unknown lands. . . ." Rev. J.T. Tucker and Rev. W.T. Gunn, in *Canada's Share in World Tasks* (Canadian Council of the Missionary Education Movement, 1920), p. 105. On Africa as a sexualized female, see Sander L. Gilman, "Black Bodies, White Bodies: Toward an Iconography of Female Sexuality in late 19th-century Art, Medicine and Literature," in H.L. Gates, Jr., ed., *'Race', Writing and Difference* (Ithaca, N.Y., 1986), pp. 223-61.

77. Booth, *In Darkest England*, pp. 19, 20.

78. *Ibid.*, p. 32.

79. *Ibid.*, p. 44. "Most of the philanthropists propound remedies which, if adopted tomorrow, would only affect the aristocracy of the miserable. . . . We have this doctrine of an inhuman cast-iron pseudo-political economy [i.e., scientific philanthropy] too long enthroned among us."

80. SA, *The Deliverer*, April, 1892, p. 166. The following month, the Eglinton Ave. Rescue Home celebrated its first anniversary, at which morality chief Staff Inspector Archibald spoke, suggesting that in a very short time the Army had managed to build close links to the police.

81. SA, *Sin-Chains Riven* [report of social work for 1896], p. 44.

82. The international magazine *The Deliverer* is the best source for SA rescue work, but unfortunately the Canadian SA archives have very incomplete holdings of this. The figures about the Toronto women's night shelter are from a report in *War Cry*, 30 May 1896, p. 10.

83. Both in *The Deliverer*, July, 1891, pp. 3, 15.

84. SA, *War Cry*, 21 April 1894, p. 1.

85. UCA, Joint Methodist and Presbyterian Social Survey of Vancouver (1913), p. 29.

86. Garland, *Punishment and Welfare*, p. 46.

87. SA, *War Cry*, 19 April 1890, p. 1.

Chapter 7

1. The main source for Alice Chown's life is her peculiar autobiography, *The Stairway* (Boston, 1921; reprinted, Toronto, 1988), which is not wholly reliable. See also Tom Socknat, *Witnesses to War* (Toronto, 1986), pp. 55, 59, for Alice Chown's peace activities in the twenties.

2. Alice Chown, "Fundamentals of Charity Organization," NAC, NCW, *Yearbook*, 1899, p. 255.

3. Alice A. Chown, "Some Criticisms of the Deaconess Movement," *The Christian Guardian (CG)*, 15 November 1911, pp. 24, 25.

4. Rev. Bartle Bull, *CG*, 22 November 1911, p. 34.

5. Alice A. Chown, "Will the Deaconess Society Adopt Modern Social Methods?" *CG*, 29 November 1911, pp. 23-24.

6. Chown, "Some Criticisms," p. 25.

7. Mrs. Morrison, *CG*, 29 November 1911, p. 25.

8. Alice Chown, "Not Deaconesses but Deaconess Training," *CG*, 6 December 1911, p. 34.

9. J.S. Woodsworth, in *CG*, 29 November 1911, p. 25.

10. For instance, after returning to Canada from a prestigious gathering of U.S. home economists in Lake Placid, Chown denounced the grandmother of Canadian domestic science training, Adelaide Hoodless, as suffering not only from a "lack of science" but also from deficient mental capacities; see Terry Crowley, "Adelaide Hoodless and the Canadian Gibson Girl," *Canadian Historical Review*, LXVII, 4 (1986), pp. 542-43.

11. Joey Noble, "Class-ifying the Poor: Toronto Charities 1850-1880," *Studies in Political Economy*, I, 2 (1979), pp. 109-27.

12. Goldwin Smith's contribution to social theory (but not his practical activity) is discussed in Cook, *The Regenerators*.

13. C. Pelham Mulvany, *Toronto: Past and Present* (Toronto, 1884), p. 62. On p. 69, Goldwin Smith is cited as the initiator of charity organization, although it is "ladies and others who do the visiting."

14. For an interesting though partisan account, see Helen Bosanquet, *Social Work in London 1869-1912: A History of the Charity Organization Society* (London, 1914).

15. NAC, NCW, *Yearbook*, 1896, p. 224. An earlier speaker had stated that attempts at charity organization societies in Victoria and Ottawa had ended up in yet more organizations that gave relief, neglecting the investigatory function; Machar agreed and said that was the case in Kingston as well. Incidentally, there is no evidence that Machar and Alice Chown worked closely together despite having similar views on charity and living in the same place; perhaps Chown's radical views on the church and on feminism shocked the traditionalist and patriotic Machar.

16. Ames, *The City Below the Hill*, p. 77. Echoing Machar, Ames said that "benevolent work overlaps with a tendency to pauperize the recipients."

17. These were Halifax, Kingston (where the secretary was Alice Chown), London, Montreal, Ottawa, Toronto, and Victoria. National Council of Women of Canada, *Women of Canada: Their Life and Work* (1900), pp. 323-24.

18. Associated Charities of Winnipeg 1912 annual report, quoted in Dennis Guest, *The Emergence of Social Security in Canada* (Vancouver, 1985), pp. 37-38. On this organization, see Woodsworth, *My Neighbor*, pp. 180-88.

19. James Pitsula, "The emergence of social work in Toronto," *Journal of Canadian Studies*, 14, 1 (Spring, 1979), p. 38; Richard Splane, *Social Welfare in Ontario 1792-1893* (Toronto, 1965), p. 115.

20. City of Toronto Archives (CTA), RG-11, Box 2, *Report of the Charities Commission, 1911-1912*, p. 6.

21. J.A. Turnbull, president of the Associated Charities of Toronto, in Rutherford, *Saving the Canadian City*, p. 120. By contrast, the province only gave $52,000 (and its Inspector of Charities and Corrections kept much better tabs on these grants).

22. Lorna F. Hurl, "Building a Profession: The Origin and Development of the Department of Social Service in the University of Toronto 1914-1928," Working Papers on Social Welfare in Canada, School of Social Work, University of Toronto, pp. 3-5.

23. NAC, NCW, *Yearbook*, 1895, p. 138. Lady Aberdeen had been, just prior to her husband's appointment as Governor-General, the president of the British Women's Industrial Council, a social feminist organization concerned with investigation and research and sharply distinguished from the reform-oriented Labour women's organizations.

24. Marlene Shore, *The Science of Social Redemption: McGill, the Chicago School, and the Origins of Social Research in Canada* (Toronto, 1987).

25. A list of headings under which to gather information was provided in the annual report of the Methodist DESS for 1911, p. 47.

26. Carolyn Strange, "The Toronto Survey of 1915 and the Search for Sexual Order in the City," in Roger Hall *et al.*, eds., *Patterns of the Past* (Toronto, 1988).

27. Map showing one block of Sydney, N.S., in *Sydney, N.S.: A Preliminary and General Social Survey* (1913). The United Church Archives has copies of this and

many other social surveys; the vast majority document "the problem of the city" but there is an interesting one comparing the rural and urban sections of Pictou County, N.S. Chapter 9 of Woodsworth's *My Neighbor* contains a very detailed plan of work for social investigation, which appears to have been followed to some degree by the social surveys done in Canada.

28. UCA, Pidgeon Papers, Box 52, File 2070, notes for a sermon on "The Church and Moral Reform" (1907).

29. Hurl, "Building a Profession," p. 21.

30. For a study of a similar process in Vancouver, see Diane L. Matters, "Public Welfare, Vancouver Style, 1910-1920," *Journal of Canadian Studies,* 14, 1 (Spring, 1979), pp. 3-15. Matters demonstrates that even as the city assumed responsibility for relief, the charity ethos by no means abated: municipal workers considered relief not a citizens' right but a state charity. Her study thus also undermines the Canadian social democratic version of Whig history, and particularly the myth of the inexorable if slow rise of welfare as a right, as developed, for instance, in Dennis Guest, *The Emergence of Social Security in Canada* (Vancouver, 1985).

31. UCA, pamphlet, [F.N. Stapleford], *After Twenty Years: A Short History of the NWA* (Toronto, 1938).

32. See *ibid.,* pp. 7-8; see also UCA, Fred Victor Mission files, Bureau of Municipal Research *White Paper No. 17* (17 October 1917) and *White Paper No. 18* (26 December 1917), for the conflict between the city and the board.

33. Horatio Hocken, "The new spirit in municipal government" (1914), reprinted in Rutherford, ed., *Saving the Canadian City,* pp. 206-07.

34. Bureau of Municipal Research, *White Paper No. 18* (26 December 1917).

35. Hurl, "Building a Profession," p. 21. Other experts also who began to teach social work in 1918 were drawn from the conservative wing of the moral and social reform movement (for instance, Lucy Brooking and Sarah Libby Carson). A planned visit by Jane Addams was cancelled by the School of Social Work in response to protests by pro-military groups.

36. Stapleford, *After Twenty Years,* p. 17. For the transformation of relief work during the depression, see Pitsula, "The emergence of social work in Toronto"; John Taylor, " 'Relief from Relief': The Cities' Answer to Depression Dependency," *Journal of Canadian Studies,* 14, 1 (Spring, 1979), pp. 16-23.

37. Stapleford, *After Twenty Years,* p. 17.

38. Quoted in Veronica Strong-Boag, "Wages for Housework: Mothers' Allowances and the Beginnings of Social Security in Canada," *Journal of Canadian Studies,* 14, 1 (Spring, 1979), p. 27; see also Brigitte Kitchen, "The Introduction of Family Allowances in Canada," in Moscovitch and Alpert, eds., *The "Benevolent" State,* pp. 222-41.

39. For instance, in 1911 the province of Ontario gave well over $300,000 in grants to private charities: A. Moscovitch and Glenn Drover, "Social Expenditures," in Moscovitch and Alpert, eds., *The "Benevolent" State,* p. 19.

40. The main liberal accounts are Splane, *Social Welfare in Ontario,* and Guest, *Rise of Social Security.* Political-economy perspectives are used by Reg Whitaker, "Images of the Canadian state," in Leo Panitch, ed., *The Canadian State*; Moscovitch and Drover, "Social Expenditures and the Welfare State," pp. 13-43; and in most of the articles in James Dickinson and Bob Russell, eds., *Family,*

Economy and State: The social reproduction process under capitalism (Toronto, 1987).

41. See Philip Abrams, *The Origins of British Sociology* (Chicago, 1967), pp. 34-37; Philip Corrigan and Derek Sayer, *The Great Arch: English State Formation as Cultural Revolution* (Oxford, 1986); Philip Abrams, *Historical Sociology* (London, 1982).

42. Garland, *Punishment and Welfare*.

Index